STANISLAVSKY AND GENDER

Edited by Mark Shields

Routledge
Taylor & Francis Group
LONDON AND NEW YORK

Designed cover image: Oksana ILIUSHCHENKOVA/Shutterstock.com

First published 2025
by Routledge
4 Park Square, Milton Park, Abingdon, Oxon OX14 4RN

and by Routledge
605 Third Avenue, New York, NY 10158

Routledge is an imprint of the Taylor & Francis Group, an informa business

British Library Cataloguing-in-Publication Data
A catalogue record for this book is available from the British Library

Library of Congress Cataloging-in-Publication Data
Names: Shields, Mark (Researcher) editor.
Title: Stanislavsky and gender / edited by Mark Shields.
Description: London ; New York : Routledge, 2025. | Series: Stanislavsky and... | Includes bibliographical references and index.
Identifiers: LCCN 2024045244 (print) | LCCN 2024045245 (ebook) | ISBN 9781032533513 (hardback) | ISBN 9781032533506 (paperback) | ISBN 9781003411611 (ebook)
Subjects: LCSH: Stanislavsky, Konstantin, 1863-1938--Criticism and interpretation. | Sex role in the theater. | Gender identity in the theater. | LCGFT: Essays.
Classification: LCC PN2728.S78 S7525 2025 (print) | LCC PN2728.S78 (ebook) | DDC 792.02/8071--dc23/eng/20240927
LC record available at https://lccn.loc.gov/2024045244
LC ebook record available at https://lccn.loc.gov/2024045245

ISBN: 978-1-032-53351-3 (hbk)
ISBN: 978-1-032-53350-6 (pbk)
ISBN: 978-1-003-41161-1 (ebk)

DOI: 10.4324/9781003411611

Typeset in Galliard
by SPi Technologies India Pvt Ltd (Straive)

CONTENTS

CONTRIBUTORS

Barry Fitzgerald (He/They) is a queer Irish performer and maker based between Ireland and the UK. Their practice is concerned with the intersections of identity. Playing with form and connecting with communities is at its heart – experimental work that is aesthetically rich, accessible, thought-provoking, and fun. Barry has worked with companies such as Complicité and Punchdrunk and devised work shown at the Arcola, Birmingham REP, Bush Theatre, Camden People's Theatre, Contact, the Glory, Hackney Showroom, and Shoreditch Town Hall. They are artist-in-residence at VISUAL Carlow and an associate artist of OUTBOX, a company of LGBTQIA+ creatives. Barry's film and video work has screened at festivals including Aesthetica, Cork International Film Festival, Galway Film Fleadh, GAZE LGBTQ+ Festival, Homotopia, Scottish Queer International Film Festival, and SHOUT. Their most recent video work, "...you should see me in the dress" was part of VISUAL's 2023 summer exhibition, Remembering the Future, and won an Artworks Award, granted to artists who demonstrate "exceptional promise". An experienced facilitator, director, and teacher, Barry has worked with the Almeida, ArtsEd London, Barbican, Gendered Intelligence, Hackney Shed, Mountview, Royal Central School of Speech and Drama, Royal Court, Unicorn Theatre, and University of East London, among others.

Maria Ignatieva (She/Her) is the Martha W. Farmer Endowed Professor at the Ohio State University, Department of Theatre, Film, and Media Arts. Ignatieva is a specialist in Russian theatre, film, and culture. Before coming to the US, Ignatieva taught at the Moscow Art Theatre School Studio, Russia, and worked as a theatre and film critic. Ignatieva is the author of *Stanislavsky and Female Actors: Women in Stanislavsky's Life and Art* (2008), and published chapters and essays about Konstantin Stanislavsky, Anton Chekhov, and Michael Chekhov, Russian female actors, and directors in various anthologies between 2010 and 2021.

Samia La Virgne (She/Her) is an early career academic, classically trained actor, director, and Lecturer in Acting and Performance Making and Course Lead for BA Drama with Acting at Royal Holloway, University of London, UK. Having received training in both the US and UK, she has earned a BA in Theatre Arts, an MFA in Acting, and a PhD in Performing Arts. Her keen interest in the representation of Black women in the performing arts industry was the inception of master's interrogatory research into the paucity of Black women playing leads roles on the professional Shakespearean stage. This was followed by PhD research that examined the social stigma of Blackness and womanhood through a comparative study of the stereotypical representations of Black women in the performing arts industry, and the effects they have on Black actresses in the UK and US. She is passionate about reframing perspectives, ideologies, and representations of marginalised groups in the performing arts industry by forging new, inclusive, and innovative twenty-first century methodologies.

Bella Merlin (She/Her) is an actor, writer, and professor of acting at the University of California, Riverside. A leading proponent in practice-based research, publications include *The Complete Stanislavsky Toolkit* (2014), the radically revised *Acting: The Basics 3rd Edition* (Routledge 2023), and *Shakespeare & Company: When Action Is Eloquence* with Tina Packer (Routledge 2020). Performances for stage, screen, and radio include her fact-based solo play, *Tilly No-Body*, featured at the United Nations Commission on the Status of Women (CSW68) (2024). With Professor Paul Fryer at the Stanislavsky Centre for Research she co-created the international series of symposia, "The S Word".

Maria Brígida De Miranda (She/Her) is a Brazilian theatre director, actor, translator, and Professor of Acting and Directing of the University of the State of Santa Catarina (2004 – ongoing). She is a pioneer in establishing the field of academic research on feminist theatres and is one of the first female directors to translate and stage feminist plays in Brazil. She has published articles, chapters, and books on actor training methods, martial and meditative practices, directing, and feminist theatres. Brígida's research includes post-doctoral research in feminist theatre at University of the State of Rio de Janeiro. She is the author of *Playful Training: Towards Capoeira in the Physical Training of Actors* (2010) and *Corpos Dóceis: Reflexões sobre métodos de treinamento de atores e atrizes no século XX* (2021), associate editor of the academic journal *Urdimento: Revista de Estudos em Artes Cênicas*, and coordinator of the working group “Women of the Stage” in the Brazilian Association of Research and Postgraduate Studies in Performing Arts.

Brígida was born in a small town in the state of Minas Gerais, Brazil, in 1970. She is the ninth child of a working-class couple who strongly believed in the power of education and academic studies. Brígida completed a PhD in theatre and drama, La Trobe University (Australia), in 2004, on a Brazilian Federal Scholarship award from CAPES/Ministry of Education. She had been appointed as a tenured Lecturer at the Theatre Department at University of Brasília, 1996–1999, after completing an MA in Theatre Practice at the University of Exeter (England) on a Federal Scholarship award from CAPES/ Ministry of Education. Her First Degree in Art Education and Theatre was gained at the University of Brasília (Brazil) in 1992. She is a member of the postgraduate programme in performing arts of University of the State of Santa Catarina, researching, teaching, and supervising doctoral and master's students.

Lisa Peck (She/Her) is a theatre-maker, teacher, and academic. She is Senior Lecturer in Theatre and Performance Practice at the University of Sussex, UK. Her research interests include actor training, theatre-making pedagogies, women in theatre, critical pedagogies, and site-based performance. Her most recent publication, *Emma Rice's Feminist Acts of Love*, was published in 2023. *Act as a Feminist: Towards a Critical Acting Pedagogy*, was published by Routledge in 2021. She is Associate Editor for *Theatre, Dance and Performance Training* where she curates an open access blog on critical pedagogy.

Mark Shields (They/Them) is a queer nonbinary Postgraduate Researcher in Actor Training Pedagogy at the School of Performance and Cultural Industries, University of Leeds. Mark is also a graduate of the Royal Central School of Speech and Drama, with an MA in Actor Training and Coaching (2016) and the University of Leeds (2011). Their research considers a queer engagement with *An Actor's Work: A Student's Diary* by Konstantin Stanislavsky, translated and edited by Jean Benedetti (2010), to elucidate the relational ethics of actor training pedagogy. Mark has also trained in teaching the Uta Hagen technique with HB Studio, New York and holds Fellowship of the Higher Education Academy.

Peta Tait (She/Her), La Trobe University, is an academic professor and playwright and a Fellow of the Australian Academy of the Humanities. She has written 70 scholarly articles and chapters and recent books include the authored *Forms of Emotion: Human to Nonhuman in Drama, Theatre and Performance* (2022); *Theory for Theatre Studies: Emotion* (2021); *Fighting Nature: Travelling Menageries, Animal Acts and War Shows* (2016); *Great European Stage Directors: Antoine, Stanislavski and Saint-Denis* (2018);

Circus Bodies (Routledge 2005); and *Performing Emotions* (Ashgate/Routledge 2002) and the co-edited *Feminist Ecologies: Changing Environments in the Anthropocene* (2018). Her current collaborative book project "Ecological Theatre and Australian Performance" is ARC funded.

Rose Whyman (She/Her) is a Senior Lecturer in Drama and Theatre Arts, University of Birmingham, UK. Her teaching includes acting courses based on the work of Stanislavsky and Michael Chekhov and the Alexander Technique. Her research focuses on the science of actor training. Her monograph publications include *The Stanislavsky System of Acting; Legacy and Influence in Modern Performance* (2008); *Anton Chekhov*, Routledge (2010); and *Stanislavski: The Basics*, Routledge (2012), and she is currently working on *Performance in Revolutionary Russia: The Art and Science of Biomechanics* for Routledge. Rose is a teacher trainer and member of the Professional Association of Alexander Teachers www.paat.org.uk.

Spencer Wood (He/Him) is a queer writer and teacher living in Leeds. His poetry has been published in *fourteen poems*; *Alchemy Spoon*; Broken Sleep Book's *Masculinity; An Anthology of Modern Voices*; *Strix and Modern Queer Poets*; amongst others. His poem "falling backwards holding glass" was highly commended in the 2023 Verve Poetry Competition. Spencer's creative non-fiction has been published in *Hinterland*.

Ray Young (They/Them) is an award-winning performance artist and writer based in London. Their interdisciplinary work is socially engaged and exists on the boundaries between contemporary theatre, live art, and dance. Their work creates space to explore and celebrate intersectional realities through alternative narratives and forms. Ray's work has been presented widely across the UK, including in London, Cambridge, Brighton, Leeds, and Edinburgh, as well as internationally including Portland, Mexico City, and Venezuela. Their groundbreaking contributions to the field of performance art have earned them numerous awards and accolades, and their work continues to push boundaries and challenge conventional notions of what art can be and do. Ray also works as a lecturer, mentor, and outside eye for other artists.

ACKNOWLEDGEMENTS

First and foremost, I want to express my deepest gratitude to the contributors of this volume, Maria Ignatieva, Peta Tait, Lisa Peck, Bella Merlin, Samia La Virgne, Barry Fitzgerald, and Spencer Wood, for your patience and generosity working with me as editor. Secondly, I would like to thank our esteemed interlocutors, Rose Whyman, Maria Brígida De Miranda, and Ray Young, for their engagement and willingness to dialogue. This volume and the "Stanislavsky And..." series would not exist without the support and kindness of the commissioning editor, Paul Fryer, who has demonstrated inspiring vision and scope in creating and guiding this collection. I am also incredibly grateful to Claire Margerison, Lucia Accorsi, and Steph Hines at Routledge for their support and direction. I also thank Oberon Books and Bloomsbury Publishing for their permissions.

The publication began as a webinar, part of *The S Word: Stanislavsky and the Contemporary Theatre* series created in 2015 by Bella Merlin and Paul Fryer, the Stanislavsky Research Centre. In December 2021, I invited panellists and moderated the *Stanislavsky and Gender* webinar, co-hosted by the School of Performance and Cultural Industries, University of Leeds and the School of Performing Arts, University of Malta. The webinar included valued contributions from Professor J. Ellen Gainor (Cornell University) and Professor Baron Kelly (University of Wisconsin Madison). The organisation of the webinar and the opportunity to edit the following publication, *Stanislavsky and Gender*, became possible because of the expert mentorship I have received in my postgraduate education. Jessica Hartley and Ian Morgan at the Royal Central School of Speech and Drama between 2014 and 2016, who led me to postgraduate research with Maria Kapsali and Jonathan Pitches at the School of Performance and Cultural Industries, University of Leeds, have both gently challenged and steered me throughout my doctoral research with care, honesty, and compassion. I also sincerely thank mentors on this academic journey: James Palm, George Rodosthenous, Aylwyn Walsh, Fiona Bannon, Tony Gardner, Alice O'Grady, Anna Fenemore, Helen Finch, and Mel Prideaux.

The research *Stanislavsky and Gender* builds upon benefits significantly from the work of many women, whom I cannot name individually (partly for fear of missing someone) but to whom I am inspired by and grateful.

Finally, I am always indebted to the grace and unconditional love of friends and family, who make anything I do possible.

STANISLAVSKY AND GENDER

Introduction

Mark Shields

Konstantin Stanislavsky: Man and Myth

The global impact of Konstantin Stanislavsky on the performing arts invites new questions informed by ongoing debates about his enduring influence as a prominent male figure of twentieth and twenty-first-century theatre and performance.

Sharon Carnicke deliberately conjures a rhetorical "mythic image" of Stanislavsky to deconstruct and dispel misconceptions of him and his legacy that are remarkably gendered (Carnicke, 2009, 3). She observes how the idea of Stanislavsky as "[a] grandfatherly figure in a pince-nez who reveals the secrets of great acting to insecure young students" (Carnicke, 2009, 40) has transcended an immediate audience within the performing arts, entering popular culture more broadly as "our archetypal image of the acting teacher" (Carnicke, 2009, 9). Often credited as a 'genius' and the 'father' and 'master' of modern theatre directing and acting, his theories and techniques are considered 'seminal'; perhaps it is this masculinised image of Stanislavsky which personifies many issues still troubling the performing arts today. Carnicke comments that although this simplified caricature is imprecise, it is often this impression of Stanislavsky which is at odds with contemporary theatre and performance scholarship because it is "too patriarchal for feminist actors and theorists, too essentialist for scholars of performance studies, and too absolute for contemporary theatre artists in a multicultural, unsure age" (Carnicke, 2009, 1). Despite this, many scholars in Stanislavsky research, including Sharon Carnicke, have determinedly deconstructed this popularised image of Stanislavsky to demonstrate that a once-living human being was much more complicated and contradictory.

DOI: 10.4324/9781003411611-1

Social Constructivism and Gender: Empire, Romanticism, Modernism, and Sovietism

Gender is not a recent phenomenon or trend. Stanislavsky was not immune to how social, political, and cultural changes influenced ideas about gender, as his lifetime spanned the last years of Imperial Russia, the Russian Revolution, the Civil and First World Wars, and the Soviet Union.

The binary gender categories of 'Male' and 'Female' are entwined with imperialism and colonialism. First Nations, Indigenous, Pre-Colonial, Global South, and Global Majority people have expressed and organised gender differently and expansively across their respective cultures outside of the narrow and strictly prescribed gender binary of 'Man' and 'Woman'. Decolonial scholars have evidenced how imperialism and colonialism imposed racialised and classed binary genders as 'universal' categories to divide and conquer nations, justified by Abrahamic religious belief systems and eugenics, to dehumanise non-white people, construct, and validate white innocence.[1]

The effects of imperialism and colonialism on gender are still felt. Victor Madrigal-Borloz, the independent expert on sexual orientation and gender identity appointed to the United Nations (UN), reported in 2023,

> Most colonial projects regulated sexuality and gender as part of their broader enterprise to dominate peoples and territories, and colonization processes account for varied forms of violence and discrimination against individuals of diverse [Sexual Orientation and Gender Identity]. Colonial oppression, inextricably tied to capitalism, imposed systems of differentiation, hierarchization and domination to exercise strict control over colonized peoples. This was done through conversion to the colonizer's religious institutions, the imposition of a rigid gender binary on colonized peoples, and the criminalization of gender and sexual non-conformity with models decided arbitrarily by the colonial authorities.
>
> *(Madrigal-Borloz, 3)*

The implications of Russia's transition from the late nineteenth century into the twentieth century for gender are manifold. Towards the end of Imperial Russia, aristocratic women engaged with philanthropy after the end of serfdom and before state-approved socialism, helping to transform the social and political mobility of working-class women who experienced gender and class oppression. Leon Trotsky considered the women's textile workers' demonstration, joined by soldier's female relatives on International Women's Day in Petrograd 1917 for food, the end of the First World War, and Tsarism, as an inaugural event of the Russian Revolution, with the abdication of Tsar Nicholas II and the provisional government permitting women the right to vote days after (Trotsky, 2008, 75).

The history of Russia during this time demonstrates that a social constructivist perspective on gender, instead of gender exclusively determined by biological sex, is not a recent social, cultural, political, or theoretical development.

The Bolshevik Revolution brought with it new ideologies of gender – the New Soviet Man and Woman. Writing in 1924 on 'Revolutionary and Socialist Art', Trotsky described,

> Man will make it his purpose to master his own feelings, to raise his instincts to the heights of consciousness, to make them transparent, to extend the wires of his will into hidden recesses, and thereby to raise himself to a new plane, to create a higher social biologic type, or, if you please, a superman.
>
> *(Trotsky, 2007, 207)*

Lynne Attwood further outlines the Bolshevik social constructivist perspective on gender:

> The notion that it was possible to create a new type of person, fully committed to the socialist cause and willing to put the interests of society above his or her personal desires, was fundamental to the Bolshevik project. According to Marxist theory there was nothing innate about human personality and behaviour; these were social constructs, formed through interaction with the social environment. It must be possible, then, to reconstruct them.
>
> *(Attwood, 1)*

Revolutionary leader Vladimir Lenin claimed that the New Soviet Woman occupied "the exact same position as men" (Lenin, 69). However, Attwood explains, "The revolutionaries were agreed that women had to be freed from domestic servitude and drawn into social production. [...] As well as being workers themselves, they also had to produce the next generation of workers" (Attwood, 1–2). These 'rationalist' and 'romantic' beliefs about womanhood and femininity created a dichotomy for the New Soviet Woman (Attwood, 3). The former considered women to be "a vital economic resource and should be involved in the public world of production", and the latter believed women were "naturally more tender, loving, and nurturing than men; they were the moral backbone of society, providing a humanising influence" (Attwood, 3).[2]

The influence of Romanticism on Stanislavsky can be detected in characteristics of his artistic ethos – originality, subjectivity, imagination, the importance of 'nature', the moral purpose of the artist, and emotion in creative expression.[3] Stanislavsky was enamoured with the romantic idea of the male genius, demonstrated in his admiration of Italian actor Tommaso Salvini and the canonical figures of Russian Literature, Gogol, Dostoevsky, Pushkin, and

Tolstoy.[4] The status of 'genius' has also been bestowed on Stanislavsky as the heir to imperial Russian actor Mikhail Shchepkin, considered the "father of Russian realistic acting" (Borovsky, 254), and mentor to Stanislavsky's teacher, Glikeria Fedotova. Stanislavsky was inspired by Shchepkin in his "near-religious devotion to acting" (Carnicke, 2009, 175). David Higgins notes that the "principle modern usage of the word 'genius'" which emerged in the early eighteenth century is reflected in the *Oxford English Dictionary* definition:

> Innate intellectual or creative power of an exceptional or exalted type, such as is attributed to those people considered greatest in any area of art, science, etc., instinctive, and extraordinary capacity for imaginative creation, original thought, invention, or discovery.
>
> *(Higgins, 1; OED, 2014)*

The romantic idea of the male creative genius gains further significance through Modernism because of "the modernists' elevation of art to the status of 'secular religion'" (Schuler, 2) and the Modernist "ideal of the God-like artist" (Lewis, 35). Moreover, the artistic male genius in Russia, the "*khudozhnik*", had a moral vocation, influenced by German Romanticism (Whyman, 15) – "an inspired artist, and a master who brings disciples together, and guides them in art and life" (Autant-Mathieu & Wautlet, 173).

Marianne Devoken discusses the intersection of gender and Modernism, observing how "[t]he radical implications of the social-cultural changes feminism advocated produced in modernist writing an unprecedented preoccupation with gender" (Devoken, 174). She elaborates further that "Much of this preoccupation expressed a male modernist fear of women's new power and resulted in the combination of misogyny and triumphal masculinism" (Devoken, 174). The reaction to growing feminism described by Devoken also produced "its dialectal twin: fascination and strong identification with the empowered feminine" (Devoken, 174).

Catherine Schuler examines Charlotte Rosenthal's (1992) claim that the Modernist's reverence of art and "concomitant emphasis on 'individual creativity' encouraged women to step outside traditional roles" (Schuler, 2). Schuler writes that conversely, "it might be argued that modernism and the attendant rise of the neo Wagerian master artist hastened the demise of starring actresses, displaced actress-entrepreneurs, and chased 'women's themes' from the stage" (Schuler, 2).

In *Women in Russian Theatre: The Actress in the Silver Age* (1996), Schuler examines the proliferation of Russian actresses at the end of the nineteenth century. The abolition of serfdom, industrialisation, the relaxation of censorship laws with developments in printing and burgeoning feminism in the West inevitably influenced the women's emancipation movement in Russia before Bolshevism (Schuler, 6–7). She notes the complexity of this growing feminism, "Although Russian women enjoyed certain privileges denied to women in more progressive nations of Western Europe, at the dawn of the twentieth century, Russia was still a rigidly patriarchal, authoritarian autocracy" (Schuler, 5). Similarly to Attwood, Schuler writes that during this time,

> The early leaders of women's emancipation movement were the first to challenge biologically based apologies for sex discrimination. Embracing Darwinian theory insofar as it sustained a constructionist point of view, they argued that environment, not biology was the chief determinant of individual development.
>
> *(Schuler, 8)*

Regarding the social construction of gender, Schuler further elaborates, "An important ideological 'side effect' of the gender war that was sparked between feminists and their detractors was the destabilization of conventional femininity, or '*zhenstvennost*', a phenomenon that had tremendous resonance in theatre" (Schuler, 8).

Zhenstvennost: The Feminine Ideal

Anke Hilbrenner examines how *zhenstvennost*, "the Soviet gender ideal" (Hilbrenner, 296), was frequently revised to serve the political developments of the Soviet Union and lasted well into the Brezhnev years after de-Stalinisation. She defines *zhenstvennost* by explaining, "It does not refer to a mere aesthetic concept but signifies a certain form of inner beauty composed of supposedly female traits, such as altruism, mental balance, compassion, grace, subordination and motherhood" (Hilbrenner, 299). Moreover, Schuler explains that Russian conservatives and opposition to women's emancipation during the nineteenth and twentieth centuries in Russia "expended tremendous energy shoring up an increasingly inadequate system of beliefs about '*zhenstvennost*' that required physical and intellectual inferiority as God-given attributes of the female sex" (Schuler, 9).

Schuler argues, "It was the debate between feminists and their detractors over 'woman's nature' that destabilized '*zhenstvennost*' as a fixed term of cultural discourse", explaining that "[t]he debate over '*zhenstvennost*' focused public attention on actresses largely because in Russia they were the most visible, concrete embodiments of gender qualities and ideals" (Schuler, 11). Consequently, according to Schuler, the debate surrounding Romantic and Modernist interpretations of *zhenstvennost* coincided with the professionalisation and proliferation of Russian actresses at the end of the nineteenth century. As a result, "actresses became highly visible representatives of, and concrete points of reference for both the preservation of old, and the construction of new models of '*zhenstvennost*'" (Schuler, 11). Celebrated actresses of the time,

Maria Gavrilovna Savina, Maria Nikolayevna Yermolova, Glikeria Nikolaevna Fedotova, and, later, Vera Fyodorovna Komissarzhevskaya, with the latter two both teachers of Stanislavsky, embodied and preserved the Russian gender ideal of *zhenstvennost* in performance, which secured their success and maintained their popularity with Russian audiences.

Both Tommaso Salvini and Eleonora Duse were idols worshipped by Stanislavsky, with Stanislavsky repeatedly referring to Salvini as a genius throughout his autobiography *My Life in Art*. He confesses to imitating Salvini as Othello early in his career and the influence of Salvini's performance on him as a young actor and director.[5] He repeatedly uses Salvini as an example for the fictional students in his pedagogical narratives to aspire to (Stanislavski, 2010a). Henry James, a key figure in Modernist literature, reviewing Salvini's performance as Othello in 1883, describes Salvini's masculinity in his "powerful, active, manly frame" (James, 379). Comparatively, described by critics as "most feminine of all women" (Kugel, 317; Schuler, 14), Eleonora Duse was akin to a theatrical Virgin Mother, with Alexsander Kugel writing that "through her suffering, she purified our souls" (Kugel, 311; Schuler, 14).

While admiring the artistry of Italian actors Salvini and Duse, Stanislavsky and Russian critics found the famous French actress Sarah Bernhardt to be a stark contrast. They considered her typical of what Stanislavsky called "the art of representation" (Stanislavski, 2010a, 22; Schuler, 13; Autant-Mathieu & Wautlet, 173). Though Stanislavsky's interest in spirituality and its influence on the system was significantly censored under Sovietism,[6] he considered the art of representation antithetical to the God-like creative state of *ya yesm*, the Supertask of the system, which Maria Shevtsova defines as "'I am in God and God is in me' in spirit and body; [...] the attitude underpinning '*ya yesm*' is 'I am attentive to my state of oneness with God'" (Shevtsova, 101).

Though Russia was sceptical of Western ideas, such influences on nineteenth- and twentieth-century Russian feminism cannot be disregarded. Schuler acknowledges Bernhardt's debut in Russia in 1881 as a landmark moment for the debate around *zhenstvennost*, describing her as the "antithesis of traditional gender/sex ideology", that "Bernhardt was correctly perceived by conservative critics as a subversive influence" (Schuler, 13). Bernhardt, Schuler argues, "offered them a model of rebellious individualism that contradicted the very essence of Russian '*zhenstvennost*'" (Schuler, 14). By comparison, Russian critics, and Stanislavsky, preferred Eleonora Duse, who, Schuler states, "at least superficially, embodied many of the sex/gender ideals" which she lists as "monogamous relationships with their husbands [...] silence, subservience, obedience, humility, modesty in dress, devotion to children, and emotional restraint" (Schuler, 14). Schuler asserts that Duse made a success of Henrik Ibsen's character Nora in *A Doll's House* when she toured Russia from 1891 to 1908, a character which had previously troubled Russian critics and audiences. Duse's interpretation was considered "less threatening than

Bernhardt precisely because the qualities of '*zhenstvennost*' she exhibited – modesty, restrained elegance, maternal feeling, devotion to her man, self-sacrifice, and elevated idealism were familiar and acceptable in the Russian context" (Schuler, 15).

Schuler explains that Bernhardt and Duse became benchmarks to which Russian actresses were frequently compared and aspired. Bernhardt and Duse also inspired Russian actresses to become entrepreneurs through their prototype celebrity (Schuler, 16). Schuler notes, however, that Russian actresses who "imitated their western counterparts, especially the French" like Bernhardt, "were often accused of contributing to the demise of Russian drama and theatre (and indirectly to the destruction of the family)" in their perceived pursuit of fame and celebrity, fashion, and money, which critics condemned as "antithetical to authentic art and traditional '*zhenstvennost*'" (Schuler, 16).

Schuler points to the misogynist depictions of actresses during this time, referring to the increasingly sensationalist "stream of articles appearing between 1890 and 1916 in major theatre journals about actresses dying from hunger, engaging in prostitution, or committing suicide" because of the lack of work or low pay, purportedly caused by the influx of women to the theatre (Schuler, 16). Schuler then observes the mimetic effect of these representations on artistic portrayals of actresses during this time, commenting, "Judging by the amount of fiction published about actresses in this period, tragical, pseudo-documentary tales of distressed young women filled with romantic illusions about service and sacrifice to art and nation were extraordinarily popular with the literate public" (Schuler, 18).

The Russian actresses of the Imperial theatres embodied and maintained the romantic Russian gender ideal of *zhenstvennost* through performance. As Russian feminists began challenging essentialist beliefs about women, the Bolshevik Revolution adopted a social constructivist perspective on gender to facilitate broader social and political reform, influenced by and influencing Russian feminism. Conservatives, however, maintained biologically essentialist ideas of women and femininity based on the romantic and nationalist notion of *zhenstvennost*. The New Soviet Woman was caught between a romantic *zhenstvennost* and becoming a more industrious, equitable comrade. Gender roles through Romanticism endorsed men as geniuses and women as naturally maternal, sacred, and subordinate to men. The status of art as an almost secularised form of religion and artists as God-like geniuses further consolidated men's power during Modernism, who feared the newly empowered feminine.

Feminist Perspectives on the Stanislavsky Tradition

The fermata in feminism between its seismic second and progressive third waves, controversially labelled 'Post-Feminism', provided opportunities for reflection on progress and to reorganise efforts for women's liberation. During this time, feminist critiques of the Stanislavsky tradition in the US emerged. Jane Ann Crum and Joel Schecter, in the afterword of the 1985 volume of the journal *Theater*, in which Linda Walsh Jenkins and Susan Ogden-Malouf's "The (Female) Actor Prepares" is published, note, "If we have now entered an era of 'post-feminism', as some commentators assert, the issues which feminists raised over the past decades are still very much alive and unsettled in the theater as elsewhere" (Crum and Schecter, 95).

Walsh Jenkins and Ogden-Malouf raise pertinent questions for a gendered examination of the Stanislavsky tradition. Although their chosen title suggests otherwise, they do not refer to Stanislavsky directly, possibly to avoid conflating Stanislavsky's system with training that cites him as a positive influence, instead, naming the Method and its variations as troubling for the female actor (Walsh Jenkins and Ogden-Malouf, 66).

Walsh Jenkins and Ogden-Malouf question the power of the acting teacher, who "frequently serves as an all-knowing guru for whom the performer must be absolutely vulnerable (opening the way to both psychological and sexual exploitation)", explaining,

> When a female is asked to align with an unhealthy gender role, to search for self-revelations that are demeaning, and to yield personal autonomy to a potentially exploitive authority figure, a syzygy occurs that usually reinforces the woman's already negative ontological development.
>
> *(Walsh Jenkins and Ogden-Malouf, 66)*

Walsh Jenkins and Ogden-Malouf suggest strategies for training and rehearsing with gender consciousness based on interviews with various feminist practitioners. In the fourth chapter of this volume, Samia La Virgne provides an insightful evaluation of these proposals from an intersectional perspective as a Black female actor. It is Walsh Jenkins and Ogden-Malouf's hope that "[i]f the journey toward production can be liberated from gender oppression, perhaps itself will be so as well" (Walsh Jenkins and Ogden-Malouf, 66).

Walsh Jenkins and Ogden-Malouf cite Sue Ellen Case in their feminist reassessment of training, who, observing the rise of feminism in academic disciplines in the 1980s, writes in *Feminism and Theatre*, initially published in 1988,

> The psychological construction of character, using techniques adapted from Stanislavski, places the female actor within the range of systems that have oppressed her very representation on stage. The techniques for the inner construction of a character rely on Freudian principles, leading the female actor into that misogynistic view of female sexuality.
>
> *(Case, 122)*

Elaine Aston (1999; 2005) repeats Case's critique of Stanislavsky to reject "the objectification of women in the realist tradition, and in particular, to the character-based, Method acting, derived from the teachings of Constantin Stanislavski" (Aston, 7). Respectively, Jill Dolan (1988; 2012) and Elin Diamond (1997; 2006) also question oppressive representations of women in realist drama and acting techniques associated with Stanislavsky.

Lauren Love (2002) also critiques the pervasiveness of methodologies inspired by Stanislavsky in US actor training that promote "so-called universal human attributes and values" in pursuit of "*Truth*" (Love, 278, original emphasis). Love argues "liberal humanist ideals that privilege dominant ideologies as 'natural'" underpin methodologies in the US Stanislavsky tradition before arguing that "Post-modern, materialist feminist and queer theory discourses (among others) problematize this essentialism" (Love, 278). She claims that such belief "fantasizes an ontological space which is untouched by ideological operations and contestations" (Love, 278). Love also identifies that "psychological processes (as delineated by Freud)" have become "the privileged, indeed exclusive, route toward creating a character" in US actor training (Love, 279). As a result, Love observes, "The experiences of the disenfranchised are then rendered invisible when the privileged class's experiences are represented as 'universal' and 'true'" (Love, 280).

Similarly to Walsh Jenkins and Ogden-Malouf, Love discusses an alternative approach of practising a heightened feminine style of Camp performance when portraying misogynistic characters to resist uncritical discourses of 'natural' and 'organic' in the rehearsal room and on stage that are often uninterrogated but commonplace (Love, 284).

These feminist critiques of the US Stanislavsky tradition raise questions about actor training that are still relevant. The unequal power dynamic between the acting teacher and their students who are vulnerable to exploitation by them, and the recurrence of sexist characters in male-dominated dramatic canon that women actors are required to psychologically and physically align themselves with in rehearsal and performance using techniques at least partly inspired by Stanislavsky are both noted by Walsh Jenkins and Ogden-Malouf and Love. Additionally, Love challenges dogmatic approaches to acting that espouse a pseudoscientific technique based on appropriated understandings of psychology, rigid opinions about 'truth', Stanislavsky's beliefs about universal human nature,[7] and the absence of critical discourse on these dominant ideologies, as detrimental to the woman actor's development and well-being.

Walsh Jenkins and Ogden-Malouf, and Love focus their arguments primarily on American interpretations of Stanislavsky's work, specifically the Method, and iterations of Stanislavsky-based practices after the work of the Group Theatre in the US during the mid-twentieth century, influenced by psychology and responding to realist innovations in drama. Despite repeated efforts to distinguish between Stanislavsky's system and the 'Method', conflations persist,[8] though that is not to say that problems similar to those identified by these feminist scholars in their respective contexts do not exist elsewhere and have occurred more recently. However, there is ambiguity about the prevalence of issues identified by feminist scholars related to methodologies and pedagogies outside of the Stanislavsky tradition in actor training, which is not to say they do not exist elsewhere.

Writing in 2008, Vreneli Farber comments that in the post-Soviet acting classes that she observed, "A number of remarks made by teachers [...] conformed to gender stereotypes" (Farber, 189). She provides several examples that she witnessed:

> [A male teacher] instructed one male student to be masculine in his activity and told male students to remove their earrings, saying that when he sees boys wearing earrings, it gives him a strange sensation, for men need to be men. Girls, on the other hand, should be pretty and wear jewelry and they need to develop these qualities.
>
> *(Farber, 189)*

It is essential to consider the previous remarks within the political context of Dmitry Medvedev and Vladimir Putin's Russia, which has demonstrated its persistent violent hostility towards LGBTQIA+ people and the impact of these policies on attitudes towards gender normativity. Since the early 2000s, Russia introduced several prohibitive regional and federal laws on the so-called "propaganda of non-traditional sexual relationships", which viewed the "international LGBT movement" as an "extremist organisation", described as predatory and corrupting of Russian minors and intended to cause "social and religious discord" in the country (Human Rights Watch, 2023). However, outside of Russia, in response to the MeToo and Black Lives Matter movements, several student and professional actors came forwards, typically on social media, and shared their experiences of discrimination in actor training. Despite Russia's recent and current politics, the nature of the comments that Farber observed in Russia could have also been made in acting classrooms in London, New York, and further afield.

Though Lauren Love (2002) criticises practices that deny ideological influences are at play in actor training,[9] these feminist perspectives on the Stanislavsky tradition in the US could also go much further in addressing the experiences of those who do not benefit from what bell hooks called "white supremacist capitalist patriarchy" (hooks, 4), who are LGBTQIA+ or otherwise queer and gender non-confirming, of the Global Majority and Global South, disabled and neurodivergent, working class and poor, who are marginalised and experience intersections in their identities and exceed these imperfect categories, experiencing less privilege than others. It is also crucial not to underestimate that the concerns raised repeatedly by feminists within the performing arts are part of a broader global context where violence against women and gender inequalities that oppress women have always been and continue to be prevalent.

Several scholars have identified that Stanislavsky's thinking about the actor's psychology predates the popularity of Freud's psychoanalysis,[10] that instead he favoured theories by French psychologist Théodule-Armand Ribot,[11] and that the similarities between Freud and Stanislavsky's ideas are largely coincidental. Instead, Freud's influence had a more significant impact on the American interpretations of Stanislavsky's work and Psychological Realism, including the Method. Sharon Carnicke also clarifies Stanislavsky's association with behaviourism and the Soviet psychologist Ivan Pavlov:

> Following Stanislavsky's death, however, those aspects of Ribot's work that link him to Yoga were wilfully ignored in the USSR, while those who anticipate behaviorism were studied more deeply than records warrant. Soviet scholars and practitioners were fulfilling expectations by providing politically correct readings of Stanislavsky. They used scant evidence to manufacture a deep connection between Pavlovian behaviorism and the System.
>
> *(Carnicke, 2009, 163)*

Carnicke comments further, "In short, Russia's acting lore promoted the System's overstated link to behaviorism as common coin. The force of this linkage was so persuasive that the Method too assumes that this scientific heritage is accurate", as Strasberg characterised the Method as Pavlovian behaviourist conditioning above Freudian psychology (Carnicke, 2009, 163).

Stanislavsky's association with Naturalism and Realism is also cause for feminist concern because he theorised "living the role" (Stanislavski, 2010a, 160), agitated further by misogynistic roles for women written and directed by men, the prevalence of Psychological Realism, and American interpretations of his work that were influenced by popular psychology.

Naturalism and Realism, however, were already popular in art and literature before Stanislavsky founded the Moscow Art Theatre in 1898 with Nemirovich-Danchenko, emerging in Europe in the mid-1800s as Romanticism gave way to Modernism. Russian writers Gogol, Dostoevsky, Pushkin, Tolstoy, Turgenev, and Chekhov, as well as Ostrovsky and Shchepkin in theatre, all engaged in Naturalism and Realism. European playwrights Henrik Ibsen, August Strindberg, Émile Zola, David Garrick, John Synge, George Bernard Shaw, to name a few men as examples, that either predate or intersect with Stanislavsky's career, also used Naturalism and Realism, respectively. Women playwrights such as British Cicely Hamilton and Americans Elizabeth Robins and Susan Glaspell also explored ideas about Modernism's New Woman using Realism influenced by their feminism and suffragist activism. J. Ellen Gainor, conducting a contextual analysis of Susan Glaspell's work, cautions:

> we do need to be aware that the term *realism*, like the term *feminism*, [...] has come to be seen by theorists as too broad. In identifying multiple forms of realism, as well as feminism, critics have realized that such designations require specific contextualizing.
>
> *(Gainor, 2001, 58, original emphasis)*

Stanislavsky and Nemirovich-Danchenko in their leadership of the Moscow Art Theatre needed to respond to realist innovations in drama and take advantage of the financial benefit international tours. Stanislavsky was also inspired by the realistic crowd scenes and popularity of the Saxe-Meiningen ensemble that toured Russia in 1890 and technological innovations in scenography early in his career (Merlin, 2004, 1–37; Carnicke, 2009, 29). The desire that Stanislavsky could resist the influence of Realism across the West would be exceptional and becomes further complicated as he was expected to conform to Socialist Realism under Stalin (Carnicke, 2009, 39). Carnicke provides a detailed overview of the Moscow Art Theatre's complicated relationship with the Stalin regime, which enhances a critical view on Stanislavsky's universal ambitions for the system:

> Under Stalin, Stanislavsky and his company garnered extraordinary privileges denied to others. [...] Such indulgences followed upon Stalin's decision to promote the Theatre's interest in nineteenth century realism as the model for twentieth century Socialist Realism [...] and Stanislavsky's System as the official curriculum as the official curriculum for all Soviet theatrical institutes. [...] The Moscow Art Theatre had walked a tightrope in the early years after the revolution, balancing severe criticism of its bourgeois repertory against insidious governmental support which threatened to stifle free artistic expression.
>
> *(Carnicke, 2009, 85)*

Stanislavsky also notably worked with other genres, styles, and aesthetics, including Symbolism, Farce, Melodrama, Shakespeare, and Opera (Merlin, 2007, 182). The publishing of *An Actor Prepares* in English, translated and edited by Elizabeth Hapgood Reynolds in 1936, also confounds the association of Stanislavsky with Psychological Realism. *An Actor Prepares*, which only tells the first year of Stanislavsky's proposed three-year fictional training, focuses on *perezhivanie* or 'experiencing' the role and included his ideas about Emotion Memory influenced by Ribot. Although chapters on action, imagination, concentration and attention, relaxation, and units and objectives appear before emotion, publishing *An Actor Prepares* in 1936 as a single volume in

English erroneously inferred the importance of an exclusively psychological approach which was no doubt further exploited. Stanislavsky's 1938 Soviet edition *Rabota aktera nad soboi*, or *An Actor's Work on Himself*, reintegrated *perezhivanie* with the proposed fictional second year of training with its emphasis on embodiment as part of his psychophysical technique, edited by Lyubov Gurevich. Twelve years after *An Actor Prepares*, *Building a Character*, also translated and edited by Hapgood Reynolds in English, was published as a separate volume in 1948 and then *Creating a Role* in 1957 (Carnicke, 1984, 2009; Benedetti, 2010, xxi).

Stanislavsky's early experiments with Realism, particularly in performing emotion, were disseminated prematurely by actors who left the Moscow Art Theatre before Stanislavsky had fully developed his system (Pitches, 2006, 88; Carnicke, 2009, 84). Despite continuing experimentation with rehearsal practices throughout his life, Stanislavsky's ideas inevitably evolved (Aquilina, 2013). Even before his arrival in the US, émigré ex-Moscow Art Theatre actors were spreading various forms of his system including Russian actress Alla Nazimova (Pitches, 2006, 88). The influence of Russian director Theodore Komisarjevsky in the UK also perpetuated myths about a purely psychological Stanislavskian approach, arguably to disparage him (Pitches, 2012; Shevtsova, 246). The work of David Belasco and Elizabeth Robins, and Susan Glaspell's work in the US also reflects a burgeoning interest in Psychological Realism in American theatre that predates the American Moscow Art Theatre tours 1923–1924.[12] Stanislavsky later clarified his notion of artistic truth in his Soviet notebooks, evidenced by Carnicke (2009, 144), writing "the actor's experiencing on stage is not at all the same as it is in life" (Stanislavski, 1991, IV, 380) and commenting further "On stage truth is whatever you believe and in life truth is what actually is" (Stanislavski, 1999, VI, 81–82).

The Stanislavsky tradition in the US has its own well-researched history and contestations. Rhonda Blair, in her introduction as editor of the 2010 edition of Richard Boleslavsky's *Acting: The First Six Lessons*, identifies Boleslavsky as the main conduit of the initial transmission of Stanislavsky's ideas in the US (Blair, 2010, ix).

Boleslavsky attended the Moscow Art Theatre in 1906, aged 17, before joining the company a year later, performing extensively, and becoming a member of the First Studio, where Leopold Sulerzhitsky and Yevgeny Vakhtangov also influenced him. He founded the American Theatre Laboratory in 1923 during the Moscow Art Theatre tours in the US, attended by, notably, Lee Strasberg and, later, Stella Adler (Blair, 2010, ix–x)

Blair notes the significant gender differences in Boleslavsky's use of a pedagogical dialogue as a narrative device for his writing, compared to Stanislavsky. She explains, "The way in which the book's 'I' (Boleslavsky's designation for his surrogate self) speaks to and of 'the Creature' has understandably been an obstacle to some of us who encountered [Boleslavsky's writing] after the rise of feminism" (Blair, 2010, xii). Though Blair counterargues, "[W]hile Boleslavsky's representation of 'the Creature' is certainly problematic, I am not certain that it is more problematic than the virtual absence of women except as supporting characters in Stanislavsky's books" (Blair, 2010, xii). Jonathan Pitches also suggests that the pedagogical relationship between 'I' and 'the Creature' in Boleslavsky's writing has some resemblance to Stanislavsky's relationship with Olga Knipper during rehearsals for the 1909 production of Ivan Turgenev's *A Month in the Country* (Pitches, 2006, 103), a relationship which Peta Tait analyses later in the second chapter of this volume. Pitches writes that "the relationship between the two ['I' and 'the Creature'] is redolent of the popular understanding of a patient's relationship with their psychiatrist – confessional, needy, private" which he argues "parallels exactly the experience of Ribot's Madame X" (Pitches, 2006, 104), one example of how psychotherapeutic relationships influenced actor training pedagogy in the US at the time and its depiction and transmission in writing.

In her editorial, Blair makes a critical feminist intervention by restoring Maria Ouspenskaya's contribution to the American Stanislavsky tradition. Ouspenskaya avoided writing about her pedagogy (Carnicke, 2009, 61). Blair observes how "Boleslavsky's work with students was primarily in masterclasses and lectures", whereas Maria Ouspenskaya "was the one in the 'trenches' teaching acting every year" (Blair, 2010, xv). Blair also mentions that Boleslavsky "is generally described by his students as being warm and approachable". In contrast, actress Blanche Tannock Hogg describes Ouspenskaya as having "a fierce, demanding quality", commenting,

> I know I for one, and I think most people were really terrified of her. Her classes were both a delight and a torture. [...] And once she had kind of broken you on the rack of this kind of horrible experience, from then on you had much more freedom, much less fear of showing emotion.
>
> *(Tannock Hogg, in Willis, 2; Blair, 2010, xvi)*

Blair's inclusion of this anecdote regarding Ouspenskaya's pedagogy as a female acting teacher offers a vital counterpoint to arguments about the gender differences of the student's vulnerability and the power of usually male teachers. Tannock Hogg's experience of Ouspenskaya shows that the intimidation and potential exploitation of the actor's vulnerability by the acting teacher and director is not exclusively a problem with male acting teachers and directors, though possibly explained by their prevalence in the field. Though, this instance does not diminish gendered perspectives on this persistent problem. Within the American Stanislavsky tradition, Rosemary Malague notes Uta Hagen's ambivalence to feminism (Malague, 2012, 169) and in a British context, Nadine Holdsworth argues that it is "inaccurate to refer to [Joan Littlewood] as a feminist", as Littlewood once declared, "I don't believe in that stuff. … I'm not a feminist" (Holdsworth, 2011). Anecdotal evidence such as Tannock Hogg's and the reputation of Joan Littlewood for her scathing admonishments of her actors, for example, challenge an essentialist belief that women acting teachers and directors are *naturally* kinder, more ethical, empathetic, compassionate, and even feminist. Perhaps Stanislavsky's belief in traditional *zhenstvennost* influenced his opinion that women are better suited to pedagogy than theatre directing as Maria Ignatieva explores in her chapter and discusses with Rose Whyman. Just as Russian conservatives perpetuated myths about the destitute and impoverished actress, the trope of the tortured artist also reinforces beliefs about actor training pedagogy being necessarily traumatic. There is also the likelihood of inevitable dissatisfaction with early actor training pedagogies because they simply do not compare well to our contemporary standards, politics, ethics, and desires.

J. Ellen Gainor, responding to earlier feminist critiques of the Stanislavsky tradition included here, asks the question,

> [I]s Stanislavskian acting theory fundamentally at odds with feminist theatre practice, or is it evidence from the application of those techniques in key historical, creative contexts that is the real—even if not overtly acknowledged—object of the feminist critique?
>
> *(Gainor, 2002, 165)*

Gainor reviews the aims of feminism and theatre in the US, and critiques of the Stanislavsky tradition (Gainor, 2002, 163). In her reply to Elaine Aston (1999), Gainor comments, "Aston ostensibly rejects the Stanislavskian tradition in preference to techniques derived from Brecht. Yet she simultaneously offers […] a number of acting exercises that originated in the Stanislavskian System" (Gainor, 2002, 164). Gainor argues for caution, stating, "[Aston's] failure to acknowledge the source of the techniques she espouses must prompt us to question the over-simplified polarization of these acting methodologies within feminist theatre criticism" (Gainor, 2002, 165).

Gainor highlights two distinct groups of women influenced by feminism in US theatre: those new to theatre, finding a platform for political agency, and those already in theatre seeking alternatives for their artistry who consequently "regarded their inherited tools and techniques with the greatest suspicion" (Canning, 33; Gainor, 2002, 164). Gainor also recognises, following the feminist arguments regarding the Stanislavsky tradition and its association with Realism:

> Some feminist scholars argue that, in other specific historical contexts (especially those that would not have been influenced by Freud, or by the same understanding of him as existed by the mid-to-late twentieth century, especially in the United States), realist drama could be a site for resistance.
>
> *(Gainor, 2002, 168)*

Onwards, Gainor quotes Stella Adler to describe her experience of misogyny while working with the Group Theatre: "The Group was really a man's theatre. [...] The theatre was aimed at plays for men. They understood men. There were really no women in the Group. The women were ruined, absolutely neglected" (Adler in Chinoy, 509, in Gainor, 2002, 166). Gainor also describes "[t]he power and inseparability [...] of scripts, directors and Method actors", how male dominance became consolidated as "[p]laywrights wrote for actors trained in Method techniques. Directors staged their script using Studio actors", commenting further that "we must not underestimate the impact of this triangular structure, which had been in place for at least thirty years, as one prompting resistance" (Gainor, 2002, 167). Though, quoting Elizabeth Stroppel's research on feminist perspectives on the Method, Gainor observes,"[M]any of the Method's tenets still worked for [these] women" (Stroppel, 113 in Gainor, 2002, 169).

Responding to Lauren Love's (2002) argument concerning the power of the often-male director who serves the usually male playwright, disenfranchising women who are required to portray misogynistic roles, Gainor contemplates,

> If, however, we disentangle acting methodologies from the texts that feminist scholars have irrefutably shown are patriarchal (not to mention racist, classist, ageist, etc.), we have the opportunity to re-examine techniques in new contexts, precisely so that we may evaluate their efficacy for performance praxis.
>
> *(Gainor, 2002, 170)*

The successful possibility of separating acting techniques from their developmental contexts to examine them from an exclusively technological perspective and whether this is the desire of feminist practitioners of theatre and performance, is, however, arguable. The examination of techniques for their contemporary efficacy must also respond to misogyny and patriarchal influences in the here and now.

Rhonda Blair, writing in the same issue of *Theatre Topics* as Gainor, draws on cognitive neuroscience to review feminist concerns about Stanislavsky. Making her argument that "we feminists must move beyond responses based on received information and routinized antiessentialism (which itself is a kind of essentialism)" (Blair, 2002, 177). Blair asserts, "Recent developments in cognitive neuroscience and neurophysiology can provide a fruitful way for reengaging issues of feeling, consciousness, and performance, and concomitantly, for reassessing Stanislavsky's contributions to systematizing the actor's process" (Blair, 2002, 177).

Blair notes, "Science is not a final or absolute authority. It is not bias-free", arguing that "it is shortsighted and parochial not to consider applications of scientific knowledge and hypotheses that might inform our understanding of theatre and performance" (Blair, 2002, 177). She shares,

> My personal investment in these issues grows out of a desire better to understand the actor's process and possibly why so many of us who are feminist actors or feminists who work with actors keep returning to the fundamentals of the system; to explore the "rightness" of skepticism about feeling and narrative; and also to counter the ways in which Stanislavsky is misread and abused by mainstream theatre practitioners.
>
> *(Blair, 2002, 179)*

Blair acknowledges the validity of feminist arguments about Realism. However, she notices that these critiques "do not extend beyond cultural, literary, or psychoanalytic studies", bringing attention to the essentialised anti-essentialism in the arguments she refers to earlier (Blair, 2002, 179). Blair summarises that for some feminists, "[Stanislavsky's system] is part of the humanist project of reductively universalizing about experience in order to erase difference; and that, along with Realism, it is inherently patriarchal and misogynist" (Blair, 2002, 179). However, Blair offers the counterargument that such critiques are contradictory because they "[misread] Stanislavsky to justify a decontextualized, hyperpersonalized, emotionalism or narcissism" through exclusively associating Stanislavsky with Psychological Realism, which "ignores the immense range and variety of his work" (Blair, 2002, 179).

Blair assesses Stanislavsky's approach to acting that preceded and yet complement more recent developments in cognitive neuroscience and neurobiology, particularly the research of neuroscientist Antonio Damasio. Blair concludes that the complementary parallels between Stanislavsky's research into actor training and cognitive neuroscience offer an opportunity for feminist actors and acting teachers "to be more rigorous in their understanding of bodies, consciousness, and feelings as they rehearse and perform" because of "the inescapability of the pull to narrativize our experience, as well as the power of engaging a self with the given circumstances of a situation" (Blair, 2002, 189). Reflecting on the continued prevalence of the system in contemporary actor training and in her assessment of how cognitive neuroscience can support and inform Stanislavsky's work, Blair argues that

> If theatre is about illuminating the human condition and making us more conscious of what it means to exist – of what it can mean to be human – then our approaches to it must accommodate our history and our experience in every possible way.
>
> *(Blair, 2002, 189)*

Rosemary Malague, in her monograph *An Actress Prepares: Women and "the Method"* (2012), gives a comprehensive feminist analysis of US acting teachers within the American Stanislavsky tradition from a pedagogical perspective. Reflecting on her own training, which she remarks as "a struggle; it was at best demanding, at worst demoralizing and demeaning" (Malague, 2012, 4–5), Malague critiques the misogyny that begins in the acting classroom which mirrors the performing arts industry: "Since the acting studio frequently serves as an entrée into the theatrical marketplace, the commercial prospects of an acting student – especially her personal attractiveness – are more than likely prejudicial factors in the training she receives" (Malague, 2012, 6), an issue Samia La Virgne also comments on as a Black female actor in her chapter in this volume. Malague notices how the acting classroom serves as a crucible for rehearsing gender normativity:

> What is perhaps unique to the acting class is that it is a setting in which lessons about what men and women "should be" – about how they should behave – are so explicitly repeated and reinforced. Where else might one find so complete and literal an embodiment of Judith Butler's oft-quoted depiction of gender as a "*stylized repetitions of acts*".
>
> *(Malague, 2012, 8, original emphasis; Butler, 270)*

As such expectations are taught, rehearsed, and presented, Malague argues, "The Stanislavskian pedagogical model places at its center a figure who functions as director coach and critic", adding that "[t]he teacher, in this model, becomes the arbiter of truth" (Malague, 2012, 13). However, Malague emphasises the instability of this pedagogic model by commenting, "But once this notion of objectively 'truthful' behaviour is destabilized, how does on the acting teacher judge the actor's 'honesty'?" (Malague, 2012, 13).

In Vreneli Farber's research, she further reported that a particular exercise was introduced "where students mimed throwing shot was a kind of 'sexual' test: some boys throw in a masculine way, some in a feminine way" (Farber, 189), justified again by a male teacher in his opinion:

> [J]ust as in ancient Russia, woman today is a protector and nurturer; in the final result, what counts for her is bearing children. He averred that as soon as a wife has a baby, the husband takes second place to the child. He explained that when a man is lonely, he wants a woman's caresses – something females do not understand – because it is a way for the man to affirm that he is a man.
>
> *(Farber, 189)*

The anecdote reveals how heteronormative and misogynist opinions about gender are reinforced in the contemporary acting class (and nationalist beliefs about *zhenstvennost* in a post-Soviet context, more specifically). Farber documents another example of misogyny: "[the male acting teacher] seemed to encourage sexual overtones in the études with the girls undoing their blouses and baring their breasts" (Farber, 189). Farber's observations on training gender normativity through acting technique and the sexual exploitation of female student actors affirms early feminist concerns on the Stanislavsky tradition and Malague's argument regarding the exploitation of the female actor's personal attractiveness and the power of the acting teacher over their vulnerable students.

Like Gainor (2001, 58; 2002, 168), Malague, who quotes Phillip Zarrilli,[13] highlights how notions of truth and authenticity determined by acting teachers are always context-dependent and, therefore, subject to change (Malague, 2012, 11; Zarrilli, 8). She also notices that Realism can be and is utilised by feminist theatre practitioners too. Malague states that ideas about truth in training and rehearsal, are "often established by the teacher and often by social convention and sexual stereotyping" (Malague, 2012, 13). This observation, Malague argues, then necessitates "expos[ing] the assumptions underlying truth claims made by and on behalf of Stanislavskian acting theory" from a feminist perspective (Malague, 2012, 11). Crucially, Malague also observes that feminist critics and practitioners, in their rejection of the Stanislavsky tradition, infer that "'non-Method' acting as some kind of panacea" but that "there is really not yet enough collected evidence or analysis to determine how 'alternative' actor training programs serve (and treat) women" (Malague, 2012, 205).

Just as Lauren Love (2002) argued that any subjective difference in the training environment can challenge so-called universal and uncritical discourses on truth, Malague contends that "A multicultural presence in the classroom challenges basic assumptions about the universality of Stanislavsky-based, 'truthful' acting" (Malague, 2012, 194). Malague is also the only scholar who challenges "another unacknowledged paradox" that, despite "the obvious fact that gay men and lesbian women have always populated" acting classes and the performing arts industry, "training presumes (or pretends) that an actor's 'natural' impulses will be heterosexual" (Malague, 2012, 13). Malague's call for more diversity is sincere. However, arguments for improved diversity must also acknowledge that any student of difference carries an extra burden when it is determined their responsibility to challenge such beliefs, even with their mere presence, as Samia La Virgne and Barry Fitzgerald also discuss respectively in their chapters. The experiences of marginalised students are recognised by Malague, who places this responsibility on the acting teacher, arguing that "teachers would do well to remember that each student brings his or her own knowledge, experience, and cultural background into the classroom. Not to acknowledge difference is to deny the multiplicity of human truth(s)" (Malague, 2012, 195).

Malague's contention is pedagogical, and the examples she gives are not easily dismissed as isolated instances of bad pedagogy, as the issues she raises are widespread and unremitting, at least across the US Stanislavsky tradition. In her conclusion, she affirms,

> The single most important factor in this tradition of actor training is the teacher. The teacher has nearly all the power. [...] Teachers, even those of us with the very best intentions, may unwittingly bring an array of biases – inherited, ingrained, or all our own – into the classroom.
>
> *(Malague, 2012, 188–189)*

Malague, like Gainor (2002, 170) contemplates the possibility to "'disentangle' Stanislavsky-based actor training from its patriarchal past" but with the caveat that both "teachers and students must heighten their awareness of the pertinent issues; they must bring feminist understanding to theatre theories, techniques, and texts and renegotiate the traditional power dynamic of the acting classroom" where it may often "seem to student actors that their only option is to comply" (Malague, 2012, 188–189).

In her 2013 chapter, "Stanislavsky's System and Women: A Feminist Reading of New Translations", Malague considers more recent edited translations of Stanislavsky's writing by Jean Benedetti (2010a, 2010b) as "the source" for a close feminist reading of Stanislavsky's fictional training narrative (Malague, 2013, 142).

Malague covers the familiar terrain of issues with translation and publication and Stanislavsky's ideas in the US, and the Method, and feminist criticisms I have also reviewed here. Commenting on Benedetti's more recent translations of *An Actor's Work: A Student's Diary* (2010a) and *An Actor's Work on a Role* (2010b), Malague is cautious, writing, "On the one hand, I am grateful to have this more 'authoritative' version of Stanislavsky's writings; on the other hand, I fear it might lead us to re-authorize a patriarchal voice, with its outmoded gender biases" (Malague, 2013, 152–153). In her earlier monograph, Malague observes that "The rhetoric surrounding feminism and Stanislavsky is full of reactions, rejections, and reconsiderations", instead calling for "What has been missing is a close reading, a careful and precise consideration of specific theories, techniques, and pedagogical practices" (Malague, 2012, 25), which she initiates in her subsequent chapter on Benedetti's translation.

Malague discusses the impact of the homosocial pedagogical dialogue that constitutes the narrative of Stanislavsky's fictionalised training in *An Actor's Work: A Student Diary* (2010a), writing, "The most vivid and detailed explorations are those of male actors exploring male roles" (Malague, 2013, 143). Identifying "the valuation of the weeping woman" in the Stanislavsky tradition (Malague, 2013, 145), Malague analyses Stanislavsky's depictions of the female characters in *An Actor's Work: A Student's Diary* (2010a) and the texts they are required to rehearse, finding that "if we return to Stanislavskian texts as the "bible" of a school of acting, there is no denying that the women are stereotyped and sidelined" (Malague, 2013, 149).

Malague's feminist reading of the female characters in *An Actor's Work: A Student's Diary* (2010a) supports her analysis of Tortsov's pedagogy, commenting, "For while Tortsov is sometimes guilty of gender bias in his teaching and unduly harsh on the women, he also offers guidance that could help them to resist objectification" (Malague, 2013, 150). Malague describes Tortsov's criticism of Varya/Sonya for "flirting with the audience" (Stanislavski, 2010, 40) and "showing off your legs" (Stanislavski, 2010a, 35). Malague also refers to the distress of the female students as Tortsov berates them as they walk up and down a corridor to demonstrate "Belief and the Sense of Truth" (Stanislavski, 2010a, 175). However, Malague offers a feminist re-reading of these troubling and oft-cited moments in Stanislavsky's fictionalised training. She comments, "Though Tortsov's treatment of Varya in this moment may be tough [...] the advice itself has potential feminist utility" (Malague, 2013, 151), suggesting that Stanislavsky, as Tortsov, is urging the female students not to rely on their personal physical attractiveness in performance but instead, his technique. Of the same moment in Chapter 8 of *An Actor's Work: A Student's Diary* (2010a) when Tortsov severely criticises Marya and Sonya, causing them to cry, Stanislavsky reveals the learning objective "[n]ever allow your art, your creative work, your methods, your psychotechnique and so on turn you into exaggerated, nit-picking critics" (Stanislavski, 2010a, 175). Tortsov continues, "To the devil with the nit-picker both outside and inside you – in the audience and even more in you yourselves. The critic is all too happy to find a home in the actor's ever doubting mind", as he urges the women to "[d]evelop a healthy, calm, judicious, understanding, true critic in your self – the actor's best friend" (Stanislavski, 2010a, 176).

Stanislavsky was motivated by his belief in the moral purpose of theatrical art, which is detected at a technical level in his pedagogy and in his discussion of 'Ethics and Discipline' (Stanislavski, 2010a, 552–578). He likely observed, in his relationship with Olga Knipper and others, that female actors experienced doubt in their abilities, especially when confronted with an entirely new, experimental approach to acting, compounded by patriarchy and misogyny inside and outside of the theatre. As Peta Tait clarifies, Stanislavsky expected his female actors to interpret emotions written for female characters by a male playwright using a new style and technique of acting unfamiliar to them and then perform emotional expression in a socially coherent way for a male director's satisfaction. Stanislavsky's ethics and ambitions for theatre are also informed by his Romanticism, ideas about *zhenstvennost* as discussed, and possibly the rhetorical images of the actresses, as Schuler (1996) described, who were vulnerable to and exploited by their physical appearance. Though Stanislavsky's depictions of his female characters are underdeveloped if not completely flawed, and though, Tortsov's pedagogy is described as 'tough', the fictionalised training conceived by Stanislavsky in these pedagogical narratives can be re-read for feminist potentiality, demonstrated by Malague.

Within the narrative of *An Actor's Work: A Student's Diary* (2010a), Stanislavsky frequently exploits moments of high emotion using female characters. As a man of the theatre with a specialised knowledge and interest in drama and dramatic literature, Stanislavsky undoubtedly constructs these moments to be emotionally compelling for the reader, his audience. However, his use of the female character's tears for emotional impact has had consequences in reality for women practising his techniques; his methodology has undoubtedly been exploited by teachers and directors who base their approach on his teachings, as feminist critics have repeatedly argued.

Among the feminist perspectives I have included here, there is consensus on questioning the power of acting teachers and recognising the actors' vulnerability in training within a complex hierarchy of the classroom and the wider performing arts industry that often relies on their objectification and subordination which protects patriarchy. The prevalence of not only misogynist but racist, ableist, and otherwise harmful stereotypical characters, depicted in a male-dominated Eurocentric dramatic canon that actors are required to embody, rehearse, and repeatedly perform both in training and the profession, reinforce uncritical beliefs about truth and nature, supported by claims of a universal human nature, which creates a narrow artistic and privileged view of human experience, that excludes and marginalises the majority of people who do not conform to such a worldview. Though Stanislavsky's relationship to Naturalism and Realism and the influences of Freudian and Pavlovian psychology have been debated and refuted, feminist scholars examining his work detect his Romantic and Modernist influences. These influences become further complicated by Stalin's politics and nationalist ambitions for the system and by Stanislavsky's depiction of female characters in his own writing, causing justified concern when practised without proper scrutiny or appropriate framing. Furthermore, the various interpretations of Stanislavsky's work and his legacy are all expressed in a broader global context that historically and currently disadvantages and oppresses women, LGBTQIA+ or otherwise queer and gender non-confirming people, those of the Global Majority and Global South, disabled and neurodivergent, working class and poor, who are otherwise marginalised by the status quo and experience intersections in their identities and exceed these imperfect categories, experiencing less privilege than others as I have mentioned. Though Lauren Love argues that our mere presence can challenge essentialist beliefs and universal claims about the human experience, such a claim must prompt the question, at what cost, personally and professionally?

J. Ellen Gainor (2002) rightfully draws attention to the polarising and oversimplification of these issues when critiquing Stanislavsky from a feminist perspective, just as Rhonda Blair (2002) notices how essentialism and anti-essentialism can become contradictory and two sides of the same coin. Though there is legitimate feminist concern about the homology of acting techniques, Gainor (2002) and Blair (2002) also warn of a homology of critique to avoid an oversimplification of complex issues and repetitions of inherited arguments and biases. Some of the feminist perspectives also appear to affirm or share Stanislavsky's belief in a great moral and universal purpose of the theatre which can seem inconsistent with their arguments. While criticising the exploitation of Stanislavsky's techniques by men to dominate women, there is also a dissimilar exploitation of Stanislavsky's ideas by feminists to further their politics.

Rosemary Malague (2012) questions the close alignment of the teaching and learning of acting with an unregulated industry where the exploitation of women, racism, homophobia, transphobia, and ableism are pervasive and often tolerated. She also warns against idealising alternative methodologies and pedagogies to the Stanislavsky tradition, given the rich and diverse scholarship on Stanislavsky's legacy, that other acting traditions have received much less careful examination. Malague (2012) proposes destabilising the acting teacher's authority as the purveyor of truth by recognising the diverse experiences of a multicultural twenty-first-century classroom, reminding teachers to develop a critical awareness of their own biases and assumptions. Like Gainor (2002), Malague (2012) also considers the possibility of disaggregating Stanislavsky's techniques from their patriarchal past. However, it is unclear that an exclusively technological perspective of Stanislavsky's work fully addresses the concerns raised by feminist scholars. Interpretations of Stanislavsky's work in new contexts are not without their problems, as various interpretations within the tradition have shown. Malague's (2013) close feminist reading of Jean Benedetti's 2010 edition and translation of *An Actor's Work: A Student's Diary* (2010a) and *An Actor's Work on a Role* (2010b) locates the source of misogyny in the fictionalised depictions of female characters that, in reality, acting teachers have further exploited, though as Malague indicates, a feminist re-reading of Stanislavsky's writing is possible.

Organising Actor Training Knowledge

At first, the pairing of Stanislavsky 'and' gender made me feel uncertain as it suggested a polemic. The name 'Stanislavsky' can elicit various feelings – excitement, curiosity, reverence, nostalgia, and weary familiarity. Conversely, or perhaps not, some may also find his name strange, outdated, offensive, and even painful. These emotional attachments might not always be as polarising or experienced exclusively from each other in a binary way.

Much of what we know now about Stanislavsky is wholly dependent on language, not only how it is written and read but also how it is translated, edited, censored, and published. Language also performs when we share knowledge about Stanislavsky, speaking his words to demonstrate or give instruction, direction, or feedback, or quoting him directly in writing to provide evidence to support or challenge an argument. Our performance of Stanislavsky's words inevitably influences how he is interpreted by others. The gender theories of Judith Butler, perhaps most notably and popularly, connects ideas about language, gender, and performance. Though, Stanislavsky scholarship can tell its own story about language, gender, and performance to demonstrate how gender can often organise knowledge.

Stanislavsky's preference for simple language to describe his approach to acting is ironically in tension with the politics and technicalities of translating his work. Fundamental terms to the Stanislavsky lexicon like *perezhivanie* and *ya yesm* seem to lose their potency when rendered in English as 'experiencing' and 'I am being'. From Stanislavsky scholarship, we might also understand how language evolves and inflects the transmission of knowledge, an understanding that could also be applied to gender. More recently, the anglophone language of gender has expanded beyond the binary sexed categories of 'Men' and 'Women' as people find new and appropriate a wider vocabulary to more accurately describe themselves and their experiences of gender, and to gain social and political recognition.

The issue of accurate translation and editing in Stanislavsky studies is in many ways personified in the female figure of Elizabeth Hapgood Reynolds, his English language translator and editor, responsible for the publication of Stanislavsky's pedagogic trilogy, *An Actor Prepares* (1936), *Building a Character* (1948), and *Creating a Role* (1957). Readers have often been guided towards preferred accounts of Stanislavsky's practice by men such as David Magarshack, Nikolai Gorchakov, Vasili Toporkov, and Jean Benedetti. As Peta Tait identifies in her chapter, some scholarship has privileged Stanislavsky's perspective on acting as the male authority over Olga Knipper's understanding of her craft, for example. Stanislavsky's Russian editor for over 30 years, Lyubov Gurevich, has also received less attention than her American counterpart. As Sharon Carnicke importantly recognises, "Without Lyubov Gurevich in Russia and Elizabeth Hapgood Reynolds in the US, Stanislavsky may never have completed his books" (Carnicke, 2009, 5). I have also noticed in a US context that Russian American Sonia Moore has received less attention than Boleslavsky or members of the Group Theatre. Moore trained at Moscow Art Theatre Third Studio in 1920 under Yevgeny Vakhtangov for three years before his death. This scarcity of recognition might be explained by the already established studios affiliated with the Group Theatre and consequently the dominance of the Method in American Theatre prior to her arrival in the US in 1940, compounded by the political tensions of the Cold War. She published *The Stanislavski System: The Professional Training of an Actor*, first titled *The Stanislavski Method* (1960). A review of her 1991 book *Stanislavski Revealed* suggests by then a scepticism of the Stanislavsky tradition, "a format that imitates the 'master' [...] based on actual classes, but in both the smug 'all-knowingness' of the teacher and the excessive naivety of the students the book becomes irritating" (Eddershaw, 399).

Yet, despite the concerns raised by feminists that advocate moving away from the Stanislavsky tradition, Stanislavsky research has significantly benefitted from the wealth of scholarship by women, to whom I am grateful, including Rhonda Blair, Sharon Carnicke, J. Ellen Gainor, Maria Ignatieva, Rosemary Malague, Bella Merlin, Maria Shevtsova, Peta Tait, and Rose Whyman, among many others, and some of whom I have been fortunate and able to include here.

In the first chapter of this volume, Maria Ignatieva explains how Stanislavsky's holistic ambitions at the Moscow Art Theatre defined the role of the modern theatre director, consequently gendering the profession in many minds as male. Alison Hodge's introduction to her edited compendium of the primarily Western European actor training canon, *Actor Training* (2010), begins with Stanislavsky as she remarks on how "[t]he relatively recent rise of the specialist role of theatre 'director' brought about a seismic shift in the process of theatre making" and in turn, actor training, positioning Stanislavsky as pivotal, at the top of this genealogy of the first formal newly conceived actor trainers (Hodge, xxi). Moreover, Ian Watson identifies that the dominant pedagogic and transmission model of actor training, the "family apprenticeship model, in which skills were passed from one generation of actors to the next", which he also terms as the "generational model of performer training", is historically prevalent in both Europe and Asia (Watson, 3). Watson also refers to the linearity of this mode of transmission, terming it as "vertical training" (Watson, 3), which Jonathan Pitches expands to include the "horizontal (synchronic)" and "vertical (diachronic) [modes of] transmission" (Pitches, 2015, 56).

Such ways of organising actor training knowledge have implicit biases and consequences, especially regarding gender. While accurate, Stanislavsky, as the progenitor of modern actor training and directing, affirms the Modernist belief in the God-like figure of the male artist genius who created more male geniuses in his image, overshadowing the contributions of his female collaborators. Moreover, the familial metaphor for actor training transmission privileges a heteronormative perspective on training histories. The pedagogic relationship between Tortsov and Kostya in Stanislavsky's albeit fictionalised training narrative is a prime example of the apprenticeship model, which excludes a female perspective. The homosocial arrangement of the apprentice model favours the heteronormative and patriarchal transmission of 'father' to 'son' based on reproduction and inheritance. That is not to discredit the value of the linear transmission model for analysing the person-to-person transmission of actor training skills and knowledge (horizontal/synchronic) and how these ideas have evolved generationally (vertical/diachronic), but to consider the effects of organising actor training knowledge in this way from a gendered perspective.

The linearity of the vertical and horizontal lines of transmission indicates a 'straightening' out of actor training knowledges. By straightening the lines of transmission (which also implies a heterosexual 'straight' perspective and logic), the messy nature of collaboration that fosters actor training methodologies and pedagogies, and their transmission, are tidied up and subsumed under a male figurehead, followed by a strict line of male heirs. In *Russians in Britain* (2012), Jonathan Pitches offers a less linear, cultural materialist approach to organising actor training legacies through "training places", "theatre spaces", and "documentation" (Pitches, 2012, 3) which begins to reveal contributions of women such as Dierdre Hurst du Prey and Joan Littlewood but still primarily concentrates on the contributions of men to the British Stanislavsky tradition. Pitches later addressed the taxonomy of actor training practitioners, precisely "the important consideration of gender, too often overlooked in writings on training and practitioners" (Pitches, 2015, 56) in *The Actor Training Reader* (2015), edited by Mark Evans. Pitches observed that out of thirteen practitioners case studied, only one female is included, Kristin Linklater. Pitches remarks, "This fact accurately expresses the depressing balance of power in actor training over the last century", as he turns his attention towards Alison Hodge's *Actor Training* (2010), which also featured few women actor trainers (Pitches, 2015, 57). Pitches does rightfully list several women practitioners, including Hodge herself, who ought to be included in future collections.

Lisa Peck, included in this volume and author of *Act as a Feminist: Towards a Critical Acting Pedagogy* (2021), citing queer theorist Eve Kosofsky Sedgwick, proposes "'thinking beside' might be a more productive way to ignite change than 'thinking beyond'" as she researches feminist lineages of actor training in the UK that have inevitably intersected with the Stanislavsky tradition (Peck, 2021, xii). Kosofsky Sedgwick asserted that 'being beside'– "there's nothing very dualistic about it; a number of elements may lie alongside one another", which she described as "a spacious agnosticism about several of the linear logics that enforce dualistic thinking" (Kosofsky Sedgwick, 8). Peck's mobilisation of Sedgwick's theory to conduct her feminist analysis opens up the opportunity for a queering of actor training traditions and their transmission.

Another approach advocated by Eve Kosofsky Sedgwick is to read reparatively, as she challenged what Paul Ricoeur described as "hermeneutics of suspicion", warning against the "unintentionally stultifying side effect" of paranoid criticism that only concerns itself with injury and intellectual, political, ethical one upmanship, creating a homology of negative criticism (Kosofsky Sedgwick, 2003, 124). In reparative reading, Kosofsky Sedgwick suggests the reader may embrace "changing and heterogeneous relational stances" instead of repeating dominant "theoretical ideologies" that presuppose one perspective, offering the reader temporary safety by protecting them from surprise (Kosofsky Sedgwick, 2003, 128). Sedgwick explains,

> Because there can be terrible surprises, however, there can also be good ones. Hope, often a fracturing, even a traumatic thing to experience, is among the energies by which the reparatively positioned reader tries to

> organize the fragments and part-objects she encounters and creates. Because the reader has room to realize that the future may be different from the present, it is also possible for her to entertain such profoundly painful, profoundly relieving, ethically crucial possibilities as that the past, in turn, could have happened differently from the way it actually did.
>
> *(Sedgwick, 2003, 146)*

Stanislavsky is full of surprises and contradictions, just as Sharon Carnicke reminds her reader, "If you consider Stanislavsky too patriarchal", before identifying Irina Rozanova, one of Stanislavsky's last female students whom he cast as Hamlet in 1937 at his last Opera Dramatic Studio (Carnicke, 2009, 1). Maria Ignatieva, too, dedicates a chapter to Stanislavsky's "Artistic Granddaughter", Rozanova, in *Stanislavsky and Female Actors: Women in Stanislavsky's Life and Art* (2008), an example of Stanislavsky's lifelong experimentation that required him to have some degree of open-mindedness, demonstrated in this instance in the cross-gender casting of Rozanova as Hamlet at the end of his life, which feminist critics have sometimes failed to recognise (Ignatieva, 2008, pp. 120–128).

It is not that Kosofsky Sedgwick completely refutes the legitimacy of paranoia and criticism rooted in negative affect, but that often, such criticism can foreclose other potential possibilities by adhering to academic conventions of criticism that are exclusively negative, which she also characterises as masculine. Reading reparatively, to remain open to encountering such surprises and contradictions, Sedgwick argues, can "[inaugurate] ethical possibility [...] providing the self with pleasure and nourishment in an environment that is perceived as not particularly offering them" (Sedgwick, 2003, 137). Just as feminist practitioners have utilised Realism and Stanislavskian techniques for their political ends, as Gainor (2002), Blair (2002), and Malague (2012), all note, Sedgwick argues that a reparative approach proposes that "What we can best learn from such practices are, perhaps, the many ways selves and communities succeed in extracting sustenance from the objects of a culture – even of a culture whose avowed desire has often been not to sustain them" (Sedgwick, 2003, 150–151).

Sharon Carnicke explains in *Stanislavsky in Focus: An Acting Master for the Twenty-first Century* (2009),

> Stanislavsky does not lay out a single right way to act. There is nothing absolute about his compendium of theory and techniques for the ephemeral art of acting that he so loved. He saw his System as offering advice to actors of different temperaments who wished to speak through different aesthetic styles. He called his System "universal" for these two reasons. Only three months before his death, he cautioned his directing students that, "One must give actors various paths".[14]
>
> *(Carnicke, 2009, 3)*

Such variation in sources, interpretations of Stanislavsky and traditions inspired by him, global applications as shown by Jonathan Pitches and Stefan Aquilina (2017), and polyvocal critique, inevitably elicits the question expressed by Maria Shevtsova, "Which Stanislavsky?" (Shevtsova, 235). Shevtsova invokes the image of a "panorama", a "*tour d'horizon* of various landmarks that the eye can grasp while others recede in the distance simply because sight cannot seize them all at once, or even on a third or fourth round" to consider the vastness of "The question of Stanislavsky's legacy and of which of its aspects and where, when how and why they were appropriated, adapted or refashioned in differing social and artist contexts" (Shevtsova, 235). Shevtsova covers the diverse and simultaneous contemporary developments of Stanislavsky's legacy in her epilogue to *Rediscovering Stanislavsky* (2020), observing the heterotemporalities of his legacy. She explains, "Time and timing are critical for legacy in so far as they determine which particular aspect of Stanislavsky – indeed *which* 'Stanislavsky' – is selected, accepted, and put into practice" (Shevtsova, 238, original emphasis).

Referring to Lev Dodin's place in the Stanislavsky lineage, Shevtsova writes that "He increasingly felt that, in order to be a 'living' presence, Stanislavsky has to be rethought with the changing times" (Shevtsova, 268). Dodin, commenting on *An Actor's Work on Himself*, remarks that it is a "rather unsatisfactory book, but with wonderful things in it", and of Stanislavsky's research into the 'laws' of nature, that "they may possibly not be solvable because laws may not exist" (Dodin, in Shevtsova, 268). Shevtsova argues, "Where Stanislavsky's legacy is concerned", based upon Dodin's comments, "this legacy finds its just value only when those who turn to it view it from the prism of the time contemporary to them" (Shevtsova, 269).

It is now so often the case that we encounter Stanislavsky's ideas, techniques, and writing outside of its original historical chronology and context, which both blurs a precise understanding of how his practice accumulated and evolved and liberates us from being bound to one particular idea over another as we also survey his work and our own horizons. Shevtsova concludes,

> This means that whatever resonates with them in Stanislavsky's work will have its own impact and leave its traces in varying depths and degrees within their time; and the part of the legacy they absorbed is bound to mutate with the changing times and their differing conditions, energies, and questions. Stanislavsky's motto for the theatre 'simpler, lighter, higher, happier' may be taken as a note to his legacy and a reminder that, while all things pass, they can pass with grace.
>
> *(Shevtsova, 269)*

Book Structure and Chapter Overview

Each contributor brings their unique expertise to engage with and respond to the relationship they make between Stanislavsky and Gender. To retain the spirit of conversation at the heart of the webinar which initiated this book and to prompt further dialogue beyond the page, following each chapter is a post-chapter discussion between the author and an interlocutor.

The first chapter, "Stanislavsky and the First Female Directors of the Moscow Art Theatre" by Maria Ignatieva, includes excerpts from unpublished and newly translated material to shed light on the complex dynamics of the Moscow Art Theatre and the first female director-pedagogues under the supervision of the founders, Stanislavsky and Nemirovich-Danchenko. Maria elaborates on how Stanislavsky's ambitions for the system were realised by its dissemination through the teaching of women, newly empowered with his acting methodology, working as director-pedagogues alongside male colleagues for the first time. The chapter highlights the professional distinction made at the Moscow Art Theatre between director-pedagogues and theatre directors, which was gendered, as women were considered the "director's comrade". In particular, Maria illustrates the courage of Nina Litovtseva, who challenged the all-male Moscow Art Theatre Collegium in 1927 to admit three female members, herself, Elizaveta Telesheva, and Kseniya Kotlubai, to its board. The women of the Moscow Art Theatre's reckoning with the male bureaucracy and their overall creative control over productions humanises and complicates the often-simplified historical narrative that champions the creative genius of men. Maria Ignatieva is joined in a post-chapter discussion with Rose Whyman from the University of Birmingham, UK.

Peta Tait's analysis of Olga Knipper's performances in her chapter, "Acting Emotional Expression and Gender Identity in Stanislavsky's Approach", offers an alternative perspective on English language scholarship that privileges Stanislavsky's analytical approach to performing emotions. Knipper's performances helped establish the reputation of the Moscow Art Theatre and realised several key female characters in twentieth-century literary theatre, receiving great acclaim. Here, Peta describes how, though close collaborators and an admirer of his work, Knipper frequently disagreed with Stanislavsky's early ideas about acting and her interpretation of the characters she was playing. In her chapter, Peta demonstrates how Knipper's performances of emotion develop in a dynamic, relational process within a social context, an approach to performing emotions which precedes later theories about emotion and has specific implications for women, especially Knipper. Peta asks to what extent a divergence in Stanislavsky and Knipper's approaches was due to gendered perspectives of emotional expression that point to broader patterns in twentieth-century theatre and have since been perpetuated in scholarship favouring Stanislavsky. Peta Tait is joined in a post-chapter discussion with Maria Ignatieva, Ohio State University, US.

The third chapter brings together Lisa Peck and Bella Merlin in a conversation that reconsiders Stanislavsky's system as a feminist practice, echoing the pedagogic dialogue that Stanislavsky uses between fictional teacher and student to narrate his ideal training in the system in *An Actor Prepares.* Lisa draws upon new feminist materialisms – namely, posthuman feminism and Black feminist love politics – to speculate on acting from a critical and feminist pedagogic perspective. In discussion with Lisa, Bella reflects on her own training, performing experiences, and pedagogic influences to consider how Active Analysis might express a feminist lineage of the Stanislavsky tradition. Lisa invites Bella to reflect on how her pedagogy resonates with bell hooks' 'engaged pedagogy' by centring the student as the curriculum and dismantling the top-down hierarchy of playwright, director, and actor.

Samia La Virgne gives an intersectional perspective as a Black female actor on the disparities in the Stanislavsky tradition and broader performing arts in the US and the UK. Samia shares her personal insight as an actor on the often casual and uncritical encounters with the Stanislavsky tradition in the training room and how, when met with the intersections of racism and misogyny, she was left dispossessed of her creative agency that such techniques promise to enhance. Drawing on Rosemary Malague's feminist analysis of the Stanislavsky tradition, intersectionality, and the work of bell hooks and Toni Morrison, Samia discusses how the racialised and gendered identity of being a Black woman is both hypervisible and invisible, which is further complicated by Stanislavsky's depiction of women and Kostya's first performance as Othello in *An Actor's Work: A Student's Diary* (2010a). Samia theorises this paradox of visibility, looking towards Black women who are innovating in actor training pedagogy. Samia is joined in a post-chapter discussion with Maria Brígida De Miranda, Professor of Acting and Directing at the University of the State of Santa Catarina, Brazil.

I first met Barry Fitzgerald when they dragged me out of the audience on stage to dance at the curtain call of OUTBOX's *And The Rest of Me Floats* at the Bush Theatre in 2019. In their chapter, "Commingling Queerness and Stanislavsky: Developing and Practising a Slippery Pedagogy to Shift Perspectives on Actor Training", Barry reflects on their experiences of training and queerness to teaching and performance-making with queer, trans, and nonbinary performers and communities, often coexisting with Stanislavsky tradition in training spaces that exclude them. Barry explains the contradiction of techniques that promise to empower the queer performer to be themselves and draw on their personal experience, and yet queer people are so often told to conceal their queerness in training, rehearsal, and performance. Barry engages an idea of a haptic perspective to make tangible the usually intangible and fluid process of performance-making and training, challenging heteronormative and cis-centred language that pervades rehearsal spaces by employing Stanislavsky's principles of physical tension and subtext. Barry also points out how homophobia and transphobia is usually rooted in misogyny and a fear of the feminine and a perceived failure to conform to social expectations that uphold a gender binary. Barry offers professional insight from their perspective as a practitioner with TransActing. This project began in 2015 between Gendered Intelligence, My Genderation, and Professor Catherine McNamara at the Royal Central School of Speech and Drama, joined by OUTBOX in 2016, with whom Barry also created and performed, *And The Rest of Me Floats* in 2019. Barry is joined in a post-chapter discussion with award-winning performance artist and writer, Ray Young, London, UK.

Finally, I am delighted to share Spencer Wood's poem, *Stanislavski's Dog*, as an epilogue, which I discovered serendipitously towards the end of my editorial of this volume. Spencer uses Declan Donnellan's anecdote from his introduction to Jean Benedetti's edited translation of Stanislavsky's *An Actor's Work: A Student's Diary* (2010a) about an actor's dog to reflect toxic masculinity and internalised homophobia, which echoes themes of queerness, masculinity, and being working class in Spencer's work more broadly. *Stanislavski's Dog* uniquely expresses how anecdotal evidence in the Stanislavsky tradition can become lore. His emphasis on the word *naturally* will resonate with students of acting who have their personhood denied them because of limited perceptions about what 'truth' and 'nature' are and can be, chiming with the feminist perspectives I have reviewed here. Hearing Spencer perform this poem reminded me of my own experiences of learning to act, frequently being told that I could never convincingly play cisgendered male heterosexual characters because of my femininity, justified by teachers practising a flawed understanding of Stanislavsky's pedagogy, which left me with a sense of shame. The poem's last section illustrates a desire and the false promise to be complicit with masculinity before reaching its visceral climax. *Stanislavski's Dog* was first published in Issue 9 of *fourteen poems*, published by Fourteen Publishing in 2022, and has been re-printed here with the permission of the poet.

Notes

1 Scholars such as Oyèrónkẹ́ Oyěwùmí (1997), Greg Thomas (2007), and Maria Lugones (2008), have all published compelling scholarship on decolonisation and gender.
2 Jonathan Pitches has similarly analysed the Stanislavsky tradition from two scientific positions, which he terms the "Newtonian" and "Romantic" – "one linear, rational and empirical, while the other is fluid, organic and intuitive" (Pitches, 2006, i).
3 On Stanislavsky's Romantic influences, see William B Worthen (1983); Rose Whyman (2008, 2; 15; 37); and Sharon Carnicke (2009, 140).
4 On Stanislavsky's literary influences, see Whyman (2008, 16; 25) and Carnicke (2009, 36; 133).

5 On Salvini's influence on Stanislavsky see Jean Benedetti (1999, 18); Jonathan Pitches (2006, 16-17); *My Life in Art*, translated and edited by Jean Benedetti, by K Stanislavski (2008, 143).
6 On Soviet censorship of spiritual influences on Stanislavsky, See Sharon Carnicke (2013; 2009); R Andrew White (2013); Sergei Tcherkasski and & Черкасский, C (2012); Gabriela Curpan (2019); and Maria Shevtsova (2020).
7 More recently, Jonathan Pitches and Stefan Aquilina (2017) have given a robust examination of Stanislavsky's influence in a global context, including how the tradition intersects with imperialism and colonialism, unpicking Stanislavsky's idealistic universal ambitions (Pitches, 2017, 12–21).
8 Many Stanislavsky scholars have worked to address misconceptions between Stanislavsky's system and the work of the Group Theatre in the US during the mid-twentieth century. For a more detailed explanation of how Stanislavsky's ideas influenced the work of the Group Theatre and the development of 'the Method', see Jonathan Pitches (2006, 86–125), Sharon M. Carnicke (2009), also David Krasner in *Actor Training* edited by Alison Hodge (2010, 144–163), Jean Benedetti's translator's foreword in *An Actor's Work: A Student's Diary* (2010, xv - xxii), and the editor's introduction to Richard Boleslavsky's *Acting: The First Six Lessons* by Rhonda Blair (ix – xxvi).
9 Maria Kapsali (2013) has argued that training disciplines that were also influential on Stanislavsky, such as yoga, need to "be viewed and explored in relation to the social, cultural and economic circumstances under which they and actor training programmes operate" (Kapsali, 73).
10 On Freud and Stanislavsky, Jonathan Pitches (2006), Rose Whyman (2008), and Sharon Carnicke (2009).
11 On Ribot's influence on Stanislavsky, see Jean Benedetti (1999, 2005) Jonathan Pitches (2006); Rose Whyman (2008, 2013) Sharon Carnicke (2009), and, of course, Stanislavski (2010a).
12 On naturalism, realism, and psychological realism in American theatre prior to Stanislavsky, see Lise-Lone Marker (2019), J. Ellen Gainor (2001), Jonathan Pitches (2006, 97).
13 "Many discourses about acting assume that they are expressing *the* truth. Most narratives foreground neither the process of constructing this 'truth' nor the voice or specific position from which this (version of) 'truth' is being constructed. To do so would reveal the fact that *this* 'truth' is a particular version authored by a particular person for a particular audience in a particular place and time and is thereby open to question and revision" (Zarrilli, 8, original emphasis).
14 Quoted by Carnicke from (Vinogradskaia, 498).

Works Cited

Aquilina, S. "Stanislavski's accumulative practice in Artists and Admirers rehearsals (1932-33)". *Stanislavski Studies*. Volume 1, Issue 2, 2013, pp. 3–47. DOI: https://doi.org/10.1080/20567790.2013.11428586

Aston, E. *Feminist Theatre Practice: A Handbook*. Second Edition. London & New York: Routledge, 2005. DOI: https://doi.org/10.4324/9780203981269

Aston, E. *Feminist Theatre Practice: A Handbook*. First Edition. London & New York: Routledge, 1999.

Attwood, L. *Creating the New Soviet Woman: Women's Magazines as Engineers of Female Identity, 1922–53*. London & New York: Palgrave Macmillan, 1999. DOI: https://doi.org/10.1057/9780333981825

Autant-Mathieu, M C & Wautlet, E. "The Journey of the Moscow Art Theatre and Its Disciples Through Europe and the United States (1906–1937)". In: *The Routledge Companion to Stanislavsky*. White, R. A. ed. London & New York: Routledge, 2013, pp. 157–178. DOI: https://doi.org/10.4324/9780203112304-14

Benedetti, J. "Translator's Foreword". In: *An Actor's Work: A Student's Diary*. Benedetti, J. trans and ed. London & New York: Routledge, 2010, xv–xxii. DOI: https://doi.org/10.4324/9780203936153

Benedetti, J. *Stanislavski: An Introduction*. New York, US: Routledge, 2005. DOI: https://doi.org/10.4324/9780203998182

Benedetti, J. *Stanislavski: His Life and Art*. Third Edition. London UK: Methuen Drama, 1999.

Blair, R. "Reconsidering Stanislavsky: Feeling, Feminism, and the Actor". *Theatre Topics*. Volume 12, Issue 2, pp. 177–190. Maryland, US: John Hopkins University Press, 2002. DOI: https://doi.org/10.1353/tt.2002.0008

Blair, R. ed. "Editor's introduction". In: Boleslavsky, R. *Acting: The First Six Lessons – Documents from the American Laboratory Theatre*. London & New York: Routledge, 2010. DOI: https://doi.org/10.4324/9780203847237

Borosky, V. *A Triptych from the Russian Theatre: An Artistic Biography of the Komissarzhevksys*. London, UK: C. Hurst & Co Publishers Ltd, 2001.

Bramwell, M "A Cup of Tea with Joan Littlewood". In: Tompkins, J and Holledge, J. eds. *Performing Women / Performing Feminisms: Interviews with International Women Playwrights*. Brisbane, AU: Australasian Drama Studies Association, 1997, pp. 103–109.

Butler, J. "Performative Acts and Gender Constitution: An Essay in Phenomenology and Feminist Theory". In: Case, S. ed. *Performing Feminisms: Feminist Critical Theory and Theatre*. Baltimore, US: John Hopkins University Press, 1990, pp. 270–282. DOI: https://doi.org/10.56021/9780801839689

Canning, C. *Feminist Theaters in the U.S.A: Staging Women's Experience*. London: Routledge, 1996. DOI: https://doi.org/10.4324/9780203991466

Carnicke, S. M. *Stanislavsky in Focus: An Acting Master for the Twenty-First Century*. Second Edition. London & New York: Routledge, 2009. DOI: https://doi.org/10.4324/9781003134381

Carnicke, S. "The Effects of Russian and Soviet Censorship on the Practice of Stanislavsky's System". In: White, R. A. ed. *The Routledge Companion to Stanislavsky*. London & New York: Routledge, 2013, pp. 249–269. DOI: https://doi.org/10.4324/9780203112304-20

Carnicke, SM. "An Actor Prepares/Rabota aktera nad soboĭ, Chast' I": A Comparison of the English with the Russian Stanislavsky. *Theatre Journal*. Volume 36, Issue 4, pp. 481–494. Washington DC, US: John Hopkins University Press, 1984. DOI: https://doi.org/0.2307/3206736

Case, S. *Feminism and Theatre*. Second Edition. London & New York: Routledge, 2014. DOI: https://doi.org/10.1007/978-1-349-19114-7

Case, S. *Feminism and Theatre*. First Edition. Basingstoke: Macmillan, 1988.

Chinoy, H. K. ed. "Reunion: A Self-Portrait of the Group Theatre". *Educational Theatre Journal*. Volume 27, Issue 4, pp. 445–552. Maryland, US: John Hopkins University Press, 1976. DOI: https://doi.org/10.2307/3206147

Crum, J. A. and Schecter J. "Afterword". *Theater*. Volume 17, Issue 1. Connecticut, US: Duke University Press, 1985, p.95. DOI: https://doi.org/10.1215/01610775-17-1-95

Curpan, G. "The Influence of Christian Orthodox thought on Stanislavski's Theatrical Legacy". *Stanislavski Studies*. Volume 7, Issue 2. Taylor and Francis Online, 2019: pp.201–217. DOI: https://doi.org/10.1080/20567790.2019.1644747

Devoken, M. "Modernism and Gender". In: *The Cambridge Companion to Modernism.* Levenson, M. ed. Cambridge, UK: Cambridge University Press, 2006. DOI: https://doi.org/10.1017/CCOL0521495164.008

Diamond, E. *Unmaking Mimesis: Essays on Feminism and Theater.* Second Edition. London & New York: Routledge, 2006. DOI: https://doi.org/10.4324/9780203358900

Diamond, E. *Unmaking Mimesis: Essays on Feminism and Theater.* First Edition. London: Routledge, 1997.

Dolan, J. *The Feminist Spectator as Critic.* Second Edition Michigan, US: University of Michigan Press, 2012. DOI: https://doi.org/10.3998/mpub.5169198

Dolan, J. *The Feminist Spectator as Critic.* First Edition. Michigan US: University of Michigan Press, 1988.

Eddershaw, M. "Sonia Moore Stanislavski Revealed". *New Theatre Quarterly.* Volume 9, Issue 36, pp.398–399. Cambridge, UK: Cambridge University Press, 1993. DOI: https://doi.org/10.1017/S0266464X00008423

Farber, V. *Stanislavsky in Practice: Actor Training in Post Soviet Russia.* New York, US: Peter Lang, 2008.

Gainor, J. E.. "Rethinking Feminism, Stanislavsky, and Performance". *Theatre Topics.* Volume 12, Issue 2, pp.163–175. Maryland, US: John Hopkins University Press, 2002. DOI: https://doi.org/10.1353/tt.2002.0010

Gainor, J. E. *Susan Glaspell in Context: American Theater, Culture, and Politics, 1915–48.* Michigan, US: University of Michigan Press, 2001. DOI: https://doi.org/10.3998/mpub.14558

Higgins, D. *Romantic Genius and the Literary Magazine Biography, Celebrity, Politics.* London & New York: Routledge, 2005. DOI: https://doi.org/10.4324/9780203963852

Hilbrenner, A. "Soviet Women in Sports in the Brezhnev Years: The Female Body and Soviet Modernism". In: *Euphoria and Exhaustion: Modern Sport in Soviet Culture and Society.* Katzer, N., Brudy, S., Köhring, A., Zeller, M., eds. Frankfurt, Germany & New York: Campus Verlag GmbH, 2010, pp.295–313.

Hodge, A. ed. *Actor Training.* Second Edition. London & New York: Routledge, 2010. DOI: https://doi.org/10.4324/9780203861370

Hodge, A. ed. *Twentieth Century Actor Training.* First Edition. London: Routledge, 2000.

Holdsworth, N. *Joan Littlewood's Theatre.* Cambridge, UK: Cambridge University Press, 2011.

hooks, b. *Writing Beyond Race: Living Theory and Practice.* London & New York: Routledge, 2013. DOI: https://doi.org/10.4324/9780203108499

Human Rights Watch. "Russia: Supreme Court Bans 'LGBT Movement' as 'Extremist': Russian LGBT Community in Dire Need of International Support". 30 November 2023. [*Online*]. [May 2024]. Available: https://www.hrw.org/news/2023/11/30/russia-supreme-court-bans-lgbt-movement-extremist

Ignatieva, M. *Stanislavsky and Female Actors: Women in Stanislavsky's Life and Art.* Maryland, US: University Press of America, 2008.

James, H. "Tommaso Salvini". *The Atlantic.* March 1883 Issue. Washington, D.C, US: Emerson Collective, 1883, pp.377–386.

Kapsali, M. "Rethinking Actor Training: Training Body, Mind and … Ideological Awareness". *Theatre, Dance and Performance Training.* Volume 4, Issue 1, 2013, pp.73–86. DOI: https://doi.org/10.1080/19443927.2012.719834

Kosofsky Sedgwick, E. *Touching Feeling: Affect, Pedagogy, Performativity.* Durham, North Carolina & London: Duke University Press, 2003. DOI: https://doi.org/10.2307/j.ctv11smq37

Krasner, D. "Strasberg, Adler and Meisner: Method Acting". In: Hodge, A. ed. *Actor Training*. Second Edition. London & New York: Routledge, 2010. DOI: https://doi.org/10.4324/9780203861370
Kugel, A. "Eleonora Duse". *Teatral'nye portrety*. Number 8, Part II. Leningrad: Iskusstvo, 1967.
Lenin, V. I. *On the Emancipation of Women*. Moscow, Russia: Progress Publishers, 1965.
Lewis, P. *Religious Experience and The Modernist Novel*. Cambridge, UK: Cambridge University Press, 2010. DOI: https://doi.org/10.1017/CBO9780511674723
Love, L. "Resisting the 'Organic': A feminist actor's approach". In: Zarrilli, P. B. ed. *Acting (Re) Considered: A Theoretical and Practical Guide*. Second Edition. London & New York: Routledge, 2002, pp.277–291. DOI: https://doi.org/10.4324/9780203991473
Lugones, M. "The Coloniality of Gender". *Worlds & Knowledges Otherwise*. Volume 2, Dossier 2. North Carolina, US: Duke University Press, April 2008, pp.1–17. DOI: https://doi.org/10.1007/978-1-137-38273-3_2
Madrigal-Borloz, V. *The impact of colonialism in violence and discrimination based on SOGI (Sexual Orientation and Gender Identity) Summary Report*. Geneva, Switzerland: Office of the United Nations High Commissioner for Human Rights, October 2023.
Malague, R. "Stanislavsky's System and Women: A Feminist Reading of New Translations". In: White, R. A. ed. *The Routledge Companion to Stanislavsky*. London & New York: Routledge, 2013, pp.139–153. DOI: https://doi.org/10.4324/9780203112304-12
Malague, R. *An Actress Prepares: Women and 'the Method'*. London & New York: Routledge, 2012. DOI: https://doi.org/10.4324/9780203144671
Marker, L. L. *David Belasco: Naturalism in American Theatre*. New Jersey, US: Princeton University Press, 2019. DOI: https://doi.org/10.1515/9781400870264
Merlin, B. *Konstantin Stanislavsky*. London & New York: Routledge, 2004. DOI: https://doi.org/10.4324/9781351117180
Merlin, B. *The Complete Stanislavsky Toolkit*. London: Nick Hern Books, 2007.
Moore, S. *An Actor's Training: The Stanislavski Method*. London: Gollancz, 1960.
Oxford English Dictionary. [Online]. Revised 2014. S.V. Genius. N. & Adj. [Accessed May 2024]. Available from: www.oed.com. Oxford, UK: Oxford University Press.
Oyěwùmí, O. *The Invention of Women: Making an African Sense of Western Gender Discourses*. Minnesota, US: University of Minnesota Press, 1997.
Peck, L. *Act as A Feminist: Towards a Critical Acting Pedagogy*. London & New York: Routledge, 2021. DOI: https://doi.org/10.4324/9781351130516
Pitches, J. "Introduction to Part III: Technique – Training the Actor's Body and Voice". In: Evans, M. ed, *The Actor Training Reader*. London & New York: Routledge, 2015, pp.55–65.
Pitches, J. and Aquilina, S. *Stanislavsky in the World: The System and its Transformations Across Continents*. London & New York: Bloomsbury Methuen Drama, 2017. DOI: https://doi.org/10.5040/9781472587916
Pitches, J. ed. *Russians in Britain: British Theatre and the Russian Tradition of Actor Training*. London & New York: Routledge, 2012. DOI: https://doi.org/10.4324/9780203146590
Pitches, J. *Science and the Stanislavsky Tradition of Acting*. London & New York: Routledge, 2006. DOI: https://doi.org/10.4324/9780203391204
Rosenthal, C. "The Silver Age: Highpoint for Women?" In: *Women and Society in Russia and the Soviet Union*. Edmondson, L. ed. Cambridge, UK: Cambridge University Press, 1992, pp.32–47. DOI: https://doi.org/10.1017/CBO9780511520877.004

Schuler, C. *Women in Russian Theatre: The Actress in the Silver Age*. London & New York: Routledge, 1996. DOI: https://doi.org/10.4324/9781315003948
Shevtsova, M. *Rediscovering Stanislavsky*. Cambridge, UK: Cambridge University Press, 2020. DOI: https://doi.org/10.1017/9781139151092
Stanislavski, K. *An Actor's Work on a Role*. Benedetti, J. trans and ed. London & New York: Routledge, 2010b. DOI: https://doi.org/10.4324/9780203870921
Stanislavski, K. *An Actor's Work: A Student's Diary*. Benedetti, J. trans and ed. London & New York: Routledge, 2010a. DOI: https://doi.org/10.4324/9780203936153
Stanislavski, K. *My Life in Art*. Benedetti, J. trans and ed. London & New York: Routledge, 2008. DOI: https://doi.org/10.4324/9781315823720
Stanislavsky, K.S. *Sobranie Sochinenii* [*Collected Works*]. Volumes 1–9. Moscow: Iskusstvo, 1988-1999.
Stroppel, E. C. "Reconciling the Past and the Present: Feminist Perspectives on the Method in the Classroom and on the Stage". In: Krasner, D. ed. *Method Acting Reconsidered: Theory, Practice, Future*. New York, US: Palgrave Macmillan, 2000, pp. 111–127. DOI: https://doi.org/10.1007/978-1-349-62271-9_6
Tcherkasski, S and Черкасский, С. "Fundamentals of the Stanislavski System and Yoga Philosophy and Practice". *Stanislavski Studies: Practice, Legacy, and Contemporary Theater*. 1 (1). Taylor and Francis Online, 2012. DOI: https://doi.org/10.1080/20567790.2013.11428590
Thomas, G. *The Sexual Demon of Colonial Power: Pan-African Embodiment and Erotic Schemes of Empire*. Indiana, US: University of Indiana Press, 2007.
Trotsky, L. *History of the Russian Revolution*. Eastman, M. trans. Illinois, US: Haymarket Books, 2008.
Trotsky, L. *Literature and Revolution*. Keach, W. ed. Illinois, US: Haymarket Books, 2007.
Vinogradskaya, I. ed. *Letopis' zhizni i tvorchestva Stanislavkogo (1863–1938) [The Life and Work of Stanislavsky (1863-1938)]*. Volumes 1–4. Second Edition. Moscow: Izdatel'stvo Khudozhestvennyi Teatr, 1971-2003.
Walsh Jenkins, L and Ogden-Malouf, S. "The (Female) Actor Prepares". *In: Theater*. Volume 17, Issue 1. Connecticut, US: Duke University Press, 1985, pp. 66–69. DOI: https://doi.org/10.1215/01610775-17-1-66
Watson, I. ed. *Performer Training: Developments Across Cultures*. London & New York: Routledge, 2000. DOI: https://doi.org/10.4324/9781315079981
White, R. A. "Stanislavsky and Ramacharaka: The Impact of Yoga, and the Occult Revival on the System". In: White, R. A. ed. *The Routledge Companion to Stanislavsky*. London & New York: Routledge, 2013, pp.287–304. DOI: https://doi.org/10.4324/9780203112304-23
Whyman, R. *Stanislavski: The Basics*. London & New York: Routledge, 2013. DOI: https://doi.org/10.4324/9780203077603
Whyman, R. *The Stanislavsky System of Acting: Legacy and Influence in Modern Performance*. Cambridge, UK: Cambridge University Press, 2008.
Willis, R. A. *The American Laboratory Theatre, 1923–1930*. University of Iowa Dissertation, 1968.
Worthen, W. B. "Stanislavsky and the Ethos of Acting". *Theatre Journal*. Volume 35, Issue 1. Maryland, US: John Hopkins University Press, 1983, pp. 32–40. DOI: https://doi.org/10.2307/3206699
Zarrilli, P. B. ed. *Acting (Re) Considered: A Theoretical and Practical Guide*. Second Edition. London & New York: Routledge, 2002. DOI: https://doi.org/10.4324/9780203991473

1

STANISLAVSKY AND THE FIRST FEMALE DIRECTORS OF THE MOSCOW ART THEATRE

Maria Ignatieva

Stanislavsky defined the contemporary understanding of the theatre director. He advised aspiring directors that the newly inaugurated profession of a theatre director should cover all aspects of the theatre – "administrative, artistic, literary, musical, staging, and finally, pedagogical and psychological" (Stanislavsky, 1999, Vol. 9, 983). From drawing sketches and creating scenographic models, including lighting and sound, to rehearsing actors and the ensemble, Stanislavsky demonstrated his extensive and unique knowledge of the theatre as a progenitor of what became known as the modern theatre director that is recognised today. The profession of the theatre director – distinct from the actor stage manager – invested Stanislavsky as an undisputed leader in all his various creative endeavours. If Moscow Art Theatre was a theatrical Olympus, Stanislavsky was its reigning Zeus, and the profession and gender of a theatre director would become closely associated with men.

Although an advocate and admirer of female creativity, be it the highly decorated and celebrated actresses of the Maly Theatre, Maria Nikolayevna Yermolova and Glikeria Nikolaevna Fedotova, or the internationally recognised performers Eleonora Duse and Isadora Duncan, Stanislavsky was no different to others in his time in believing that a woman's sacred mission was to nurture, support, and follow men.

Stanislavsky's artistic career and the careful cultivation of his system benefitted from his collaborations with women, for instance, in his family, his sisters Zinaida and Anna, his wife and actress Maria Lilina, and professionally, the actresses of the Moscow Art Theatre, including Olga Knipper, Maria Andreyeva, Olga Gzovskaya, Lidia Koreneva, and Maria Ouspenskaya, who was influential in the transmission of his ideas in the North America, and Maria Knebel, custodian of his final rehearsal methodology, Active Analysis.

DOI: 10.4324/9781003411611-2

Stanislavsky's relationship with Lyubov Yakovlevna Gurevich, one of his most trusted friends and colleagues, demonstrates his appreciation of his female collaborators. An accomplished journalist, philosopher, and critic, Gurevich was a historian of the Moscow Art Theatre since she wrote her first reviews of Moscow Art Theatre productions in 1904 before formally joining the theatre in 1905. She authored a book about Stanislavsky and a further article on him for the collection "Masters of the Moscow Art Theatre" and became his personal literary assistant and editor. Stanislavsky expressed his gratitude and praise for her editing in a letter addressed to the "beloved and highly esteemed" Gurevich:

> Personally, I needed a lot of support from people who were competent, impartial, and sincere about art. I have always found such support in you. You were the filter and test through which I passed all my searches, research, and works. Your high level of culture, your exceptional artistic sensitivity to all that is real and artistically valuable, your vast experience as a writer, your critic, your knowledge of contemporary theatre, the history of the past, but above all your sincere sympathy and pure heart were an extremely valuable element in my work as an actor, director, and researcher.
>
> For me, your work remains unforgettable, based on excerpts from old books concerning the work of acting, which you and I produced every day in Marienbad, despite the fact that storm clouds were gathering all around. This work comprehended a lot and helped to "put on the shelves of the mind" all the knowledge that the experience gave me. You were the first to enthusiastically accept my timid attempts to create a so-called system, and throughout the rest of your work you have approved, evaluated, and criticized all my research in this field.
>
> *(Stanislavsky to Lyubov Gurevich, 4 March 1928, 157)*

Stanislavsky held his learned female friends in high regard, and Gurevich was no exception, as expressed in his concluding comment showing his appreciation to her: "I sincerely love you, appreciate you, thank you deeply, and bow to you and embrace you in a friendly way" (Stanislavsky to Lyubov Gurevich, 4 March 1928, 157).

Stanislavsky's achievements and global influence are inconceivable without the contributions of women. For example, without Gurevich's American counterpart, Elizabeth Hapgood Reynolds, translations of his writing in English may have appeared decades later. I have previously published research on Stanislavsky's female creative partners in my book *Stanislavsky and Female Actors: Women in Stanislavsky's Life and Art*, including his relationship with one of his last students, Irina Rozanova, with whom he rehearsed the role of Hamlet for what would be the final two years of his life at the Opera-Dramatic Studio. But did Stanislavsky believe that women could be theatre directors?

For the first time, young women expressed their interest in directing while studying the system at the Moscow Art Theatre's First Studio. Studying the system and working on their characters and scenes, both male and female students joined an ensemble under the guidance of Stanislavsky and Leopold Antonovich Sulerzhitsky. The First Studio offered a more gender-equal creative endeavour, encouraging female students to volunteer to direct scenes. Women began to teach the system after learning it themselves first-hand. By the early '30s, many of those women became experienced teachers of the system, among them Serafina Birman, Sofia Giatstinova, Lidia Deikun, Olga Pyzhova, Elizaveta Telesheva, Kseniya Kotlubai, and Maria Knebel. Stanislavsky encouraged his former students to teach the system despite its constant evolution. It was Stanislavsky ambition for the system to become the foundation for the Soviet theatre of the future and for the theatre director to develop the actor's organic creativity through the system. Thus, initially believing in the pedagogical talents of female actors, now pedagogues, Stanislavsky further empowered them with the system and envisioned a female actor pedagogue director eventually preparing a theatre production based on the system. Stanislavsky might not have lived long enough to start believing that a woman could be a theatre director, but he certainly greatly valued the role of women in theatre as actors, students, collaborators, and teachers.

Stanislavsky's Artistic Mother: Glikeria Nikolaevna Fedotova

The formative influence of one woman who taught Stanislavsky acting, Glikeria Nikolaevna Fedotova, whom he named his artistic mother, had herself trained with Mikhail Shchepkin and was the acclaimed actress of the Maly Theatre. Fedotova inspired Stanislavsky's view that women could act as pedagogues in theatre. Stanislavsky describes her influence on him "artistically and ethically" and that Fedotova was "enormously gifted, a real artist, who could express the very essence of the play, and create the inner and outer shape of a role. She was masterly in artistically embodying a role and a virtuoso with a dazzling technique" (Stanislavski, 2008, 32). Working synergistically with her husband, director Aleksandr Fedotov, "[h]e saw the whole picture, the characters and drew them. She sensed our feelings and tried to reproduce them. Fedotov and Fedotova complemented each other" (Stanislavski, 2008, 117). Together, they were "the heirs and successors" of canonical figures of 19th Century Russian Theatre, like Shchepkin, who "handed down the vestiges of these simple, unwritten traditions and teaching methods" to Stanislavsky (Stanislavski, 2008, 60). Stanislavsky notes how Fedotova "managed to convey the inner essence of these traditions", remarking:

> Less gifted people copied Shchepkin from the outside and imagined that they were teaching *à la Shchepkin* but in fact they merely demonstrated a

> row of clichés and taught how to play this or that role or explained what the final result should be when performing it.
>
> *(Stanislavski, 2008, 60, Original emphasis)*

Stanislavsky's description of Fedotova explains her significant influence on him and what would become the system and the Moscow Art Theatre. During their time at the Moscow Society of Art and Literature, Maria Petrovna Lilina, Stanislavsky's wife, recounted,

> For many years to come, [Fedotova] worked with us for free, generously, and completely devoting herself to this work, thus helping form the venture that geared up towards the creation of a group of actors ready to join the Moscow Art Theatre.
>
> *(Maria Lilina in Leontievsky, 164–165)*

Fedotova advised on staging, teaching voice, and correcting amateurs' diction and pronunciation, becoming chair of the Moscow Society of Art and Literature in 1891, sitting at the director's table. She also taught Stanislavsky to analyse his roles. Vladimir Ivanovich Nemirovich-Danchenko also noted her potential as a director:

> She was not only busy with her own roles, but she also followed the whole performance. She was on the sidelines, near the backstage, listening to rehearsals of scenes she did not participate in [....] And Fedotova [...] sometimes very harshly interfered with the work of all the actors. [...] We felt that every scene was being watched closely with her keen and demanding eye, that did not allow us to relax or become lazy.
>
> *(Nemirovich-Danchenko in Goyan, 348)*

It was Stanislavsky imitation of Fedotova and her husband Fedotov's demand for precision and the "control and sangfroid" of Ludwig Chronegk, director of the German Saxe-Meiningen Company, that inspired him to become a "dictator-director" early in his career (Stanislavski, 2008, 115).

Fedotova encouraged Stanislavsky to find psychological drives for his characters' behaviours. However, Stanislavsky disagreed with Fedotova's interpretation of Don Juan in Aleksandr Pushkin's *The Stone Guest*, performed at the Moscow Society of Art and Literature in 1889. Fedotova found Stanislavsky's performance "overly dramatic and passionate" (Vinogradskaya, Vol.1, 132–133). Traditionally, Don Juan was portrayed as dishonest and amoral on the Russian stage. Stanislavsky felt it was important for his character to fall in love at the end of the play. When Stanislavsky attempted to follow Fedotova's directions for Don Juan, which continued the Maly Theatre's tradition of the character, he became dissatisfied. As a student of Shchepkin, Fedotova strove to continue the tradition of Russian realism. When Stanislavsky shared with her his ideas to systematise the art of acting, she objected. Fedotova did not believe in systems, only in personal work with individuals and the continuation of tradition from an experienced actor to their younger apprentice. She insisted that all great actors learned from their predecessors and thus ought to be the source of the actor's education, not textbooks. Despite their differences, Fedotova demonstrated to Stanislavsky the pedagogical power of the experienced female actor (Stanislavsky, 1999, Vol. 5, 219).

Stanislavsky's Sister: Zinaida Sokolova née Alekseyev

Stanislavsky's sister, Zinaida, was among the first women who wanted to be responsible for working with actors, staging plays and operas, and becoming a theatre director. Considered an expert teacher of the system, Zinaida Sokolova née Alekseyev received her education at home; knew various traditionally feminine crafts, such as sewing and embroidery; was fluent in French, German, and English; and proficient in singing and music, with a passion for Opera and Drama much like her family. She assisted Stanislavsky in many of his home productions recounted in *My Life in Art* and had acted with him since they were teenagers. Sokolova shared Stanislavsky's belief of theatre as a vital source of cultural enlightenment. With her husband, a doctor, she opened Russia's first peasant theatre, The People's Theatre, in 1896 in the village of Nikolsky, not far from Voronezh.

The Sokolovs built a school where they taught peasants reading, writing and traditional crafts, which was part of their extensive education programme for the local population. The Sokolovs directed various plays by Gogol, Ostrovsky, and Chekhov in their village theatre. Stanislavsky visited Nikolsky in 1901 and admired his sister and her husband's work. The amateurs of Sokolov's provincial theatre were nervous about Stanislavsky's presence, though he assured his sister he understood the nature of their work (Stanislavsky, 1999, Vol.7, 401–402). When Sokolova moved to Moscow, she expressed interest in joining the Moscow Art Theatre as an actor. Stanislavsky highly valued Sokolova's professional acting skills. Nevertheless, she was placed as one of the students in the First Studio to study the system under the guidance of Vakhtangov, Sulerzhitsky, and her brother, Stanislavsky.

From 1912 to 1913, she attended her brother's lectures and followed the same exercises as the other students. She was admitted to the Moscow Art Theatre only after she passed her exams on the system and played roles such as Libanova in Ivan Turgenev's *Where It Is Thin, There It Breaks*, Gertrude in Shakespeare's *Hamlet*, which she rehearsed with Stanislavsky, Mrs Pernel in *Tartuffe*, and Belina in *The Imaginary Invalid*, both by Moliere. Stanislavsky intended for Sokolova to play Olga in Anton Chekhov's *Three Sisters*, but she left the Moscow Art Theatre prematurely to look after her sick daughter in Yalta. During this time, though, she observed Stanislavsky's approach to directing, which inspired her.

Later in her life, Sokolova taught the system as Stanislavsky taught it at the First Studio. She believed in the system dogmatically, even criticising her brother for his later revisions. After the death of her husband in 1919, Sokolova dedicated herself to pedagogy and directing, working at the Opera Studio first and then, from 1935, the Opera-Dramatic Studio. Sokolova's pedagogical skills were truly unique; she taught movement and voice, including diction and recitation, and, most importantly, the system. Some students felt she followed the system too strictly, though Stanislavsky defended her, insisting she was among the most knowledgeable and dedicated theatre professionals. A disagreement erupted between Sokolova and Victor Sadovnikov, a well-known tenor, at the Bolshoi Theatre Opera Studio in 1921; Sadovnikov wrote to Stanislavsky, insisting he dismissed Sokolova or Sadovnikov would leave the Studio. Stanislavsky responded to Sadovnikov, defending his sister, that in his entire life, he had only known two other people who worked as tirelessly and selflessly as him: Sulerzhitsky and Sokolova (Stanislavsky, 1999, Vol.9, 39). Stanislavsky refused Sadovnikov's demand, telling him he would rather close the Studio. Working at the Bolshoi Theatre Opera Studio, Sokolova had prepared scenes for several operas and hoped to direct them independently. Stanislavsky, however, explained that his sister was not a theatre director as he envisaged the profession:

> If Sokolova wanted to be a director in our theatre? – I would have answered no. Therefore, I view *The Country Honor* and *Sheloga* by Rimsky-Korsakov as your pedagogical work. That production was neither staged nor included as part of the theatre repertoire or season [...] I don't have any doubts that when your work is presented professionally, they would be happy to welcome you back as one of the directors.
>
> *(Stanislavsky, 1999, Vol.9, 581)*

Unfortunately, the Artistic Council of the Bolshoi Theatre Opera Studio did not welcome Sokolova back, and they did not give her further opportunities to rehearse operas. However, Sokolova remained irreplaceable in her pedagogical work during Stanislavsky's life and after his death, strengthening what he saw as one of the weakest areas of the system, voice and speech, to which, with her brother, she dedicated years of life.

The Female Director-Pedagogues: Nina Litovtseva, Elizaveta Telesheva, and Maria Petrovna Lilina

Nina Litovtseva was among the first female directors at the Moscow Art Theatre. Once a successful provincial actress and wife of fellow Moscow

Art Theatre actor Vassily Kachalov, she joined the Moscow Art Theatre in 1901. Litovtseva turned to pedagogy and directing after experiencing a sudden illness. In 1907 and 1908, she had several surgeries, which left her with a physical disability. She successfully made a career of teaching and directing, drawing on her experience as an actress and favourite student of Nemirovich-Danchenko at the Philharmonic School in 1896 and was an expert of the Moscow Art Theatre's repertoire. Litovtseva first began teaching and was hired as a pedagogue at the Studio of the Three Nicholas (also known as the Schools of Three Nikolais), which became the Moscow Art Theatre's Second Studio. Litovtseva still portrayed minor roles that did not require her to move around the stage excessively, and she could disguise her limited mobility by sitting in chairs. In 1916, together with Vakhtang Mchedelov, she co-directed as a pedagogue working with the actors on *The Green Ring* by Zinaida Gippius and appeared in a supportive role as Elena Ivanovna, the mother of the protagonist, Uncle Mika, played by Alexey Stakhovich, and as Voinitskaya in Anton Chekhov's *Uncle Vanya*, which she played during the Kachalov Group's tour and later at the Moscow Art Theatre, and was praised greatly by critics.

In her directing and pedagogical work, Litovtseva preferred smaller stages and chamber theatres, working in a realistic style with deep psychological analysis of the characters' inner lives and their inner psychological drives for their behaviour. Although encouraged to direct by Stanislavsky, Litovtseva faced hostility from her male colleagues as the younger generation of the Moscow Art Theatre competed as directors. While Stanislavsky thought of Litovtseva primarily as a pedagogue, it was her ambition to have the responsibility of a whole theatre production as a theatre director. However, Stanislavsky once mocked Litovtseva openly during her time at the Second Studio, in front of the actors as she rehearsed Leonid Andreyev's play *The Youth* in 1918. Stanislavsky allegedly asked Litovtseva sarcastically, "So, what is the name of the play, Nina Nikolayevna?" to which she replied, "Leonid Andreyev's *Youth*, if you insist". Stanislavsky cruelly remarked, "What I have just seen should not be called *Youth*. It should be called 'old age'. The author is someone else, not Leonid Andreyev" (Vinogradskaya, Vol. 3, 28). The actors laughed at Stanislavsky's comments about their director, Litovtseva. Stanislavsky had ridiculed her work, and he diminished her authority.

During the tour of the Kachalov Group, which continued to perform outside of Russia in Europe from 1919 to 1921 after being cut by the White Army, Litovtseva worked as a director and co-director recreating famous Moscow Art Theatre productions for smaller stages. In Zagreb in 1921, Litovtseva was trusted to re-direct *The Deluge* by Henning Berger – a well-known production directed by Evgeny Vakhtangov that premiered at the First Studio in 1915. Litovtseva had painstakingly analysed the characters, rehearsing the play for eight months. This venture was significant progress in her career as a director. Unfortunately, the Croatian, Serbian, German, and Russian émigré critics considered the production a failure, causing Litovtseva public humiliation, which she remembered for the rest of her life. She included elaborated backstage explosions using a real cannon to amplify the performance's climax, which did not help its reception.

During the Moscow Art Theatre Tours of North America between 1922 and 1924, Litovtseva assisted Stanislavsky in rehearsing crowd scenes and preparing new actors for the Moscow Art Theatre's classical repertoire. Litovtseva worked with Olga Pyzhova on her role as Mirandolina in *The Mistress of the Inn* by Carlo Goldoni, which was especially important for Stanislavsky as he reprised his role as the male lead, Ripafratta. Although grateful for her assistance, Stanislavsky still did not believe women could be theatre directors, and Nemirovich-Danchenko, who agreed with him, called female directors, director's comrade (*товарищ режиссера*) – a woman who could help prepare roles but not stage full theatre productions. Olga Bokshanskaya, Nemirovich-Danchenko's secretary, quoted Stanislavsky in a letter to Nemirovich-Danchenko to say, "[Elizaveta] Telesheva and Litovtseva could by no means be considered anything else but the directors working with actors. They cannot stage plays and must always be paired with male directors who can" (Nemirovich-Danchenko in Bokshanskaya, 2005, Vol. 2, 375).

Litovtseva resumed her work in Moscow in 1924 and was given greater freedom in choosing her directorial projects at the Moscow Art Theatre, although under the close supervision of either Stanislavsky or Nemirovich-Danchenko. One of her most successful productions, *Nikolai I and the Decemberists* by Alexander Kugel, based on Dmitry Merezhkovsky's writing, was performed in 1926. The performance celebrated the Decembrist's insurrection in 1825 for a select audience of the Bolshevik elite and was a unique event at the Moscow Art Theatre. Litovtseva's production was so successful that the theatre commissioned a full production. The renowned Moscow Art Theatre actor Vasily Kachalov, Litovtseva's husband, played Czar Nicholas I with a strong ensemble of actors with stage design by Dmitry Kardovsky. The production was an inordinate success, and Stanislavsky wrote to thank Litovtseva and Kachalov "for the great and wonderful work that gives the theatre a true, good and noble tone. This is very important. We must continue this work and create a whole performance" (Stanislavsky, 1999, Vol. 9, 207–208). After the success of *Nikolai I and the Decemberists*, Litovtseva was appointed to work on *The Armoured Train* by Vsevolod Ivanov with Ilya Sudakov, joined later by another female director, Elizaveta Telesheva.

Litovtseva, Sudakov and Telesheva led 76 rehearsals of *The Armoured Train*. Ilya Sudakov was known for his extravagant staging, while Litovtseva and Telesheva rehearsed with the actors. Over the next 25 years, the collaboration of the two to five directors working on a production, where male directors took charge of staging and female directors worked with actors, would become the creative model at Moscow Art Theatre and Moscow Art Theatre II. The Moscow Art Theatre Collegium appointed the groups of directors to create an outline of the productions that Nemirovich-Danchenko and Stanislavsky would finish later or even significantly revise. Because of these unique collaborations, it is difficult to determine the individual contributions to each performance and the tense group dynamics (Kudriavtsev, 163).

Litovtseva next directed a play about the revolution, *Our Youth*, adapted from Viktor Kin's novel *On the Other Side*, produced for the Moscow Art Theatre's smaller stage. It provided Litovtseva with an opportunity to direct in her favourite style in a smaller venue with minimal mise-en-scène and set and a strong focus on the psychology of the characters. However, critics mentioned that the production lacked an overall dynamic in the otherwise enthusiastic reviews. Litovtseva's position in the theatre did not progress compared with her male colleagues despite her apparent successes as a director, which humiliated her. In April 1927, Litovtseva wrote a letter to the all-male Moscow Art Theatre Collegium, which included Nemirovich-Danchenko and Stanislavsky. Her remarkable letter described her humiliation but also demonstrated her passion and tenacity:

> I am writing to the Collegium because I am not allowed to attend the meetings, and thus I am deprived of the right to present and defend my thoughts about my directorial works and the revivals. In those rare cases, when I am invited to a meeting, the questions related to my work are limited to a ridiculously short time and I don't have a chance to express my opinion at all. But even if I were given enough time to say anything, it would not have mattered at all. I am always invited after my future productions have been discussed and the shows I am scheduled to direct have been cast. Please note that all of them, always promise me to discuss it with the whole Collegium, but the situation remains the same. Therefore, I decided to write because I must be heard.
>
> *(Litovtseva to the Moscow Art Theatre, 1927, 11405)*

In response to her letter, in 1928, the Moscow Art Theatre included three female members to join the Collegium: Nina Litovtseva, Elizaveta Telesheva, and Kseniya Kotlubai. Indeed, it appeared to be a progressive decision. However, it proved to be an empty gesture of concession because eight years later, in 1935, during a meeting of Moscow Art Theatre directors, Litovtseva raised the same concerns. This time, she was supported by a male colleague, as she described the theatre's unacceptable policy of casting the performances without the director's consultation and barring them from the casting process.

Despite her persistent frustrations with the male bureaucracy of the Moscow Art Theatre, Litovtseva and Stanislavsky collaborated in 1932. Though this union demonstrated that Litovtseva had standing in the Moscow Art Theatre, it also showed her powerlessness as a director. Artists at the Moscow Art Theatre generally accepted that Stanislavsky and Nemirovich-Danchenko had ultimate artistic control over every production. Litovtseva accepted all the changes with the absolute belief that Stanislavsky knew best, which she understood from the outset when she proposed to direct Alexander Ostrovsky's play *Talents and Admirers*. Stanislavsky approved her proposal, agreeing, "Let her do it all by herself: choose the actors, work with the designer, lead all of the rehearsals" (Vinogradskaya, Vol. 3, 489). Though already identified by Stanislavsky as the principal director, Litovtseva still required a male assistant, thus indirectly confirming the firmly established working model of the female directors working with actors and the men creating every other aspect of the production, which would still be finalised later by Stanislavsky and Nemirovich-Danchenko. In 1932, Litovtseva presented Stanislavsky with models of the scenery for his approval, and in 1933, Litovtseva showed Stanislavsky the first, third, and fourth acts of the play at his home. Stanislavsky thanked Litovtseva for her thorough preparatory work. However, he asked the actors to forget the existing mise-en-scène, revising the concept of the production and the interpretation of several characters. Stanislavsky continued rehearsing *Talents and Admirers* for six more months.

Alexander Ostrovsky's *Talents and Admirers*, written in 1881, is perhaps the most 'Chekhovian' among his plays. The character, Alexandra Negina, is a talented provincial actress who, to become successful, must leave her lover, Pyotr Meluzov, and pursue a career in theatre by becoming the mistress of Velikatov, a wealthy merchant. Before the revolution, actresses portrayed Negina as a victim who sacrificed her great love for art, most notably by Maria Yermolova who originated the role at the Maly Theatre in 1881. Litovtseva tried to preserve Ostrovsky's ironic impartiality while emphasising Negina's tragic parting with her love, Meluzov. Stanislavsky, however, clearly disagreed with this tradition, as evidenced by the rehearsal diaries. He disregarded any moralising of the character Negina's choice and insisted that, for art's sake, she must betray her love for Meluzov without any regret but enthusiasm. It was Stanislavsky's interpretation that the character of Negina serves what he believed to be the higher purpose of the art of theatre. In May 1933, he changed the scenery, though he approved of the music and personally examined every actor's makeup and props. The new production of *Talents and Admirers* opened in September 1933 and received harsh criticism from Soviet critics for the directors and actors' inability to condemn the merchant class. It was, however, loved by audiences and remained in the theatre's repertoire for 24 years. In his letter to Litovtseva, Stanislavsky stated that she achieved excellent results as a pedagogue and supported five new actors to professionalise. Stanislavsky's rehearsal diaries and letters to Litovtseva show the dynamic of their creative relationship:

> *Talents and Admirers* is over [...] abused [by theatre critics] as never before and was a great success with the audience [...] A lesson for you [....] If you want your play to be praised, never work with me. It does not matter that my name is hidden – critics will spy, find out, and blame me, but remember, they are not scolding you, but me. These days they won't and can't praise me. I seem to be almost the only one left – quite old, not recognising any 'tricks' that are 'protective screens' for the directors who are hurrying to fit contemporary trends. Once, they scolded my system – now they recognise it. They also admit that I stand for pure art [...] But here is what you, in my opinion, did not appreciate, both in your own work and the work of the actors. Do you remember how the play was staged? It was meant for the Small stage [...] but it was performed on the Big stage and became an exemplary performance of the Moscow Art Theatre [....] Maybe not perfect but appreciate it pedagogically. In this performance, you discovered new sides to these actors: Verbitsky, Zueva, Dorokhin, and partly Shulga; move something in Tarasova and Kudryavtsevo and show the real case of Prudkin (although he had shown his characteristic features in other roles before). And Ershov, whose role is beyond his strength, did a lot in his work and technique. Bad decoration. Maybe I don't argue. Never before has criticism revealed so strongly and clearly its insignificance, mediocrity and lack of taste.
>
> *(Stanislavsky to Nina Nikolaevna Litovtseva, 12 March 1934, 295)*

Talents and Admirers became Litovtseva's last attempt to stage an individual production at the Moscow Art Theatre. She became a highly respected director-pedagogue, a person who could restore the Moscow Art Theatre's classical productions accurately and contributed to the Moscow Art Theatre's most renowned productions of *Resurrection* and *Anna Karenina* – dramatisations of Tolstoy's novels and *Three Sisters* and *Uncle Vanya* by Anton Chekhov. But unlike other female director-pedagogues, Litovtseva did not direct elsewhere and remained faithful to the Moscow Art Theatre despite their hardships and rewards.

Twenty-one years her junior, Elizaveta Telesheva was a successful actress and director who established herself as an independent director in the late 1930s. Telesheva studied with Aleksandr Adashev at his theatre school from 1912 to 1913, where Vakhtangov attended in 1909, taught by Sulerzhitsky. She joined the Second Moscow Art Theatre Studio in 1916, where Nina Litovtseva taught and directed, and joined the Moscow Art Theatre in 1924. Telesheva became a prominent actress from the beginning of her career and aspired to become a theatre director. An enthusiast of the system and with Stanislavsky's wishes, she taught the system at several institutions throughout her life, including the State Theatre Institute and the State Institute of Cinematography, and lectured around the country. Later in life, she acted as assistant director and acting coach advising Sergei Eisenstein.

She became a renowned pedagogue, working first with the Soviet film star Lyubov Orlova and then with German American film star Marlene Dietrich. In her memoirs, Maria Knebel fondly recalled lessons with Telesheva about Stanislavsky's system:

> Breaking my desperate resistance, she forced me to deal with the elements of the system, have exercises on communication with a partner, to lead action without objects. Telesheva would harshly comment, "You don't know how to listen to your partner, you don't know how to communicate, you are too nervous, you can't perform the simplest tasks". Sometimes she gently but persistently reminds me that "every actor is an acrobat who cannot immediately perform a difficult number without developing his physical apparatus first".
>
> *(Knebel, 145)*

Over the years, Knebel fully understood and appreciated Telesheva's advice. A passionate supporter of the system and Moscow Art Theatre acting, unlike Litovtseva, who was raised as an artist in the environment of the pre-directorial and early directorial theatre, Telesheva was two generations younger, a great admirer of the Moscow Art Theatre performances, and a firm believer in the Stanislavsky's system. Stanislavsky insisted that Telesheva and Litovtseva were both director-pedagogues, though Telesheva went much further than Litovtseva in her career. Litovtseva was considered an outsider, not quite a part of the Moscow Art Theatre ensemble and not trained in Stanislavsky's system. Telesheva was part of the Moscow Art Theatre Second Studio with fellow talented actors who would later become the core of the Soviet-era Moscow Art Theatre. Telesheva's collaborations with her male colleagues, for example, with Ilya Sudakov, one of the most extravagant creators of the visual performances (with whom Stanislavsky was fighting for years, accusing Sudakov of degradingly shallow productions), were certainly very productive. While Sudakov was responsible for the extravagant staging, she was able to discuss, criticise and suggest something new, which was not possible for Litovtseva, who was senior in age and status but had less experience with directing, and whose every suggestion was often treated as a personal attack.

At the Moscow Art Theatre, Telesheva was one of the co-directors of such performances as *The Marriage of Figaro* by Pierre Beaumarchais *Sisters Gérard* by Vladimir Mass (based on *The Two Orphans* by Adolphe d'Ennery and Eugène Cormon); *Three Stouts* by Yuri Olesha; *Dead Souls* by Nikolai Gogol, adapted for the stage by Mikhail Bulgakov; *Woe from Wit* by Alexsander Griboyedov, newly directed and premiered in 1938; and *The Last Sacrifice* by Alexander Ostrovsky. Stanislavsky congratulated Telesheva on her 15th anniversary at the Moscow Art Theatre, presenting her with the theatre's famous seagull pin:

> The most difficult years of the civil war and the first years after the revolution [the Socialist Revolution in 1917] were when you entered in the art, the time when your creative energy was shaped and strengthened. During those hard years, you were [...] together with the theatre. A new era of creativity has come, and truly great work awaiting [you]. This new time expects you to dedicate ten times more to the Art Theatre at the new stage of its life. Be as understanding and truthful in art as you have been for the past 15 years.
>
> *(Stanislavsky to Elizaveta Telesheva, 27 October 1931, 236)*

In 1934, Telesheva was again one of the collective directors, with Nikolai Khemlev and Victor Konsky, working on Alexander Ostrovsky's play *The Last Sacrifice*.

Litovtseva and Telesheva's experiences at the Moscow Art Theatre might seem very different. Unlike Litovtseva, Telesheva was a dedicated teacher of the system. She was considered nearly equal to her male colleagues who belonged to the collective of directors at the Moscow Art Theatre. However, their work bore similar results. In 1935, Stanislavsky assigned Alexander Ostrovsky's *The Ward*. Telesheva led 119 rehearsals, implementing Stanislavsky's system and trying to achieve realistic acting. He followed his recommendations to avoid creating mise-en-scènes that would distract from the actors' impulses and truth of feelings. Although the production never entered the Moscow Art Theatre repertoire, it toured as a satellite project. Stanislavsky wrote to Telesheva, to assure her:

> What happened with *The Ward* should not embarrass you and your young actors. I think that neither you nor they were expected to give [...] the 'experienced' acting at once. But in such 'inexperienced' performances for me bring a very special charm to youth. Vladimir Ivanovich [Nemirovich-Danchenko] never liked an immature actor. [...] You have done a marvellous job and done it all by yourself. Continue walking along this path.
>
> *(Stanislavsky, 1999, Vol. 9, 292)*

However, before the production of *The Ward* was cancelled, Telesheva made the most important decision of her life: to direct elsewhere. Unlike Litovtseva, between 1934 and 1936, Telesheva successfully directed two productions at the Central Red Army Theatre: *The Philistines* in 1935 and *Vassa Zheleznova* in 1936, both by Maxim Gorky, while simultaneously working at the Moscow Art Theatre. Stanislavsky did not see Telesheva's productions at the Central Red Army Theatre, but Nemirovich-Danchenko did. He wrote that *The Philistines* proved to him that Telesheva had become a theatre director in the full meaning of the title (Bokshanskaya, 2005, Vol. 2, 375).

In the late '30s, before his death, Stanislavsky's focus was on pedagogical work to develop the young actor's technique, which led to changes to the system. Nemirovich-Danchenko, as usual, expressed his disagreement with Stanislavsky:

> Your requirement is that the actor does not learn the role before rehearsal, while I demand that he knows the text as soon as possible. Behind this disagreement, as you understand, is a long chain of all sorts of pedagogical differences between us [...] Or you deny the importance of the director's "showing" (the actors how to play their characters) [...] while I consider this to be a very important moment influencing the growth of an actor. [...] How many wonderful characters matured their technique after the older and more experienced actors showed them [how to play their parts].
>
> *(Nemirovich-Danchenko to K.S Stanislavsky, 24 January 1936, 514)*

In the same letter, Nemirovich-Danchenko defends Ilya Sudakov, the director, who, according to Stanislavsky, should be dismissed once and for all. Nemirovich-Danchenko's view was very practical: Sudakov, he wrote, could finish every play on time, while all the preparatory work was Telesheva's domain. Perhaps his radical disagreement with Stanislavsky about directing at the Moscow Art Theatre influenced his evaluation of Telesheva's production of *The Philistines* at Central Red Army Theatre. Telesheva had worked successfully as a director at the Central Red Army Theatre but did not finish her work on *The Ward* at the Moscow Art Theatre. The never-ending pedagogical preparatory work of the play did not help its direction; rather, it stultified its staging.

Although the actress and director Kseniya Kotlubai is listed among the Moscow Art Theatre directors and joined the Collegium with Litovtseva and Telesheva in 1928, her work with Stanislavsky was minimal, and she worked more so with Nemirovich-Danchenko at the Moscow Art Theatre Third Studio, later the Vakhtangov Theatre, becoming his most devoted follower. Initially a devotee of the Stanislavsky system, she learned it in practice at the Third Studio, taught by Vakhtangov. In her short life and career, Kotlubai became a great advocate of the system. She was not involved in the debates between Stanislavsky's system and Vakhtangov's interpretation of it. After Vakhtangov's death, Kotlubai swore her allegiance to the Moscow Art Theatre and, in 1922, joined the group of young actors and directors as one-half of the theatre toured North America, assisting Nemirovich-Danchenko with directing and teaching at the Moscow Art Theatre Musical Studio. Together with Leonid Baratov, she directed Aristophanes' *Lysistrata* in 1923 under Nemirovich-Danchenko's supervision. She also participated in the productions of Bizet's *Carmen* and *Aleko* by Rachmaninov, with Nemirovich-Danchenko writing its libretto based on the poem *The Gypsies* by Alexander Pushkin. She prepared *Uncle's Dream* at the Moscow Art Theatre with Vasily Sakhnovsky, which was adapted from Fyodor Dostoevsky's novel, again under Nemirovich-Danchenko's general supervision.

The pedagogical aims of the system and the practical needs of the Moscow Art Theatre could not seem further apart, as demonstrated by Nemirovich-Danchenko's disagreement with Stanislavsky. In 1936, Maria Lilina, the Moscow Art Theatre actress and Stanislavsky's wife, began to rehearse Anton Chekhov's *The Cherry Orchard* as a director-pedagogue, leading 59 rehearsals. Lilina's unique position was that she could rehearse at her home with Stanislavsky under his direct supervision as a director-pedagogue. While instructing her before rehearsals, Stanislavsky gave her the same advice as he did to the group of teachers at the Opera Studio, including Maria Knebel. Stanislavsky forbade the actors from reading the play before rehearsals; they were all to be 'blindfolded' and follow their teacher for their improvisations of scenes and the characters. This practice was a unique experience in the theatre: Stanislavsky put his entire trust in the director-pedagogue's understanding of the play and its characters. By approaching rehearsal this way, the students would base their improvisations entirely on the teacher's perspective on the play and not Chekhov's writing as they read it. Stanislavsky was unmoved by any of the student's requests to read the play and recommended that they be reprimanded if they read the play against his instruction. Lilina brought a note from Stanislavsky to rehearsal that clearly stated the actors should not read the play. However, after Stanislavsky watched the last rehearsal of *The Cherry Orchard*, he noted that the improvisational acting was fresh but that the production was not adequately staged, and so, in its current form, could not be performed on a professional stage (Maria Lilina in Leontievsky, 262).

Stanislavsky never imagined women could become professional theatre directors in the same capacity as he saw himself. Analysing his working experiences with female directors on the Moscow Art Theatre productions, as well as other studios such as the Opera-Dramatic Studio, he did not teach them the skills of creating mise-en-scènes or expressing the play's themes through staging or reflecting the genre of the play in its visual presentation. However, Stanislavsky did not teach his male students directing skills either. Both men and women learned theatre directing 'from the inside'. However, as I described with Litovtseva, the Moscow Art Theatre Director's Collegium was entirely male until 1928 and only changed after her intervention. Accounts of Stanislavsky's directing, such as Nikolai Gorchakov's *Stanislavsky Directs*, provide compartmentalisations and summations of Stanislavsky's rehearsals, which Stanislavsky himself did not consider lessons in directing.

Stanislavsky's belief that women should be theatre pedagogues never changed. Although he might not have believed in the female director's ability to oversee and direct an entire production successfully, he certainly did everything he could to encourage them and foster their learning, with later generations of women honouring his efforts.

Post Chapter Discussion: Maria Ignatieva with Rose Whyman

Rose Whyman Maria, I am delighted to discuss your chapter on *Stanislavsky and Gender* with you and to continue our collaboration. I very much enjoyed co-writing our chapter for *The Palgrave Handbook of the History of Women on Stage* (2020) on the 'Second Wave' Moscow Art Theatre actresses Serafima Birman, Sofia Giatsintova, Alla Tarasova and Olga Pyzhova. I admire your dedicated work in uncovering and analysing the achievements and stories of women of the Moscow Art Theatre. These are hidden histories not just because of historical neglect of study of women in theatre but because of the fact that in the revolutionary and Soviet period, there was censorship, manipulation of information, revisionism and the destruction of valuable materials. Your work involves much painstaking archival and other research. In the current chapter, you continue to unearth information on Stanislavsky's female collaborators that is not only of interest in terms of recognising and celebrating the work of these women but also in terms of how we continue to work with Stanislavsky's legacy and methods in contemporary theatre, where of course, attitudes to gender differ enormously.

You open your chapter with the statement that Stanislavsky defined our contemporary understanding of the professional theatre director as one who should cover all aspects of the theatre – "administrative, artistic, literary, musical, staging, and, finally, pedagogical and psychological". And though Stanislavsky changed his approach from that of the "dictator-director" to one that supported the actor's creativity, he remained the "master" and as you write, he and Nemirovich-Danchenko had "ultimate artistic control" over Moscow Art Theatre productions. It is interesting that a working model was set up, as you describe, with the female directors working with actors and men creating every other aspect of the production.

Can you comment further on what were the implicit qualities in the female directors that made it seem like women could contribute to rehearsal processes of psychological realism (for example, being nurturing, emotionally attuned) and what were the male characteristics or qualities of the 'master-director'? And though Stanislavsky clearly made great moves forward for a man of his time in assisting the emergence of the female director, to what extent did the female director have to embody those male characteristics in order to work?

Maria Ignatieva Dear Rose, I have greatly valued our past collaborations and look forward to working together on new projects in the future. Your practical work as an actor and director before becoming an academician has given you unique insights into the professions of actor and director, as well as pedagogy. You have been one of the most knowledgeable scholars in Russian theatre; your professional training has allowed you to have a wider look at the different theatre training schools in Russian theatre. Your questions and comments are so deep and essential that it would have taken me many pages to answer them. Forgive me in advance for the incompletion of my responses.

I believe that the tragic aspect of his theatre experience in the last years of Stanislavsky's life is the inability to fuse the advanced development of the system with practical directorial work. Stanislavsky himself faced bitter disappointments in Nina Litovtseva's directing (while finding interesting moments in the characters' relationships, she was unable to find convincing mise-en-scènes that would express the essence of the play in actions.) A similar story happened to Maria Lilina, who was working on *The Cherry Orchard* at the Opera-Dramatic Studio: the actors convincingly 'lived their characters' lives', but the play needed to be *staged*. Something along these lines happened to Elizaveta Telesheva when she directed at Moscow Art Theatre. Telesheva later proved herself a successful director when she staged plays outside the Moscow Art Theatre (unfortunately, she never had a chance to further develop her skills because of her early death). The first woman who was able to successfully merge the system in acting with the staging, was Maria Knebel (I believe her work with Mikhail Chekhov in his studio played a pivotal role in her becoming a director).

Rose Whyman It is also interesting that contemporary directors in the UK and elsewhere who acknowledge that they work in the Stanislavskian tradition now emphasise collaborative ways of working. For example, Declan Donellan writes:

> I make it very clear that I'm not in the position of a teacher towards an actor, but I am maybe in the position of coach towards an athlete. For me theatre is always at its best when I'm learning as well.
>
> *(in Ledger, 52)*

And Katie Mitchell "sees her role primarily as that of a facilitator, emphasising listening, offering choices and setting up a democratic situation" (in Manful, 75).

While my own experience is of teaching acting rather than directing, the basis for my classes tends to be the work of Stanislavsky and Michael Chekhov (with other elements). As Ross Prior identified, "Western actor training has grown without a clearly articulated philosophy of teaching and learning practice due essentially to the kinds of trainers employed who do not come from a teaching background" (Prior, xix). In *An Actor's Work*, Stanislavsky/Tortsov describes practices and processes rather than pedagogy. In teaching student-actors how to 'experience' a role, in Stanislavsky's terminology, questions of well-being are very important for me, and I rely very much on pedagogy of the Alexander Technique in my work in enabling students to be emotionally expressive without strain or harm.

From this, I have two related questions:

1 In your own directing work with students, how do you draw on your experiences with the Moscow Art Theatre and Stanislavsky's work, and how do you see your own role as a female director?
2 In working with young people, are there pedagogical strategies you adopt, particularly around the area of emotional expression?

Maria Ignatieva Regarding the pedagogy, I agree that "Western actor training has grown without a clearly articulated philosophy of teaching and learning practice due essentially to the kinds of trainers employed who do not come from a teaching background". Would it be possible to change it? There is a great interest in Stanislavsky's pedagogy these days; however, I do not know how far contemporary theatrical practice and actual training are from theoretical studies.

The cult of creating "here and now" and instant discoveries on stage during rehearsals (and acting classes) have been THE guiding principle for many Russian directors, both male and female. The process of immediate, live creativity during rehearsals is greatly expected on the Russian professional stage. Even on the level of pedagogy in various actors' training institutions, every master teaches the system to the best of their understanding of it. Estelle Parsons, who was the head of the Actors' Studio then, visited the Moscow Art Theatre School Studio in 2003, angrily exclaimed afterwards: "What I saw is purely presentational theatre training. It has nothing to do with the Stanislavsky System". (She, her husband, I, and my husband had dinner in Moscow right after her observations). Knowing the style of the master of the class she attended, I would completely agree with her.

As for Declan Donnellan and his Stanislavskian modes: yes, he took the Russian actors whom he directed to the isolated forestry in Russia to experience "togetherness" while working on their productions. However, although very interesting from the directorial point of view, his productions did not always bring new depths in them (it was especially clear in *The Three Sisters*).

My own directing. I am hopelessly Russian in the way I direct. I come prepared for the rehearsal, but then it's time for magic, improvisations, and discoveries. Finding the mise-en-scènes that express the essence of the text is of the greatest importance to me. The intuitive togetherness that is built during rehearsals allows us to tune in to each other. The form, the movement, the gesture, and the rhythm are vital. When I direct or write, I don't feel my gender at all.

In terms of pedagogical approaches. My lyrical answer: I believe we have to infect students with our passion. For practical pedagogy, I have used Vygotsky's zone of proximal development, which is based on similar principles as the Stanislavsky system.

Rose Whyman Thank you for your responses, Maria. It is very interesting that you point out that in Stanislavsky's last years, there was no way to fuse successfully the advanced development of the system with practical directorial work and that Maria Knebel was the first woman to be able to do this, later on. It seems from what you say that Litovtseva and Lilina were skilled enough to work with actors to develop their roles but lacked the artistic vision and skill needed to stage plays that Telesheva began to develop before her untimely death. Knebel's experience in Michael Chekhov's Studio before joining the Moscow Art Theatre, first the Second Studio then the main theatre, and working closely with Stanislavsky in his later years gave her a unique experience. Chekhov always acknowledged his debt to Stanislavsky and said his own work was rooted in the system but from the time of the First Studio and the beginnings of the system, felt free to play, to challenge the ideas and develop them in his own way. Perhaps this sense of freedom was what was lacking in others wanting to develop as directors. Serafima Birman, also a member of the First Studio and one of the first women to direct was seen often as constrained by a rigid adherence to the system in her work as a Soviet director. As is well-known, in Soviet times, the system became ossified with a particular emphasis on the so-called Method of Physical Actions seen the be all and end all of the system.

With these considerations of freedom, re-invention and play, I love your description of the creation of "here and now" and instant discoveries on stage during rehearsals and acting classes as THE guiding principle for many Russian directors. As you say the process of immediate, live creativity during rehearsals is expected on the Russian professional stage and so it should be on all professional stages! The how of achieving this is what interests me – what the director or pedagogue brings to that process that means no matter what has been prepared and planned they can respond to what is going on in the group in the moment, excite and inspire and take the work in new directions.

Vadim Shcherbakov discusses the aims of Stanislavsky's First Studio of the Moscow Art Theatre and Meyerhold's Borodinskaia Studio in St Petersburg, both set up in 1912/1913, writing that despite the differences,

> the Studios had the *same aim* – of educating the actor of the new directors' theatre, of distinguishing what is the creative freedom of the actor and how this freedom

> can be combined with the with the score of the production created earlier, the aim of defining the optimal relationship in the new stage art of *zadannost'* (what has been set) and *improvisation*.
>
> *(Shcherbakov, 178–179)*

Perhaps the test of whether that 'optimal relationship' is being achieved is in that sense of immediate, alive creativity that is palpable to those engaged in the performance and to audiences, where the process, in your words, of finding the mise-en-scènes that express the essence of the text, working with what is set or in the process of becoming set in rehearsal in terms of form, movement, gesture, and rhythm is founded in that aliveness.

I find your mention of your pedagogy based in Vygotsky's zone of proximal development and comparison of it with the system intriguing. I'm aware of the influence of Stanislavsky on Vygotsky's ideas of the psychology of the actor (and his contact with Gurevich), as well as his contact with Meyerhold and Eisenstein and proposal of a new response to Diderot's paradox, but how to work with actors using the zone of proximal development sounds like a big discussion for another time!

Works Cited

Bokshanskaya, O. *Pisma Nemirovich-Danchenko* (*Letters to Nemirovich-Danchenko*). Volumes 1 & 2. Moscow: The Moscow Art Theatre Publishing house, 2005.

Goyan, G. Fedotov's Glyceria. Moscow: Iskusstvo, 1940. Available Online: http://teatr-lib.ru/Library/Nemirovich/stat/#_ee0010182 [Accessed January 2024].

Ignatieva, M. *Stanislavsky and Female Actors: Women in Stanislavsky's Life and Art*. Plymouth: University Press of America, 2008.

Knebel, M. *Vsia zhizn* [*All of Life*]. Moscow: VTO, 1967.

Kudriavtsev, I. *Diaries*. Moscow: Navona Publishing Group, 2019.

Ledger, A. *The Director and Directing*. London: Palgrave MacMillan, 2019. DOI: https://doi.org/10.1057/978-1-137-40767-2

Leontievsky, N. ed. *Maria Petrovna Lilina: ocherk zhizni i tvorchestva* [*Maria Petrovna Lilina: Life and Art*]. Moscow: VTO, 1960.

Litovtseva, N.N. *Letter no. 11405 to the Moscow Art Theatre*. April 1927. Moscow: The Museum of the Moscow Art Theatre, 1927.

Manfull, H. *Taking Stage: Women Directors on Directing*. London: Methuen Drama, 1999.

Nemirovich-Danchenko, V.I. Letter no. 514 to K.S Stanislavsky. 24th January 1936. Moscow. Available Online: http://teatr-lib.ru/Library/Nemirovich/letters_2/#_Toc163558824 [Accessed January 2024].

Prior, R. *Teaching Actors: Knowledge Transfer in Actor Training*. Bristol: Intellect Books, 2012.

Shcherbakov, V. *Pantomimy Serebryanogo Veka, St Petersburg: Peterburgskii Teatral'nyi Zhurnal*, 2014.

Stanislavski, K. *My Life in Art.* London: Routledge, 2008. DOI: https://doi.org/10.4324/9781315823720

Stanislavsky, K.S. Letter no. 236 to Elizaveta Sergeevna Telesheva. 27th October 1931. Moscow. Available Online: http://az.lib.ru/s/stanislawskij_k_s/text_0070.shtml [Accessed January 2024].

Stanislavsky, K.S. Letter no.157 to Lyubov Yakovlevna Gurevich. 4th March 1928. Moscow. Available Online: http://az.lib.ru/s/stanislawskij_k_s/text_0070.shtml [Accessed January 2024].

Stanislavsky, K.S. Letter no.295 to Nina Nikolaevna Litovtseva. 12th March 1934. Nice, France. Available Online: http://az.lib.ru/s/stanislawskij_k_s/text_0070.shtml [Accessed January 2024].

Stanislavsky, K.S. *Sobranie Sochinenii* [*Collected Works*]. Volumes 1–9. Moscow: Iskusstvo, 1988–1999.

Vinogradskaya, I. ed. *Letopis' zhizni i tvorchestva Stanislavkogo (1863–1938)* [*The Life and Work of Stanislavsky (1863-1938)*]. Volumes 1-4. Second Edition. Moscow: Izdatel'stvo Khudozhestvennyi Teatr, 1971-2003.

2

ACTING EMOTIONAL EXPRESSION AND GENDER IDENTITY IN STANISLAVSKY'S APPROACH

Peta Tait

Olga Knipper and Konstantin Stanislavsky acted together to acclaim in the early Moscow Art Theatre productions such as Anton Chekhov's *Three Sisters*, which established the company's reputation and Stanislavsky's reputation as a director. This chapter considers comments about Knipper's approach to performance and Stanislavsky's acting and directing in instances during Knipper's career when her interpretation of the character's emotions had to be adjusted. It asks: To what extent was a divergence in their approaches due to gendered expectations for emotional expression that are indicative of wider patterns in twentieth-century theatre and society? Scholarship finding disagreement between them implicitly values Stanislavsky's analytical approach over Knipper's interpretation. Knipper, however, emphasises how the character's feeling arises in relation to the circumstances and expression of others; that is, it develops within a dynamic process. Knipper describes a relational performance of emotional feeling.

Knipper was the first female performer to interpret some of the most notable female characters in twentieth-century theatre history – namely, those in Anton Chekhov's major plays. A fuller recognition of her contribution to the history of realistic acting has implications for pedagogy supporting a metanarrative of twentieth-century theatre. By implication, female collaborators need to be accorded more significance, and Knipper is one of Stanislavsky's key collaborators (Schuler, 1996; Ignatieva, 2008). The analysis here does not set out to denigrate Stanislavsky, whose work I value highly, but to question gendered assertions and assumptions within working relationships and approaches to acting emotions. It reaffirms theatre as a collaborative undertaking by highlighting Knipper's contribution to early realist acting since it may have assisted Stanislavsky's exploratory shifts. It contends that Knipper's descriptions point

DOI: 10.4324/9781003411611-3

to an actor's cognitive awareness of feeling within performance to belie claims of instinctive acting. In their theatre work, both Knipper and Stanislavsky offered perspectives on emotional experience in advance of later approaches developed in psychology.

Incomplete Histories and Relational Acting

When Oliver Sayler claims that the three great moments in the Moscow Art Theatre's production of Anton Chekhov's *Three Sisters*, first staged in 1903, were between Olga Knipper and Stanislavsky as Masha and Vershinin, he attributes these moments to Stanislavsky's "genius" (Sayler, 52). The high points of the production that Sayler saw in 1917 were the Act Two entrance and declaration of love by the characters, the Act Three exchanges of 'Tra-ta-ta', and the "most unaffected, most deeply moving farewell of the modern theatre" towards the end of Act Four (Sayler, 52). Sayler acknowledges Knipper's unique capacity, albeit through a comparison. While the lovers in the first Moscow Art Theatre production became a recognised part of theatre history (e.g. Brockett and Ball, 157), Knipper's interpretation of these emotional interactions is less recognised; Knipper as Masha and Stanislavsky as Vershinin created these dynamic moments of emotional relations. Knipper's contribution to theatre history is supported by those claiming that she was the Moscow Art Theatre's "greatest actress" (Toporkov, 221).

This chapter considers interpretations of Knipper's acting in accounts available in English that describe Stanislavsky's acting and directing and particularly those instances in which Knipper's contribution is undervalued, and criticised. I am asking whether a gender bias underlies praise for Stanislavsky's work and takes Knipper's contribution as a female performer for granted and how such a discrepancy might be explained. These accounts perpetuate values evident within the Moscow Art Theatre when criticisms of other highly accomplished female actors reveal inappropriate and mistaken prejudices (Ignatieva and Whyman, 2019). Such bias arises from beliefs about gender difference which are supported by long-standing binary values in Western culture that esteem analytical thought as masculine over emotional expression as feminine (Lutz, 1988). Since acting is emotional, it is often accorded an association with femininity. Yet theatre has long reflected Diderot's paradox of sustained technique rather than reliance on spontaneous feeling to arouse audience responses. The consideration of the emotions in theatre allows for distinctions between its expressive language and actual feeling, and recent affect theory suggesting that bodily felt sensations need not be emotional (Tait, 2022).

In Knipper's account of her work with Stanislavsky, she describes a dynamic of responding to the looks and emotional intonations of Stanislavsky's character while performing (Magarshack, 192–194). Knipper describes an approach to acting in which she responds to the embodied expressions of others.

Knipper's description of an interactive dynamic elaborates on a preparatory process undertaken in rehearsal. The description conveys how emotional feeling develops as a response to someone or something and through exchange. It suggests that emotions are relational, arising in relation to others. Knipper's understanding exists in advance of later twentieth-century analysis of emotions in social relations (Parkinson et al., 2005).

Knipper admitted that working with Stanislavsky was especially evocative for her (Magarshack, 256–257). Her relational approach is compatible with Stanislavsky's innovative encouragement of physical restraint and minimal gesture. She was part of the theatre movement which rejected melodramatic nineteenth-century demonstrating with gestures and bodily positions to signal the emotions and often accompanied by direct address to the audience. Jean Benedetti writes that instead, Stanislavsky saw the voice coming from the physical manifestation of inner impulses and the controlled pacing and adjustment of tempo for delivering strong emotions (Benedetti, 144). As Benedetti suggests, the Moscow Art Theatre became successful at seemingly "doing nothing", including with emotions (Benedetti, 97). Both Knipper and Stanislavsky sought new modes of emotional expression in theatrical contexts.

The Moscow Art Theatre was striving for realism. In social situations, someone responds emotionally, although not mechanically, and not necessarily transparently, so that this can be discerned by others either in behaviour or through bodily agitations (Parkinson et al., 13–17). Later psychological approaches would recognise that emotional feelings are responses to stimuli in the surroundings shaped by a pre-existing orientation. Hence the stimulation of feeling repeats patterns. The Moscow Art Theatre acting would seem to have sought a replication of bodily agitation insofar as it elaborates on the play's context, narrative, and staged movement. The approaches of both Knipper and Stanislavsky involve repetition in rehearsal but the primacy of bodily feeling – pioneered by James-Lange theory in the late nineteenth century – proves less helpful to the performing of emotions with minimal gesture and restraint than it might first appear (see Tait forthcoming). Both cognitive and bodily processes underpin theatrical expression.

A female performer may have been especially attuned to how emotional expression happens within social situations and conditioned to understand its gendered selectiveness. Anthropologist Catherine Lutz explains that, in Western culture, "emotion is seen as a component of individuals rather than of social situations or relationships" (Lutz, 1988, 41). The prevailing Western orthodoxy failed to appreciate how emotion and its languages are culturally specific. At the same time, gender identity arises within the embodied practices of social institutions and their knowledges (Butler, 2004), which include theatre. Lutz (1990) and Butler (2004) delineate how the feminine self is socially constituted and becomes intelligible through discursive disclosure and embodied practices. Lutz, however, finds that, historically, gender identity is reliant on exchanges about emotions in Western culture. Beliefs about gender differences are enforced by how a feminine self remains vigilant about which emotions are appropriate to express. For example, anger may have been far less socially acceptable at the turn of the twentieth century for women, whereas tears were acceptable but far less so for men. The performer enacting a female character in early realism is caught up in a dual process of having to interpret the emotions of the theatrical text in the new style of acting, as well as expressing them in socially intelligible ways.

While Knipper's approach might seem to be a precursor to an interactive approach between performers, such as that of Sanford Meisner, it can also be aligned with studies of emotions in the second half of the twentieth century that describe emotional experience as being relational and, importantly, configured within a power imbalance so it is political (Ahmed, 2004). Emotional feeling arises in relation to other people and the surroundings in response to stimuli and social cues. Hence, theatrical processes draw on prior patterning to replicate realistic social relations.

Knipper's Interpretations of Characters

Stanislavsky and Knipper each expressed respect and admiration for the other's acting. In an insightful analysis of Knipper's performance career and her well-developed professionalism and commitment to the Moscow Art Theatre, Maria Ignatieva elaborates on differences in their first years due to age and Stanislavsky's existing reputation, experience, and unpredictability that intimidated Knipper. In her first major Moscow Art Theatre role as Tsarina Irina in *Tsar Fyodor* by Aleksey Konstantinovich Tolstoy in 1898, Knipper drew respect for how she acted the character's reserve and concealed feelings while releasing tears in a crucial moment (Ignatieva, 74). Knipper's performance as Arkadina in Anton Chekhov's *The Seagull* was a complete contrast, creating sincerity in her character and a broad range of expressive emotional changes. In acknowledging this capacity, theatre critic Nicolai Efros wrote that he thought Knipper showed technical brilliance and virtuosity (Ignatieva, 75). When Stanislavsky compared Knipper in 1905 to another female actor, he praised Knipper, describing her as a "major key actress" who could "command" while the other performer could not communicate her emotional responses (Stanislavski, 1966, 44). Knipper performs emotional responses that are perceptible.

Stanislavsky directed Knipper in several formative Moscow Art Theatre productions, so it seems reasonable to ask what aspects of Stanislavsky's direction in rehearsal proved difficult for Knipper. During the rehearsals, her interpretations of the character often had to be adjusted to reflect what he sought from her performance. Some of his adjustments are about how performers need to work with the director to shape the rhythm of a whole production and therefore artistically valid. However, several examples suggest that Knipper could not interpret female characters based on her understanding and observation of female emotional experience. An ideal that early realist theatre seem realistic was also at stake for a female performer.

Benedetti reports that Knipper wanted to act Masha's confession of her love for Vershinin to her sisters "on a note of high, almost desperate emotion – a penitent woman pouring out her heart" (Benedetti, 107). Stanislavsky felt that at this point in Act Three, her delivery should be subdued to reflect exhaustion and to fit into his director's plan for emotional progression. Laurence Senelick writes that Knipper was "right" about the character while Stanislavsky was right about "the curve of the play" (Senelick, 61). In Benedetti's account, they disagreed so vehemently that he believes Stanislavsky considered removing her from the play. Their disagreement was resolved when the playwright and director and Stanislavsky's co-founder of the Moscow Art Theatre, Vladimir Nemirovich-Danchenko, agreed with Stanislavsky and imposed a physical limitation. Subsequently, Anton Chekhov concurred with Nemirovich-Danchenko. Chekhov and Stanislavsky also suggested that Knipper downplay Masha's sadness.

This difference in approach was not simply a disagreement over Knipper's general approach to acting emotions, nor was it indicative of her style. It was her interpretation of a particular character's emotions in the specific social circumstances of the play, which in *Three Sisters* involve a woman engaging in an extra-marital affair. Masha confesses a life-changing event to her sisters, who are close companions and monitor how one another feel. Masha's affair might have been exhilarating for her, but it was emotionally, socially, and morally confronting for these characters, so it was fraught. Conversely, prior to this role, in 1899, Knipper had found great difficulty acting the "anguish" of the "highly-strung" interpretation of Helena in Chekhov's *Uncle Vanya* imposed on her by Stanislavsky and Nemirovich-Danchenko (Pitcher, 192). Instead, she wanted to create a cool and impassive character. The dynamic between Stanislavsky as director and Knipper as a performer in their earliest rehearsal work on Chekhov's plays was no doubt complicated by Knipper's allegiances within the Moscow Art Theatre as well as her negotiations between the director's and the playwright's varying interpretations of the characters. But in this instance, Knipper had her own views that challenged the director's perspective over the emotional choices for the circumstances. Knipper may have subsequently become nervous and possibly inhibited in her first performances of Helena because of divergent interpretations of Helena between the two male directors – and between the characters in the play (Ignatieva, 77). Regardless, she describes acting Helena in response to the emotional undercurrents of Stanislavsky's performance as Astrov (Ignatieva, 76).

Aside from the validity of Stanislavsky's aim to create an overall tempo for a production through the direction, his interpretation of some of the reactions of female characters was questionable. His instruction for Knipper as Arkadina in *The Seagull* to pace the stage with her hands behind her back when she is angry after Treplev stops his play, strikes John Styan as inappropriate for an actress-character accustomed to commanding attention (Styan, 36).

In the Moscow Art Theatre's work, the male performers were commonly perceived to be better than the female performers. Sayler observed the Moscow Art Theatre in 1917 and writes, "The Art Theatre is weaker, comparatively, in its women" (Sayler, 23). At the same time, Sayler compliments Knipper and other Moscow Art Theatre female performers. Sayler also acknowledges Knipper's and Stanislavsky's performances in Chekhov's *The Cherry Orchard* as accomplished (Sayler, 56). He esteems Knipper's Madame Ranevskaya because she can shift from depicting a worldly woman to a caring mother (Sayler, 57). Knipper's artistic range is appreciated when her character is a lover or displays nurturing behaviour. Despite the differences between Knipper as a determined, independent woman with a career and the emotionally dependent character of Ranevskaya, Pitcher describes similarities in their emotional reactions and adherence to love (Pitcher, 197). By implication, Knipper can become Ranevskaya because she is like her rather than because she is a competent performer creating a character. Knipper perceptibly manifests Ranevskaya's uncertainty through her gestures. A critical reception that assumes an effective performer resembles her fictional female character, so her character is assumed to be like herself, undermines recognition of the performance skill. Female performers were therefore less recognised for their accomplished acting of emotional expression.

Senelick is critical of Knipper's emphasis on the "irritability" of Ranevskaya, which detracted from the depiction of charm and frivolousness (Senelick, 70). By implication, the character was less likeable. He reports that Stanislavsky describes Knipper as acting sentimentally (Senelick, 70). Ignatieva, however, recognises Knipper's capacity to convey the sensual sexuality of a character, notably with Ranevskaya. Significantly, Efros acknowledges Knipper's skill and capacity to alternate tears and laughter when she played Ranevskaya, a challenging oscillation to act for any performer. Knipper performed this role hundreds of times over 30 years.

Knipper was also experimenting with how to act in the new style of early realist theatre. Was Knipper approaching her character from within the circumstances as might be expected in realism? Social expectations influenced the reception of acting, and a female performer was expected to be emotional – perhaps more so than a male performer. At the same time, a female actor's acting of emotions was less valued because it appears to replicate (natural) female behaviour. Lutz (1988) contests the belief that emotions are natural because of selective association with women in Western culture and because of the ongoing effort to monitor and manage emotional expression to remain feminine. The self-managing of emotions seems relevant to the interpretation of female characters in performance. Hence emotional expression becomes socially complicated for female performers.

The interactions in Chekhov's texts suggest an underlying theatricality in expressing emotions to others. The characters draw on literary expressions and theatre to explain their feelings, as if fictional emotions help make sense of their experience. Chekhov's drama also resists the dramatic convention of having characters say what they feel by sometimes suggesting an inherent contradiction in what a character says.

The Moscow Art Theatre productions of Chekhov's plays suggest how one emotion supplants another, so that the character seems to subdue and/or suppress an unruly emotional feeling with another emotion. An impulse to laugh or to cry appears to be stopped by the character. While this becomes a performance of emotional control in social interaction, it has greater social significance for female identity (Tait, 2002). The feminine self is expected to engage in self-control because it is presumed to be more emotional.

It can be argued that female performers must negotiate social expectations and the imperatives of the theatre director, so they doubly discipline emotions in realist theatre. When Knipper performed the role of Anna (Sarra) in Chekhov's *Ivanov* in 1904, critic Efros expected sadness rather than "'an ironic smile'" from Anna, while also appreciating that Knipper could become almost unrecognisable as a "'masterful character actress'" (Ignatieva, 81, 85–86, 93). Also, Efros had been unsure about a previous change in Knipper's performance involving heightened expressiveness. Whether Knipper's emotional choices are innovative and less predictable or not, they were scrutinised. Yet Stanislavsky also acknowledged her capacity for character parts when, for example, Knipper transformed her appearance and performed to acclaim in *The Lower Depths* by Maxim Gorky.

Despite her success in reproducing the Moscow Art Theatre style and appearing to be inwardly experiencing, Knipper did not seem to adapt easily to Stanislavsky's ongoing experimentation with acting techniques, particularly with respect to the emotional emphasis. Other female performers also had difficulties. Maria Lilina, Stanislavsky's wife, did not find Stanislavsky's directions helpful for her work on Maurice Maeterlinck's *Blue Bird* in 1908 (Benedetti, 182). However, there was a wider resistance to the early implementation of the system. Meyerhold had found the rehearsals for *Three Sisters* when Stanislavsky began to impose his directorial style and ensemble approach laboured and "unproductive" (Worrall, 6). By the time of the full implementation of the analytical approach of the system in 1909, rehearsals were tense and performances strained (Mitter, 14). The reticence of the Moscow Art Theatre performers, male and female, to the formal adoption of Stanislavsky's system in 1911 is attributed to his inability to explain his ideas simply and clearly (Edwards, 91). Performers reliant on interactive engagement in rehearsal found Stanislavsky's analytical focus challenging, and he subsequently conceded this by adopting a more conciliatory collaborative approach in his direction.

Through his work with the Moscow Art Theatre actors, Stanislavsky developed practical ways of working with plays that proved invaluable and remain unequalled in their usefulness for performers everywhere. He approached scripts by dividing them into sections and analysing each character's objectives and actions. These separate components were then unified within the director's overall plan. He encouraged the performers to draw on their own observations in ways that could be used for their interpretation of a character's emotions, and he first referred to "'emotion memory'" in 1908 (Benedetti, 174; Stanislavski, 2010).

Early realist theatre sought a life-like effect on the stage, so the fictional character's emotional temperament and reactions needed to appear socially credible. While this relied on a performer's capacity to manifest emotional expression seamlessly, acting is also a cultural phenomenon with historical variation between cultures (Sewell and Smout, 2019). A divergence in Knipper's and Stanislavsky's approaches to the acting of the female characters' emotions continued to impact on productions. For example, Knipper was widely praised for acting Gihle in Knut Hamsun's *In the Grip of Life*, as a lonely and betrayed woman in a production that Stanislavsky did not direct. But Knipper had difficulty with Stanislavsky's psychologising of Gertrude for *Hamlet* in 1911 (Ignatieva, 99). In 1932, on their last production together, Stanislavsky removed Knipper from his cast for his production of Alexander Afinogenov's *Fear* because she could not capture the coarse, serious tone he wanted (Benedetti, 305). Ignatieva explains that Knipper was miscast as an ageing Bolshevik character (Ignatieva, 102). While Knipper's interpretation of the character's emotional reactions needed to reflect particular sociopolitical circumstances, she was once again unable to fulfil the male director's expectation for the emotional expression of a male-authored character. This example reiterates that the emotional impressions of female characterisation remain central to the meaning of realist theatre, as well as a source of tension between Knipper and Stanislavsky.

Director's Judgement

Stanislavsky provides several clear examples of the hierarchical values of gendered emotional expression in practice. His fictional acting teacher, Tortsov, sets a trap for young female performers, albeit on the premise of teaching them a significant point about discipline. He instructs Marya and Sonya to walk up and down, and he criticises their movement to such an extent that Sonya freezes completely and starts to cry, which the watching men laugh at (Stanislavski, 2010, 174–175). The performer's experience of being looked at and criticised for simply walking becomes demoralising, pointing to a pattern in social behaviour in which female physicality is scrutinised. Elsewhere,

Stanislavsky delineates gender differences in emotional reactions when he refers to "feminine feelings" and a woman's "cunning tricks" (Stanislavsky, 1961, 244). In one exercise, he says, "Let us take an example that anyone will understand – women's tears" (Stanislavsky, 1961, 245). He explains that a married female character should cry out of self-sacrificing love for another man and also cry out of anger because she is ageing and, therefore, losing her power to attract men (Stanislavsky, 1961, 246–248). In another example, Stanislavsky's student actor Dasha uses a stick as a prop to look like she is holding a baby, and her accompanying emotional expression fulfils expectations of maternal feeling (Stanislavsky, 1955, 156; 160–161).

Although not analysing Stanislavsky's work directly, Rosemary Malague (2012) explores the gendered implications of its twentieth-century legacy in 'the Method' in detail. The interpretation of emotional feeling in theatrical performance continues to be complicated by gendered values about female physicality and expressiveness. The historical and cultural specificity of gender difference in emotional expression went unquestioned for much of the twentieth century, including in the theatrical enactment of emotions. Yet the broad principles of questioning and experimenting that Stanislavsky specifically encouraged in acting remain valuable for guiding change, including for those challenging the gendering of emotions.

Knipper was described as having difficulties sustaining the character and finding a satisfactory style of speech playing Regina in Ibsen's *Ghosts* in 1905 (Benedetti, 143–144). Stanislavsky, as director, tried to solve the problem of Knipper's expression by demonstrating how the character should physically move coquettishly in a predatory manner. (Did Knipper perceive Regina's social interactions this way?) Knipper's English-language biographer, Harvey Pitcher, claims that Knipper could not copy, and once she found "the kind of feelings which that person was experiencing", then the details of the performance would follow, which he calls acting "from within" (Pitcher, 183). It does suggest beginning with a need to understand the character's situation. Knipper was actually having difficulty making her characterisation of Regina's emotional expression match the director's judgement.

By all accounts, Knipper tended to realise her characterisation fully in the performance. In partial resolution, Sharon Carnicke explains that Stanislavsky withdrew when his direction of Knipper was not working, such as with the non-realistic production of Knut Hamsun's *The Drama of Life* in 1907. Stanislavsky writes to Knipper that he gives "full freedom in the treatment of your role" (Carnicke, 2009, 2). Carnicke elaborates that Knipper had difficulty complying with his coaching in the system's structured techniques during rehearsals, although, as mentioned, there was a general resistance in the Moscow Art Theatre (Carnicke, 2009, 32). Knipper did worry about what an audience would think of her and in her mature years and was unwilling to rehearse familiar roles or to look foolish (Benedetti, 262; 281–282, 184).

Although Stanislavsky reputedly changed his dictatorial style of directing from a prepared vision after 1906 to that of a "mid-wife", eliciting greater understanding through the process and questioning (Jones, 43), he continued to hold "paternalistic attitudes" (Carnicke 1984, 482). Throughout his working life, he questioned what actors, both male and female, presented in rehearsal and instructed them until he was satisfied (Gorchakov, 1985). Stanislavsky was also pioneering how a director worked with performers as he created a vision for a production (Whyman, 2019). Clearly, Knipper supported Stanislavsky's broad purpose.

Difficulties Acting Self-Feeling

As indicated, a crucial innovation was the way in which the Moscow Art Theatre performers were encouraged to minimise their gestures in the acting of emotions and appear composed (Balukhaty, 35). As the director of Turgenev's *A Month in the Country* in 1909, Stanislavsky removed all movement and gestures in order to maximise the focus on the characters' inner impulses (Edwards, 90). He gave detailed instructions on the emotional reactions of Natalia Islaieva, played by Knipper, emphasising the female character's trickery and mockery. Knipper had difficulty developing "duty to her husband, affection for Rakitin and love for Belyayev" (Magarshack, 307). Was this emotional variability difficult to act? The rehearsals did not progress to Stanislavsky's satisfaction. Benedetti attributes fault to Knipper:

> The main problem was Knipper. She had begun well enough but she was completely thrown when Stanislavski started to apply his new method. He had been in conflict with her before. He had accused her of being lazy, of never being ready on the first night. This was a little unfair since he himself was far from being a first night actor.... But the difference between them was that he had a working method and she had none. She was an instinctive actress but her range was limited. When her instinct failed, as it had in this case, she was lost, and since she found Stanislavski's new ideas too 'intellectual' she was not prepared to be helped. She was attempting, as Stanislavski had suspected she would, to approach the role from the outside. Psychological analysis was lost on her.
>
> *(Benedetti, 183)*

This harsh criticism seems contradictory as it sets up a binary between psychological thinking and instinct. Benedetti's claim of instinctive would seem to contradict Pitcher's statement about Knipper acting from her understanding. On this occasion, Knipper could reproduce social behaviour but could not act from introspection. Knipper's process of relational interaction with other performers was being undermined by reliance on psychological analysis.

The production and the acting of Stanislavsky and Boleslavsky were considered successful, but – almost predictably – Knipper was thought to have failed. Yet interestingly, she played the character as reserved and undergoing an inner struggle, although this was less appreciated.

There seems to be some confusion here over whether the perceived problem with Knipper's acting in this example resulted from the director's rejection of her emotional interpretation of the character – her chosen expression of feeling – or her inability to develop inward psychologising. Moreover, Stanislavsky's encouragement of analytical thought, particularly from 1909 to 1911, presupposes the autonomy of an actor's thinking self. On this occasion, Stanislavsky is seen to have healed the rift by praising Knipper's capacity without making concessions to her, saying, "'I promise not to frighten you with technical jargon'. He advises her to use her own personality, her own psychology" (Benedetti, 183–184). Notwithstanding Stanislavsky's condescending compromise, he encourages Knipper to use her own approach to the character. Perhaps an instruction to draw on her own psychology created an inherent contradiction if a female performer understood that emotions were also performed in social situations outside theatre. The emotions expressed in society were not necessarily those that were being felt.

In Benedetti's description of the working process, Knipper is blamed, like other Moscow Art Theatre actors, for the problems because she does not understand the new system. There is no allowance for the possibility that she might have disagreed with this approach because it seemed to inhibit rather than enhance her performance. Benedetti's interpretation of what happened presumes a hierarchical positioning of thought and careful analysis and dismisses all other approaches as intuitive. Similarly, Pitcher's commentary on their conflict also reiterates that Knipper realised "the limitations of her intuitive approach to acting" while he quotes her saying that there is much at stake with an annual or biannual role "when one's whole life seems to depend on that role" (Pitcher, 188). Knipper was seriously dedicated to her work but not to Stanislavsky's process of acting through self-inquiry. Yet Knipper was clearly developing roles through her embodied practice.

The divergence seems to be about the difficulty of enacting socially credible expression and relational exchanges based on personal self-reflection. Admittedly, in 1909, Knipper was undergoing a period of what Pitcher describes as "acute self-doubt as an actress" – which had happened before (Pitcher, 184). She described her own inner state as chaotic and recounted her anxiety at what she termed "'listening to myself on stage'" (Pitcher, 187). Knipper's awareness of herself while acting confused her. Knipper felt self-doubt because she could act only a fraction of what she experienced. This realisation apparently immobilised her reactions in rehearsal in 1909. She found it difficult to select and sustain felt responses from self-psychologising, and it seemed to have the opposite effect from that intended by Stanislavsky. Knipper either found it hard to interpret what she experienced as instructed, or she found it inappropriate and confusing to act her characters' responses from examining her own felt experience. Whatever the explanation, the assumption that a performer is acting what is inwardly being felt becomes questionable.

Knipper's uncertainty in 1909 coincided with listening to herself, which meant she could not extract the required emotional expression in performance. At other times in her career, Knipper admitted difficulty maintaining inner concentration. When Stanislavski (2010) advocates both observations of social behaviour and self-inquiry as the basis of an actor's preparation and imagining, he assumes these two strategies cohere rather than cause consternation. The instruction to probe self-experience may have been incompatible with a socially expressive self. It may have exposed a gap between what is felt, and the expression expected of women.

Moscow Art Theatre performers developed ways of embodying dynamism. It is clear from various comments about the Moscow Art Theatre's production history that Knipper became accomplished in acting embodied emotions with minimal external movement. In her role as the Countess de Lenier in his 1927 production *The Sisters Gérard*, Stanislavsky describes Knipper as "'perfectly right in using extreme economy of external movement'" (Gorchakov, 295). This restraint made her performed intention with the words stronger. Stanislavsky acknowledges how Knipper limited physical movements and gestures to focus attention on her emotional expression in the delivery. In this instance, her voice expressed her emotions, creating an audible emotional presence. Knipper was also observed communicating emotional expressions and thoughts in silence to a male actor. Nikolai Gorchakov writes that Knipper "looked at her partner and then looked aside with mistrust and wonder. We immediately guessed from the expression of her eyes the first line of her part" (Gorkachov, 316). Her performance involved visual expression and a relational process in that she looks and responds to the other character.

Undoubtedly, by the 1920s, Knipper had mastered the physical restraint associated with the Moscow Art Theatre's realism, its premise of 'being' on stage, and innovative subtly to suggest felt responses. She conveyed the character's underlying emotional motivations and impulses through what Sayler observes as her "rhythmic control, her poise, her reticence, her intellectual as well as her emotional mastery of a scene" (Sayler, 52–53). In this way of working, a performer such as Knipper is considered to be most effective when she appears to harness emotional responses in an embodied way, which is consistent with many of Stanislavsky's ideas in the later years of 'the method of physical actions' and 'active analysis' (Carnicke, 2009, 189–194; 211).

Knipper continued to act in Soviet Russia and became known for her interpretation of Polina in *Enemies* by Maxim Gorky in the mid-1930s. New Zealand theatre director Richard Campion met Knipper in Moscow when she was 87 and described her as looking about 60, upright with "Grey and white hair. Dark eyes alert" (Campion, 5). When he asked, "How did you play the roles?" She replied, "As I felt them". Knipper continues that there is "no one 'right way'" (Campion, 5). Her approach to female characters can be said to come out of engaging with how her character responded to others in the theatrical context.

Conclusion: Imagining Emotion

Knipper clearly remembers how she responded emotionally in performance to Stanislavsky's acting as Vershinin. In the acting of Masha, Knipper explains, "I cannot recall the scene of my parting from this Vershinin without tears" (cited in Magarshack, 223). She describes emotional reactions in relation to Stanislavsky's character in the scene. It is evident that Knipper imaginatively recalls the emotions that the characters expressed with each other.

Knipper describes imagining a performance in response to an emotional other. This suggests an approach to acting emotions in keeping with Stanislavsky's emotional memory but located in the performance itself. By implication, it might be difficult to imagine acting emotions severed from a process of imagining an interactive exchange. In another example, while watching a performer on stage, Knipper was observed off stage undergoing seemingly involuntary responsiveness, emoting, and moving to a young woman's role (Pitcher, 183). Knipper was responding to the emotions being displayed in the performance. This mimicry corresponds with ideas about embodied emotion in the twenty-first century.

Scholarly speculation that denigrates Knipper's contribution to Moscow Art Theatre productions reveals some of the contradictions of performing female identity in theatre. Knipper puts into practice the expectation that acting at the Moscow Art Theatre should involve a heightened expression of selected emotions executed effectively with minimal external gestures and movement. But this is not necessarily the same process as the performer drawing on his or her analysis of self-feeling and personal psychology as the source of a character's emotions – given the relative devaluation of the female self in society. Instead, Knipper is reacting to stimuli, to what happens around her in the enactment. Even though she mastered the Moscow Art Theatre approach of acting emotions so they appear to be happening inwardly, Knipper may well have been confused by the requirement that she draw on her own feelings. At the same time, emotional expression was delivered through bodily agitations that were made meaningful within culturally specific contexts.

The instances of Stanislavsky's dissatisfaction with Knipper were also a difference over perceptions of which particular emotions were to be reproduced for her fictional character. Early realism reveals gendered precepts within the selection of emotional expression. Stanislavsky would revise his approach after 1917 and encourage an actor to physicalise the action and let the emotional aspects emerge more gradually through action and movement with others in rehearsal. His later approach seems closer to the relational process that Knipper describes happening in her approach from her earliest roles. Emotional expression develops as he or she (or they) experiment with and rehearse relational interactions.

Knipper's description of reacting emotionally while imagining the performing of emotions confirms Stanislavsky's instructions on imagining in acting and the active doing of emotions, but with a significant addition. Knipper also delineates how these arise as (remembered) responses to previous performances. It suggests that the self's emotions are derived from remembering social performances and are conceived of as unfolding in relation to those of others. Moreover, emotional reactions in this discussion are being framed in a social space that sanctions the performance of emotions – namely, theatre. An evocation of a theatricality of embodied emotions suggests that emotions circulate through imagined performances. Given that emotions can arise in response to a performance, then the acting of emotions is also the performance of a social self.

Post Chapter Discussion: Peta Tait with Maria Ignatieva

Maria Ignatieva Peta, in your chapter about Olga Knipper, you examine what psychological, emotional, and social mechanisms were involved in the actor's process of creativity at the Moscow Art Theatre, investigating how it depended on Stanislavsky's rehearsal tactics and became intertwined with the development of his system, his pedagogical and artistic searches. Referencing the well-known duet from *Three Sisters*, with Stanislavsky as Vershinin and Knipper as Masha, you invite the reader to reflect upon the Western European social, cultural, and political expectations of feminine and masculine emotional expression while the newly established Moscow Art Theatre was exploring realistic acting. You discuss the expectation that female performers interpret the emotions of a performance text for a new style of acting and express them in a socially coherent way. Olga Knipper was among the first female actors in this newly established directorial theatre. She was a recent Philharmonic school graduate, and Vladimir Nemirovich-Danchenko, her teacher, formed her acting methodology. At the Moscow Art Theatre, she experienced two radically different rehearsal practices, one of Vladimir Nemirovich-Danchenko and the other of Konstantin Stanislavsky. Nemirovich-Danchenko and Stanislavsky's co-creativity and their artistic and personal disagreements were unsettling for all the Moscow Art Theatre actors, but especially for Knipper – Lilina and Andreyeva joined the Moscow Art Theatre with Stanislavsky and knew his rehearsal process; Knipper was only familiar with Nemirovich-Danchenko's rehearsal style. Sometimes, she felt torn between two directors' contradictory suggestions and expectations; ironically, she benefitted greatly from working with both. It is important to remember that the Moscow Art Theatre was a cultural melting pot that may not have shared the same culturally specific theatrical language, with quarrels between Stanislavsky and Morozov on one side and Nemirovich-Danchenko on the other, often supported by Chekhov. Such disagreements were not solely because of organisational politics but also on casting, play interpretations, and performance modes.

As we know, Nemirovich-Danchenko never fully accepted the system wholeheartedly. How would you describe his role in Knipper's subtle fight for her creative independence?

Peta Tait I am really pleased to have such an expert like you, Maria, taking the time and effort to comment on my work in a detailed way. As my article indicates, I am reliant on English-language scholarship and benefit from your own extensive knowledge and scholarly publications. You are right that the influence of playwright director Vladimir Nemirovich-Danchenko as Knipper's first acting teacher is not signalled in this article, which focuses on Stanislavsky and the gendered interpretation of emotion in theatre. Knipper does recognise them both as developing her acting capacity, but English-language sources make Knipper's ongoing difficulties with Stanislavsky evident as they imply a gendered bias about emotional expressiveness. I was trying not to repeat points from *Performing Emotions: Gender, Bodies, Spaces, in Chekhov's Drama and Stanislavski's Theatre* (2002) including those about the co-founder of the Moscow Art Theatre, Nemirovich-Danchenko. The book's more extended discussion includes his disagreement with Stanislavsky over the emotional interpretation of Masha's confession in *Three Sisters* and his defence of Knipper but also, then, her problems with the physical restrictions imposed by both of the directors. The book mentions that Knipper did find the psychological interpretation of Nemirovich easier to follow and more subtle. Until your book, *Stanislavsky and Female Actors: Women in Stanislavsky's Life and Art* (2008) was published, I was reliant on Harvey Pitcher's biography of Knipper that has Nemirovich-Danchenko's quote that she was "one of the most gifted pupils in recent years", and since Knipper's acting is barely mentioned in the English-language version of Nemirovich-Danchenko's autobiography (Pitcher, 20).

Maria Ignatieva Olga Knipper developed and practised the habit of working on her roles by herself (before the beginning of the rehearsal period). When Stanislavsky actively incorporated the system into the rehearsal process, Knipper resisted. You note how she found it difficult to rehearse and perform characters exclusively from an inwardly felt experience.

Knipper was profoundly influenced by rehearsing with Stanislavsky, yet her work on roles remained highly individualised and followed her own creative process. And if so, to what extent?

Peta Tait I am pleased that you confirm my view that Knipper developed her own way of working while helping to create and uphold the Moscow Art Theatre style of acting. While I hesitated to make this type of claim without more direct evidence in English, I do claim Knipper's contribution to what becomes Stanislavsky's 'evolving' system. Her perspective came across in the scholarship as not simply the difference over how to act the character, but how to interpret the emotional qualities of a female (character) in the specific social circumstances. My article is interrogating the way a woman actor might have found the male director's instructions on emotional reactions limited by his presumptions and/or stereotypes and/or even preference for theatrical expression over life-like realism with the exploration of commentaries on Stanislavsky and Knipper. This facilitates questioning the function of gender difference in the emotional interpretations of twentieth-century realist theatre.

Maria Ignatieva I completely support your assessment of Jean Benedetti's unfair judgement of Knipper's co-called 'inabilities'. He certainly shares Stanislavsky's opinion (for which Stanislavsky apologised) while ignoring Knipper's point of view on the same situation. As with other female actors, Knipper was often confused or completely lost after Stanislavsky reprimanded actors and passionately demanded they follow his directions. He occasionally was unable to explain precisely what he had envisioned. Additionally, Knipper, under Nemirovich-Danchenko's influence, thoroughly analysed the psychology of her characters. You explain that though Knipper mastered the Moscow Art Theatre approach, her personal approach was more relational. Knipper returned to playing Ranevskaya in *The Cherry Orchard* in 1928. This time, as Chekhov intended in 1903, an older actress played Ranevskaya, though it was still Knipper. The audience did not take seriously the love stricken Ranevskaya who returns to her lover in Paris. By the 1930s, the characters in the play were considered *former people* who had lost their aristocratic high social status after the Revolution. They were either eradicated or fled from Soviet Russia, and during many performances, healthy laughter replaced the pre-revolutionary tears.

There is footage from 1946 of Knipper as Ranevskaya and Vassily Kachalov as Gayev. What is your impression of one of her final performances?

Peta Tait The filmed footage is a valuable record of Knipper's mature acting and that of Vassily Kachalov, although of course it is theatre captured on film, which is always qualitatively different to the live performance. Nonetheless the first sequence between them lends credibility to the play's narrative about a woman growing older who has been abandoned by her lover and someone unable to accept all the changes happening in her life – including her ageing and impoverishment. In the subtext, the character can seem to ask, "Has my life come to this?" Ranevskaya is trying to convince herself that she is needed – which implies finding a reason for living. As I have argued elsewhere, Ranevskaya is unable to make a (rational) decision because of her emotionally contradictory responses to everything, which Knipper confirms through the filmed footage as she conveys confusion in her distress. The sequences with Gayev evoke sadness and loss but while he comes across as strong and jovial – and able to move forward – Ranevskaya seems less sure of herself and possibly self-pitying about her circumstances. She can still laugh and enjoy the moment, but her underlying sorrow surfaces again in looking out the window, and these moments of Knipper's performance are moving in combination with Kachalov's crying at the end.

Works Cited

Ahmed, S. *The Cultural Politics of Emotion*. London & New York: Routledge, 2004. DOI: https://doi.org/10.4324/9780203700372

Balukhaty, S. D. ed. *The Seagull Produced by Stanislavsky*, translated by David Magarshack. London: Denis Dobson Ltd, 1952.

Benedetti, J. *Stanislavski*. London & New York: Routledge, 1988.

Brockett, Oscar G., and Ball, Robert J. *The Essential Theatre*. Tenth edition. Boston: Wadsworth, 2014.

Butler, J. *Undoing Gender*. London & New York: Routledge, 2004. DOI: https://doi.org/10.4324/9780203499627

Campion, R. "Richard Campion's Reminiscences: Mme Chekhova – Olga Knipper and a Kiwi in Moscow." *New Zealand Slavonic Journal*, 1997, pp. 193–197.

Carnicke, S. "An Actor Prepares/Rabota aktera nad Soboi, Chast' I: A Comparison of the English with the Russian Stanislavsky." *Theatre Journal*, Volume 36, Issue 4, 1984, pp.481–494. DOI: https://doi.org/10.2307/3206736

Carnicke, S. *Stanislavsky in Focus*. Second Edition. London & New York: Routledge, 2009. DOI: https://doi.org/10.4324/9781003134381

Diderot, D. *The Paradox of Acting*, translated by Walter H. Pollock. New York: Hill and Wang, 1957, pp.11–71.
Edwards, C. *The Stanislavsky Heritage*. London: Peter Owen, 1966.
Gorchakov, Nikolai M. *Stanislavsky Directs*, translated by Miriam Goldina. Westport, Connecticut: Greenwood Press, 1985.
Ignatieva, M. *Stanislavski and Female Actors*. Lanham: University of America, 2008.
Ignatieva, M., and Whyman, R. "Serafima, Birman, Sofia Giatsintova, Alla Tarasova and Olga Pyzhova: "Second Wave" Russian and Soviet Actresses, Stanislavsky's System and the Moscow Art Theatre." In: Sewell, J. and Smout, C. eds. *The Palgrave Handbook of the History of Women on Stage*. London: Palgrave Macmillan, 2019, pp.397–423. DOI: https://doi.org/10.1007/978-3-030-23828-5_18
Jones, D. *Great Directors at Work*. Berkeley: University of California Press, 1986.
Lutz, C. *Unnatural Emotions*. Chicago: University of Chicago, 1988.
Lutz, C. "Engendered Emotion: Gender, Power and the Rhetoric of Emotional Control in American Discourse." In: Lutz, C. and Abu-Lughod, L. eds. *Language and the Politics of Emotions*. Cambridge: Cambridge University Press, 1990, pp.69–91.
Lutz, Catherine, and Abu-Lughod, Lila. eds. *Language and the Politics of Emotions*. Cambridge: Cambridge University Press, 1990.
Magarshack, D. *Stanislavsky: A Life*. Boston: Faber and Faber, 1986.
Malague, R. *An Actress Prepares*. London: Routledge, 2012. DOI: https://doi.org/10.4324/9780203144671
Meisner, Sanford, and Longwell, Dennis. *Sanford Meisner on Acting*. New York: Vintage Books, 1987.
Mitter, Shomit. *Systems of Rehearsal*. London: Routledge, 1992.
Parkinson, Brian, Fischer, Agneta H., and Manstead, Antony S. R. *Emotion in Social Relations*. New York: Psychology Press, 2005. DOI: https://psycnet.apa.org/doi/10.4324/9780203644966
Pitcher, H. *Chekhov's Leading Lady: A Portrait of the Actress Olga Knipper*. London: John Murray, 1979.
Sayler, O. *The Russian Theatre*. New York: Brentano's Publishers, 1992.
Schuler, C. *Women in Russian Theatre: The Actress in the Silver Age*. New York: Routledge, 1996. DOI: https://doi.org/10.4324/9781315003948
Senelick, L. *The Chekhov Theatre*. Cambridge: Cambridge University Press, 1999.
Sewell, J., and Smout C. eds. *The Palgrave Handbook of the History of Women on Stage*. London: Palgrave Macmillan Cham, 2019. DOI: https://doi.org/10.1007/978-3-030-23828-5
Stanislavsky, C. *An Actor Prepares*, translated by Elizabeth Hapgood. London: Geoffrey Bles, 1955.
Stanislavsky, K. *On the Art of the Stage*, translated by David Magarshack. London: Faber and Faber, 1961.
Stanislavski, C. 'Director's Diary, 1905.' In *Stanislavski and America* edited by Erica Munk. New York: Hill and Wang, 1966, 30–45.
Stanislavski, K. *An Actor's Work*, translated by Jean Benedetti. London: Routledge, 2010. DOI: https://doi.org/10.4324/9780203936153
Styan, J. L. *Chekhov in Performance*. Cambridge: Cambridge University Press, 1971.
Tait, P. *Performing Emotions: Gender, Bodies, Spaces*. London: Ashgate/Routledge, 2002. DOI: https://doi.org/10.4324/9781315247120
Tait, P. *Circus Bodies: Cultural Identity in Aerial Performance*. London: Routledge, 2005. DOI: https://doi.org/10.4324/9780203391303
Tait, P. *Fighting Nature: Travelling Menageries, Animal Acts and War Shows*. Sydney: Sydney University Press, 2016.

Tait, P. et al. *Feminist Ecologies: Changing Environments in the Anthropocene*. New York: Springer International Publishing, 2018.

Tait, P. ed. *The Great European Stage Directors: Volume 1: Antoine, Stanislavski, Saint-Denis*. London: Bloomsbury Publishing, 2021.

Tait, P. et al. *Theory for Theatre Studies: Emotion*. First Edition. London: Methuen Drama, 2021.

Tait, P. *Forms of Emotion: Human to Nonhuman in Drama, Theatre and Performance*. London: Routledge, 2022. DOI: https://doi.org/10.4324/9781003124832

Tait, P. "From Performing to Feeling: Stanislavski Interprets Emotion and Affect." In: Antoniou, M. and Jones, J. eds. *Stanislavski and Emotion*. London & New York: Routledge, forthcoming.

Toporkov, V. O. *Stanislavski in Rehearsal*, translated by Christine Edwards. New York: Routledge, 1998.

Worrall, N. "Stanislavsky's Production of Chekhov's Three Sisters." In: Russell, R. and Barratt, A. eds. *Russian Theatre in the Age of Modernism*. Basingstoke: The Macmillan Press, 1990, pp.1–32.

Whyman, R. "Stanislavski: Contexts and Influences" In: Tait, P. ed. *The Great European Stage Directors: Antoine, Stanislavski and Saint-Denis: Volume One*. London: Bloomsbury, 2019, pp. 67–89.

3

RE-THINKING STANISLAVSKY'S SYSTEM AS FEMINIST PRACTICE WITH LISA PECK AND BELLA MERLIN

Lisa Peck and Bella Merlin

Stanislavsky's *An Actor Prepares*, originally published in English in 1936 and arguably the most seminal text on acting, narrates a fictionalised Socratic dialogue between a male teacher and his students in their first year of actor training in Stanislavsky's system.

Feminist practitioners and scholars (Carnicke, 2020; Malague, 2013; Blair, 2002; Gainor, 2002), responding to the legacy of critique of Stanislavsky's practice (Aston, 1999; Diamond, 1988; Case, 1988) have offered persuasive counterarguments to what they see as reductive interpretations of the system, pointing to its potential for a feminist practice. At this cultural moment, when seismic shifts force us to re-evaluate what being human means, questions of identity, agency, and well-being in actor training have never been more urgent. If feminism is "The Mother of All Questions" (Solnit, 2017), how might re-thinking Stanislavsky through contemporary feminisms position this practice as liberatory pedagogy? Whilst studies consider the ways that feminist directors and pedagogues have reinterpreted Stanislavsky's approach (Malague, 2012; Fowler, 2020) there has been limited scholarship into the teaching and learning exchange itself, *how* you teach as opposed to what you teach, and the impact of gender on this exchange.

Echoing the fictional Socratic dialogue between the characters Tortsov and Kostya in *An Actor Prepares*, the conversation in this chapter offers an alternative female perspective on acting pedagogy and gender between Bella Merlin, actor, Stanislavsky practitioner, and actor trainer, currently teaching at the University of California Riverside in the USA, and her ex-student Lisa Peck, theatre-maker and feminist educationalist, teaching at the University of Sussex in the UK. Bella has spent her professional life integrating practical acting with written reflection and classroom dissemination of her findings with students,

DOI: 10.4324/9781003411611-4

actors, and teachers. Lisa's monograph *Act as a Feminist: Towards a Critical Acting Pedagogy* (2021) maps a female genealogy of training as an alternative to traditional male lineages. In problematising the relative absence of women in the field, she speculates on the feminist underpinnings of acting knowledges, working with the practices of women to shape a critical acting pedagogy fit for purpose in the twenty-first century.

This discussion evolved over several months (April–August 2022). During this time, Bella was performing live for the first time since COVID-19 at Shakespeare & Company (renowned for their playful actor-audience aesthetic) and Lisa was researching the feminist practice of UK director Emma Rice (Peck, 2023). Together, we consider Merlin's practice as feminist pedagogy including the dynamic between teacher and learner, how to teach personal and social knowledges and how Active Analysis can operate within a feminist praxis as "a method of feminist action" (Peck, 2021, 211).

We are aware that we speak from the position of white, straight, Western women, considering gender as inscribed and femininity/masculinity as constructed behaviours; we see woman/man as expansive categories that include anyone who identifies as such. When we refer to male and female, we acknowledge that some people exist outside of this binary and that sexuality includes all aspects of sexual orientation. At this cultural moment of unprecedented change, conversations like this, where we help each other to reconsider shifting professional identities, knowledges, values, and practices, are vital.

Gender, Femaleness and Feminism in Acting

Lisa Peck: Bella, I have experienced your teaching a number of times between 2009 and 2018 as a student and researcher. I'd like to invite you to consider your work from a gendered and sexed position. My research thinks about gender and actor training through a feminist lens in two ways: I speculate on acting from the perspective of female knowledges/epistemologies that foreground the body: being in a process, working with relationality, mutuality, empathy, vulnerability, pleasure, and the erotic. I come to these acting knowledges through new feminist materialisms, particularly the posthuman feminism of Rosi Braidotti (2021) and, more recently, Black feminist love politics (Nash, 2013; hooks, 2016; Lorde, 2019; Peck, 2023). I research feminist pedagogy within the umbrella category of critical pedagogy, pioneered by Brazilian philosopher Paulo Freire, concerned with questions of power and identity (Peck, 2021). bell hooks' "engaged pedagogy" (hooks, 1994, 2010)[1] is evident in the practices of the women acting practitioners I have worked with. This approach pursues transformation for both teacher and student, enabling well-being through love and hope. Whilst hooks isn't working directly with embodiment, her ideology seems so relevant for the relational learning exchange in acting. I've experienced this embodied and engaged pedagogy in your approach, but I've not heard you explicitly ally yourself with a feminist practice of actor training.

Bella Merlin: It's true that as an actor trainer, I've never called myself a feminist. In many respects, everything that you've described in your book as a feminist practice, I would describe as a 'being human' practice. I believe we're a balance of male and female energy. And I've never thought of what I'm doing as in any way pushing against power. So, the language you're using is not necessarily familiar to me in my experience. But then I've been embedded in an industry that is so much about power and representation, and where there are never enough roles for women.

Furthermore, when I was at a British drama school in the late 1980s, I assumed that the archetypal actress was tall, thin, very beautiful, and had long blonde hair, and that's how you became successful. I thought, "Well, I'm short, not particularly slim, not particularly beautiful. The only thing I can change is my hair!" So, I already felt that I was a type that wasn't going to succeed, and my experience entailed constant reminders from my acting teachers that I wasn't this archetype. They foregrounded the body in the *wrong* way, which was very detrimental to my career for a long time because it never occurred to me to acknowledge and value what I *did* have. My agent would say, "Bella you're quirky. We put you up for quirky characters". And it was hard for me to accept 'quirky' as anything other than plain, dumpy, comic, you know. So, that was a very gendered part of my early career. My backlash against that gendered architecture has, therefore, been a huge contributor to my pedagogy. When I see the students in front of me who have chosen to be in my acting class, I encourage them to celebrate how they look and how they identify: they are their own instrument with their own process. It's my responsibility to help them value what they already have – which I guess could be framed as 'engaged pedagogy'.

I have two particular actor-training mentors who have guided my teaching methodology, and they're both feisty women: Katya Kamotskaya,[2] who taught me at the Moscow State Institute of Cinematography (VGIK), and Tina Packer, who set up Shakespeare & Company with Kristin Linklater in Lenox, Massachusetts, in 1978.[3] Curiously, Packer and Linklater were both pushing against British actor training at that time, and they came to America to do so. Both experienced certain kinds of rebuttal or personal 'attacks' in their training, which might actually have galvanised their pedagogies. One of the ways in which Katya and Tina have influenced me is to dispel any gendered archetype: as pedagogues, they work directly with the material (i.e., the people) in front of them. I think they're part of the reason that I say to my students, "You *are* the curriculum. So, if you don't show up to class, you're not just missing the content of the session, you're missing the chance to evolve your own instrument".

I mainly teach practical acting. And I'm interested in how acting practices reflect the complexity and the chaos of being human. At the moment, my passion is teaching human interaction: compassion, community, empathy, and inclusion. I also believe that ultimately, we're all plagiarising Mother Nature: whether it's Maria Knebel or Stanislavsky or Michael Chekhov or Sanford Meisner or Luis Valdez's *Vibrant Being*[4] or Cristal Chanelle Truscott's *Soulwork*,[5] we're all peering through different facets of the crystal of being human. However, now that I understand more deeply how you, Lisa, are framing feminism, I see that's in the DNA of what I do, and I'm not even sure that it's what I've evolved myself. I think it's what I learned from my teachers in Russia in the 1990s, even though – besides Katya – two of them were very strong *male* presences in the room: Albert Filozov and Vladimir Ananyev. I do think that what they were teaching us about Stanislavsky was (what could be termed) a feminist practice.

Lisa Peck: I love your expression "You *are* the curriculum" because this connects so directly to feminisms. I've experienced your teaching as feminist pedagogy. By that, I mean a teaching exchange that foregrounds relationality – recognising that we come into being *with* others, human and non-human, which allows or disallows for agency. This attunes our sensitivity to better ways of being in the world – a learning that happens *beside* technique.[6] For me, a feminist acting pedagogy foregrounds the positivity of difference – sex, gender, race, class, age, and disability. It nurtures critical hope, working with an ethics of affirmation, which I see as a politics of love.

People can be nervous of the word feminism. Whilst you "don't think in terms of power", I see your work as a feminist act pushing against many power structures. For example, the accessible way you write as a practitioner pushes against academic conventions and is so valued for that. I also think you're giving voice to the actor when it tends to be scholars and critics who write about acting. So, in all sorts of ways, you're a feminist icon pushing against the constructed walls of male tradition!

Bella Merlin: Gosh! I'm humbled and flattered!

Lisa Peck: Before we dig into *how* your work is a feminist practice, can you reflect on other ways that you experience gender as an actor and director?

Bella Merlin: I come to directing as an actor, so I don't want a top-down hierarchy. As a director, I really don't know what the production is going to look like beforehand, though I've usually done a heap of research. But the image I use when working with Active Analysis is that my role as the director is like a gardener. There's the trellis of the play; there's the ivy of the actors. All I have to do is make sure the tendrils of the ivy don't stray too far from the trellis; otherwise, we're not serving the writer or the audience.[7] The connection to the audience has come to me strongly from Tina Packer and her deeply feminist sense of listening and relationality. For a long time, I was afraid of the audience, and it was only when I took Shakespeare & Company's month-long intensive in 2016 (which focuses on the actor-audience relationship) that I truly began to *feel* the audience. They are my 'spiritual tuning fork', as Stanislavsky might say. If I'm not taking them on a journey, I have no right to be on that stage. The same if I'm directing. If my actors aren't connecting to the material in a way that ignites their hearts – and through which they can ignite the audience – we, none of us, have any right to be in that space. Time is a precious economy, and we're asking our audience to spend their life force in our presence, so we have to take them on a journey that's relevant. We have to give them an experience that, ultimately, will be transformative – with a certain playfulness and maybe an element of hope, whatever that might be.

As for 'feminist knowledges' in regard to actor/director/playwright/audience, you catch me at a very specific moment where I'm revisiting a play that I'd devised 12 years ago: *Tilly No-Body*. It's about Tilly Wedekind, the wife of German playwright Frank Wedekind, who wrote the original *Spring Awakening*, and the material is sensual, vulnerable, all about male-female relationships. I'm redoing the piece at Shakespeare & Company this summer, post #MeToo, with a body that's 12 years older, and with material that sits differently in that body. My husband, Miles Anderson, is directing, and in rehearsal this past weekend (May 2022), I began to truly feel, in a way that I'm not 100% sure I've ever experienced before, what it means to get out of my own way as an actor. I have quite 'male' tendencies: I like linear structures; I like to know what has to get done and when. So, to some extent, Stanislavsky's 'score of physical actions' sits comfortably within me. I like understanding the overall picture, the geography, the architecture.

Meanwhile, I have a brilliant actor-director-husband, who's very connected to his feminine side. Yesterday in rehearsal, he was subtly inviting me to let go: "You have the structure, you have the text, you know what you have to do". He was almost saying, "Practice what you preach. You say that the actor is the instrument and through the instrument comes the music, so let that happen. Stop trying to control everything". This feels like a feminist, feminine, approach to acting. In fact, yesterday's rehearsal was… (at the risk of sounding pretentious) …a kind of spiritual moment. I suddenly understood everything to which I've aspired as a director, actor trainer and actor – the merger of text and performer, past repetition and present experience, speaker, and listener. I was suddenly like, "Wow! It's taken me all these years to realise that this is what service to the audience means?" And it was all about transformation. As a human being, I felt transformed by the material. I felt this incredible love for Tilly. I bizarrely felt this incredible love for Frank (though he's a total manipulator). It was the complete synthesis of a score of physical actions and a constant state of improvisation. And those are two things that I really cling to from Active Analysis. In rehearsing a script as an actor, you create this very thorough score (possibly a masculine process?). In performing it, you relax into that score and let the physical and verbal actions of the script play upon you (possibly a feminine process?). Even though I was getting my words wrong in places and I screwed up the props, that was part of the chaos of the moment, the journey. I can't deny there was a certain female power, an enjoyment of the eroticism of performance – and pure fun! I've no idea if I'll ever repeat it, but the experience was very clear. While I don't necessarily want to gender the different stages of the creative process, I'm aware that a particular linear, structured part of my creative brain is in action towards the end of the rehearsal period (galvanising the physical score ready for performance) and then a female, relational aspect is at the fore in performance. Not that I've thought about it in that way until now.

Active Analysis as a Feminist Practice

Lisa Peck You introduced me to Active Analysis at Drama School and later at the National Theatre. It seemed to me that you were responsible for bringing Active Analysis to the UK through your teaching and books (2001; 2003; 2007; 2010; 2014). I'm interested in why it is that we attribute this practice wholly to Stanislavsky when it was documented and interpreted by Maria Knebel and then reinterpreted by predominantly female scholars and practitioners. Whose Active Analysis is it, and why does that matter? Can we speculate on Active Analysis as a feminist practice?

Bella Merlin I revisited your list of what makes for feminist practices. You say it is relational, situational, communal, focussed on the particularity of the person (their gender, race, class, sexuality, culture, age, ableism), resistant to structures, somatic, nonlinear, chaotic, processual, transitory (Peck, 2021, 26). Well, you're describing Active Analysis. When Katya Kamotskaya directed me in Anton Chekhov's *The Seagull* in California in 2010, I experienced a much stronger sense of the two threads: *the line of thought* and *the line of action*. The four steps in Active Analysis include: step (1) read the text and step (2) discuss the text, and these first two steps essentially uncover the first thread – the line of thought, "Why is my character saying this? What's going on for them?" Meanwhile, the improvisations (steps 3 and 4) uncover the second thread – the line of action. And these two threads weave together through Active Analysis. Both threads are necessary; they combine the cerebral text analysis with the chaos of improvisations. They're not oppositional; they just inevitably require slightly different processes to get to a place whereby you're creating something that is completely particular to *you* but absolutely rooted in the *playwright's text.* So yes, Active Analysis is *situational* (what are the Given Circumstances?). And it's *relational* (I only know what this event is going to be when my action and your counteraction rub up against each other). Everything you describe as your interpretation of feminist practice happens in Active Analysis.

I'd like to address the way that Active Analysis came into UK training because there are various aspects that link to a broader understanding of what might be feminist.

Before I went to Russia in the 1990s, I'd studied some Stanislavsky at Birmingham University, but I'd never heard of Maria Knebel, Active Analysis, or the Method of Physical Actions. And although I don't remember 'Knebel' or 'Active Analysis' or the 'Method of Physical Actions' being overtly named in class at VGIK, I do remember feeling that what we were learning had a system to it. We would read a scene; we would talk about how it landed on us; then we would get up and improvise it. Even Shakespeare. Our first acting project in Term One was *The Tempest*, and the idea of suddenly getting up and improvising Shakespeare felt acutely terrifying. But it made perfect sense in terms of unlocking the basic relationships and needs within each scene, 'owning' the action and the words, and listening to each other.

The process really sank in for me during Term Two, when we were working on *Crime and Punishment* as our final 'showcase'. I started to sense that there was a method in the improvisations, it wasn't random. I remember on the first day of rehearsals, we'd just read a scene and Filozov said, "Now get up and improvise it". And I said, "But I don't know enough about the scene!" He and Katya stated this process wasn't anything different from what we'd been doing for the past six months. But I kept thinking, "I don't have enough information about this character or this scene". Then suddenly – in the situation, in relation to others, in the chaos of the reciprocity – my fellow actors and I embarked on this 25-minute improvisation. And I came out thinking, "I didn't even know I knew that much about the scene or the character. This is coming from somewhere other than the critical judgmental mind". Once I'd silenced the inner critic saying, "I'm going to make a fool of myself", my imagination grasped what it *needed* to grasp in order to get through the first étude and that was the information I built upon.

After that experience with *Crime and Punishment* – which was seminal for me as an actor-researcher – I began asking questions about what we were doing in this process. It was only later, when I was doing my PhD research, that I formally came across the term 'Method of Physical Actions' – but *not* Active Analysis. When I then asked Filozov if our classroom improvisations had been the Method of Physical Actions, he was categorical: "No, this is different!" He was very clear that there had been two approaches in Soviet Russia: the Method of Physical Actions which was disseminated by Stanislavsky's assistant director, Mikhail Kedrov. (It was very materialist and became the standard training method in Soviet acting schools: I write about this in *Beyond Stanislavsky: The Psycho-Physical Approach to Actor Training* (2001)). And this other method, which Filozov's own acting teacher, Evgenia Maryes, had been taught by Maria Knebel. So, I knew that what we were getting from Filozov was two degrees of separation from Knebel, three degrees from Stanislavsky. It was a female lineage, you could say.

Thereafter, Ananyev gave me a copy of *On the Active Analysis of Plays and Roles* by Maria Knebel in Russian. So, with Filosov saying, "This practice is not the Method of Physical Actions", and Ananyev saying, "Read the Knebel book", I understood the path of research needed. Mike Pushkin, a senior lecturer in the Russian Department at the University of Birmingham, helped me with a very raw translation, and much of the gold dust from that translation went into *The Complete Stanislavsky Toolkit* (2007), in which I say Maria Knebel was Stanislavsky's seminal assistant in the last days of his life. Once I'd understood the gold dust of Knebel's writing, I contacted Talia Rodgers, then senior editor for drama at Routledge. She told me of an edited version, ongoing with Anatoli Vassiliev, with (subsequently) Irina Brown translating. That was twenty years ago and, at last, in 2021 the book came out.[8] I think this is going to shift radically Knebel's global positioning as a seminal actor trainer, work which Sharon Carnicke has been promulgating for some years (Carnicke, 1998, 2009, 2020).

I should state that my early practice-based research was predominantly embodied and personal, rather than archival and historical. And the material was controversial. Even Jean Benedetti, as the preeminent British Stanislavskian at the time, told me in the late 1990s that there was no distinction between the Method of Physical Actions and Active Analysis. I'm deeply grateful that Sharon Carnicke, Maria Shevtsova, and Rose

Whyman so carefully trace the lineage. They're Russian-speaking scholars who have trawled the MXAT archives, whereas I'm primarily going from what I learned as an actor in 1993 to 1994 with limited Russian language. It's interesting how many women are engaged in this work's translation and dissemination.

Lisa Peck Yes, I agree! Rosemary Malague's chapter in *The Routledge Companion to Stanislavsky* (2013) also points to this question – why don't we recognise the authorship of this work and its potentially feminist influences? Maria Knebel, in a male dominated Soviet environment, must have negotiated power structures from her minoritarian position.[9] Whilst she doesn't explicitly situate herself, we interpret Active Analysis through a female lens. Equally, the way you choose to map Active Analysis through your experience in *The Complete Stanislavsky Toolkit* (2007) offers a female perspective, and the scholarship and translation of Stanislavsky is notably gendered. It isn't unreasonable to speculate that a feminist perspective underpins the authorship and practice of Active Analysis.

Bella Merlin Yes! As I mentioned, the descriptors that you use for 'feminist practices' absolutely underpin Active Analysis. The top-down hierarchy is essentially dismantled: instead, the process is collaborative. There's an equal valuing of perspectives; it's actually what might be termed 'decolonised', where communal creativity is valued. There's no authoritarian director with a concept or vision into which everyone must fit. Furthermore, it's not a question of, "Learn your lines by this day or you're shamed!" Active Analysis meets every actor where they're at. As a director using Active Analysis, I seek ways to adjust whatever an actor may be actually feeling to their character's Given Circumstances; this way, they're never at a distance from the character. The actor-character process is *intra*relational, so to speak.

Lisa Peck The first model of theatre-making that you described places the text at the top, with a director up there as well and the actor serving from below. Whereas, in Active Analysis, the text, the director and the actor work on the same level with the material, passing it between each other. It makes me think of your analogy of director as midwife, helping the actor to birth themselves in the role. To my mind, the way that shifts the power exchange is at the heart of what makes Active Analysis a feminist practice. And that approach – coaching, encouraging, guiding, protecting, holding – creates an environment that allows for vulnerability.

Bella Merlin Exactly. You want to be able to take risks as an actor. You want to go into a rehearsal room that feels safe, non-judgemental, non-shaming enough to try something adventurous. For example, with Tina Packer at Shakespeare & Company, you can offer her anything and she goes, "Let's try it". And afterwards she asks, "How did that feel?" "It felt terrible". "Well, don't make that choice then. How about a different choice?" I have integrated Tina's feminist practice with my use of Stanislavsky in my acting processes over the last six years.

Lisa Peck Another feminist approach is working from pleasure: pleasure through play or pleasure in not knowing, that willing vulnerability that allows you to be uncertain, in the unknown with someone else, pleasure in relationality. And then, the idea of the positivity of difference. Being with a director who is open to choices that resist the expected representation and challenge stereotypes.

Bella Merlin Absolutely, and my pedagogy inherently comes out of my experience of Active Analysis, too. Given that I say to my students, "You are the curriculum", I don't necessarily use the word 'difference', because that might imply one thing should be like another thing. Instead, I'll say, "Every single one of your stories is valued. Your story is significant. Your experience is valuable". If as a teacher you've worked to create a space in which the participants feel safe and brave, they can then inform and transform the space. I feel like actor training is not necessarily training anything. It's actually freeing the human being.

Acting Pedagogy: Gender, Spirit, and Eros

Lisa Peck Focusing on pedagogy, how has yours shifted over your career?

Bella Merlin As with directing, I come to everything in the classroom as an actor. I'm actually happier as an actor than a teacher. So, I'm constantly interweaving existences. And those existences are very much in relation to – and in evolution with – each other. So, the biggest change in my pedagogy largely came with my move from the UK to the USA in 2008. In the UK, I experienced a tension between practical acting and institutionalised teaching. I couldn't do both. Interweaving careers wasn't accepted at that time – I was either a teacher or an actor, and that just wasn't my MO. So, I went back to being freelance. When I discovered that in a US university it would be expected that I continued acting as part of my creative research, that felt like a much better fit. And it was much closer to the experience I'd had at VGIK, where all our actor trainers were working in theatre and film. It was quite usual for our schedule to be arranged in chunks of two or three weeks, based on their availability. That in itself was very flexible, very relational, if you like. In the US, I'm expected to act when I'm not teaching, and my creative activity is significantly valued. This reality in itself adjusted my pedagogy because – as I say – the two aspects of acting and teaching nourish each other.

Another way in which my pedagogy has evolved is by virtue of the system in which I'm based. The University of California is a very large public university, and at UC Riverside we have a very 'open door policy': whoever shows up to my classroom, I teach them. There's no audition or selection process. One of the courses I teach is a foundational class called *Acting: The Process*. So, in addition to actors, the cohort includes filmmakers, screenwriters, stage managers, designers, dramaturgs: people who would probably rather not act, but it's a required class for their programme. Therefore, I conceptually changed the course from being an 'introduction to acting' class, to an 'introduction to being human' class. I think really all I'm teaching them is to question how to be human. And they've already got all the answers inside them. Over a ten-week course of very structured classes, I give them the environment in which they can listen to their own heartbeat, breathing pattern, physical experience of the world, imagination, how words land on them, how their words land on other people, how they interact with props, soundscapes, sets, etc. So that's been a huge change pedagogically, certainly from how I experienced being at drama school in the UK and definitely how I initially taught in the UK. It's probably far closer now to what you cite as bell hooks' 'engaged pedagogy', not least because it's very reciprocal: as a teacher, I'm learning all the time from my very diverse student cohort.

Lisa Peck So, would you ever say that you teach Stanislavsky or indeed Maria Knebel?

Bella Merlin I'm always using Stanislavsky's tools, whether I'm teaching or acting, probably even when I'm living through a situation. For example, if I'm about to go into a meeting involving a very complicated conversation, the chances are that beforehand I've considered what's the 'problem' of the situation; what's my 'objective' or desire for the meeting; what do I hope we have achieved by the end; how do I actively listen to what the other people are saying? Because Stanislavsky was essentially taking human behaviour and pulling it to bits in order to put it back together systematically for an actor, I personally can't get away from Stanislavsky. His toolkit to me is like ABC. And my students are so glued to their screens, I want to unhook them from the information 'out there' and let them feel where the information is 'in here', inside them.

To be honest, this dialogue with you has really got me thinking. And now that Knebel's book *Active Analysis* (2021) is finally in print in English, I will definitely be returning to the classroom in September 2022 with Maria Knebel overtly on the curriculum. It's not that I don't teach Knebel now. It's just that, in many respects, I'm fundamentally teaching what I learned at VGIK, and it's all interwoven, relational. I'm probably teaching as much Katya Kamotskaya, Albert Filozov, Vladimir Ananyev, as Stanislavsky or Knebel. I use many of Ananyev's tools in classes where there's neuro and physical diversity, with the emphasis being on,

"What does your unique instrument do? We don't expect the flute to do the same as the guitar. We don't expect the trombone to do the same as the piccolo. Let's honour what each part of this particular instrument that is 'You' does for you. How does it feel for you to raise your shoulder? How does it feel for you to turn your head? Bend your wrist?"

That's all essentially from Ananyev's scenic movement classes.

My Russian teachers were steeped in Knebel, Chekhov, and Grotowski. And underpinning all of these, I feel, is 'spirit', however we express that: whether it's something esoteric or energetic, it certainly needn't be anything religious. I think this is a profound part of Knebel's practices. That's what Stanislavsky was trying to explore, but he was suppressed by the Soviet regime. He was also under house arrest for the last few years of his life, conveniently too ill to be able to leave. Yet, even as he was facing his own mortality, he still sustained his research laboratory into acting.

Lisa Peck I'm wondering how sexuality, pleasure, and the erotic sit in relation to 'spirit' in acting? Audre Lorde asks that we reclaim the erotic as a female power (Lorde, 45), and bell hooks' celebrates the erotic in pedagogy (hooks, 2010, 160). It feels like an important material in connection with spirit. Can you reflect about pleasure and the erotic from your experience as an actor, director, and actor trainer?

Bella Merlin I don't know how to say this really, and I don't know if our delicate times have shifted something inherent in actor training. However, I will use this opportunity to say that, for me as an actor, we have to address the whole instrument: body (which includes sexuality and gender), identity, imagination, emotion, intellect, spirit – all these things. I've found the last few years as an actor trainer to be complex as to how we give people permission to value their erotic expression in an environment where, all too often, that has become such a hot bed. I use that term deliberately because so many actor-training disciplines over the years have been exploitative. And that's the last thing *I'm* ever going to do. I don't ever want to exploit anybody! It's of no interest to me. At the same time, how do we create a safe, brave place for healthy, mindful, sexual, or erotic expression? When I'm directing, I want the actors to be very clear, at the entry point of audition, what the writer's script entails, and if an individual does not want to do a particular role, they are under absolutely no obligation to audition for it. Once they're cast, I will do all I can to create an environment in which everyone feels safe and creatively liberated – to tell the story that the script tells, to affect the audience in the way the writer imagined, while also navigating the collective energies in the room. Before we had intimacy directors or the 'Pillars of Intimacy' (first created by Intimacy Directors International in 2016),[10] I directed several sexually specific plays – including *The Children's Hour*, *Spring Awakening*, *Richard III* – and my students never indicated, nor did I feel, that the space was unsafe. I hope they would have been able to tell me if they felt unsafe. As I say, Active Analysis invites people to meet the play's material from where they are at in their lives.

Lisa Peck Stanislavsky wrote about the writer as the father, the actor as the mother pregnant with the part, and the child as the role that is born (Stanislavski, 2008, 344). That piqued my interest early on – that Stanislavsky sexed the actor as female! Feminist scholarship theorises the womb, the chora, as the space of creation. I would have loved to ask Stanislavsky about this! What do you make of this familial metaphor?

Bella Merlin I have no issue with the image of the playwright as the father because there's a kind of straight line: here's your play and, unless it's a new script, it's not likely to change much. The actor is the mother because, as an actor, I'm going to take that play into me and it's going to morph into something new. The director is like the *doula* helping the baby to be born. And hopefully it's a baby that mutually represents what the writer intended, the actor authentically manifested, the director envisioned, and the audience will bless at the performance. As an actor trainer, my 'gendered' perspective is to nurture. If possible, I typically bring down the lights in the auditorium; the lights are up on the stage area, where we create a kind of womb (I don't know how else to describe it), and we work a lot in a circle, maybe because it feels like a birthing chamber. Pre-#MeToo, I was not as overtly tuned into the possible 'dangers' of the rehearsal space as I am now. However, times have changed and with them so has my pedagogy. I now use 'open scenes' much more than I did in the past so that the students can create the Given Circumstances for themselves according to what interests them. I'm far more attentive to the process of casting these scenes, partnering people together in an increasingly conscious way: I look to see who's hanging out together in the classroom, who seems to be comfortable with whom. I want people to feel safe. A lot of attention goes into nurturing the safe space because I want them to feel they can be their full selves, and their full selves includes their sexualities. We can't get away from it, acting is erotic, as in Eros, the god of love. We have to love what we're doing, or it's hard to be creatively free.

Lisa Peck Feminist philosopher Erin Gilson talks about "force in fragility" as an antidote to ideas around vulnerability as female weakness (Gilson, 95). Your work invites actors to access emotion. How does gender play out in this?

Bella Merlin Maybe being a female enables people to feel safer exploring emotions with me – males, females, non-binary, and transgender people – I don't know. As I mentioned, I start by saying to everybody, "You are the curriculum, so you'll get as much out of this class as you want to put in. No experience is wrong, no answer is wrong. All you're doing is listening to what's going on inside you". So, of course, emotions come up all the time, and typically somebody will say, "I'm sorry I'm laughing or crying or whatever". And I say, "No need to apologise. Emotion is your raw material as an actor". Any emotion is given space if that's where the students want to be, as they listen to themselves each day. In terms of acting, expressing emotion is far from being a female weakness. It's absolutely like the pliers or chisel or saw, etc. You've got to have emotion in your toolkit as an actor. But it's only *part* of your kit, along with your intellect, imagination, body, spirit, whatever.

Lisa Peck I thought it might be interesting to share the moments in your teaching that have had the greatest effect on my practice. You mention these in your first book, *Beyond Stanislavsky: The Psycho-Physical Approach to Actor Training* (2001). The first is a silent étude to help actors embody the exchange between their characters. You call it 'the Empty Space exercise' or 'coiled spring'. Two actors stand opposite each other with eye contact and an imaginary coiled spring linking them, solar plexus to solar plexus. This exercise just breaks everything down. Everything drops away. It immediately takes students off the page into their bodies, into what's really going on – the push and pull between these two actors/characters (Merlin, 2001, 120–127). But what's interesting in my memory of this is the way my body felt. And that had to do with who I was working with. And I remember I was paired with a male student who I had a difficult relationship with, and I think the feeling was mutual. And so 'the Empty Space exercise', strongly imprinted in my felt sense, had so much to do with the dynamic between us that I was experiencing in the exercise. There is, inevitably, a huge amount of information about gender, sexuality, and agency in the exchange and sometimes that subsumes your focus on the text.

Bella Merlin That's Katya Kamotskaya's exercise, which I've evolved over the years. At VGIK, we must have done it almost every day for at least three or four weeks as the foundation of our ensemble training. And it took me a while to get it. I really thought I was supposed to 'do' something (my masculine side?), and I found it really hard to understand that it was about relinquishing blocks, not acquiring skills.

The other thing I'd note is eye contact. Eye contact is less socially or culturally common, particularly for non-Western students and particularly post-Zoom learning. I've actually had Black male students in my class say, "We've learned not to give people eye contact because they might be threatened by us". Or Asian students say, "It's not socially polite". And I say,

> "I completely understand, and anything you do in this classroom does not have to be a tactic or strategy for your everyday life. But see what happens if you give yourself permission in this exercise to look somebody in the eye if you can".

And I frame it in terms of my beloved dog, Dempsey. Dempsey is my best acting teacher: She will look me in the eye for ages. And the minute the students consider the exercise in terms of a pet – in terms of the trust of a dog to a human, rather than an intimate, sexual, or threatening act – they relax. But the credit has to go to Katya for the 'coiled spring' exercise. It's genius. I don't know if she's manifested it herself, which is highly likely because she spent so much time investigating her own creative blocks. Or whether it emerged from her time with Grotowski's 'Tree of Life Laboratory' in Poland, I don't know (Merlin, 2001, 103). It's so simple and its essentially Katya: maybe her own powerful feminine connection to acting unfurled the exercise to her.

Lisa Peck It's fantastic. And the other exercise I remember experiencing as incredibly sensual was an exercise where we, as a group, became amoebas. We had to imagine waking up on the planet as if for the first time as non-humans, exploring how we moved in space, in contact with the environment (Merlin, 2001, 110–111). We had our eyes closed, swarming and squirming all over each other and being free to use touch as a way to try to relate. I felt it was incredibly affecting for us as a group because it gave permission to be in relation in a non-human way, and it loosened some of our competitive dynamic. Rosi Braidotti calls for a posthuman feminism (Braidotti, 2021), turning to the non-human to expand our understanding of how to be in relation in the world; to break free of the typical power structures of gender, sexuality, age, class, race, but to recognise our mutuality in relation to the earth, planet, time, space, object, and animal (Braidotti, 2002). It's interesting that your students become open to eye contact through the example of your dog.

Bella Merlin I love 'posthuman feminism'. What I call the 'waking up on the planet' exercise is again from Katya, combined with some of Ananyev's movement work and evolved over the years by me. This exercise was one of the foundations of both ensemble training and scenic movement at VGIK, taking ourselves back to a place where we don't have assumptions about how our body moves, we've literally just woken up on the planet. How do we defy gravity? How does one movement lead to the next and on to the next? How does a shoulder lead to an elbow lead to a wrist? Nor do we have assumptions about social or physical contact. As creatures or amoebas, we've just woken up to our existence; how do we experience every moment of it, without expectations or assumptions: just curiosity? Again, this was an exercise that we would do over and over at VGIK. I hate to admit it, but I don't use it in classes anymore. I'll do the solitary 'amoeba' stage of the exercise, but I don't do the evolution of 'creatures coming into contact with each other'. Maybe I would if I were in a drama school, where I know that that group of twenty people are working together all the time and they've had some kind of intimacy training. But I'm not going to do it in the liberal arts environment where this is the only class in which those people are all together. You know, what you're saying is making me sad because I know these exercises are brilliant. I know that they are fundamentally taking us back to childhood innocence, where we would roll around with our pals like puppies in a pen and no one ever assumed anything. And I don't find that anymore. I'm sad.

Lisa Peck I think it is a real challenge for us as teachers. How can we work with the essential need to move through an experiential discovery process with actors when we're scared to allow them to fully experience and to bring their full selves into the room? How can we allow sexuality, pleasure, and desire to be explored as vital materials? At this time of 'gender revolution', how we work with Stanislavsky's practices is shifting. We need to find ways to make what was once implicit, explicit in our pedagogies, otherwise we are foreclosing the potentially liberating knowledges that, as you say, are at the heart of an acting curriculum. It's exciting to be working at this point of renewal and rebirth in actor training.

Bella Merlin Yes, maybe we can be each other's nurturing doulas.

Notes

1 bell hooks introduces her notion on "engaged pedagogy" in the first chapter of her 1994 book *Teaching to Transgress: Education as a Practice of Freedom*, explaining its roots in the critical pedagogy of Paulo Friere and Buddhism of Thich Nhat Hanh. It advocates "To educate as the practice of freedom [...] To teach in a manner that respects and cares for the souls of our students" centring principles of active participation, "mutual recognition" that regards both students and educators as "'whole' humans" and emphasises wellbeing to guide and empower students' "self-actualization" (hooks, 1994, pp.3-22). hooks further elucidates this concept in *Teaching Critical Thinking: Practical Wisdom* (2010).

2 Katya Kamotskaya and Bella Merlin co-author a chapter in *Russians in Britain* (2012) edited by Jonathan Pitches.

3 See *Shakespeare & Company: When Action is Eloquence* by Bella Merlin and Tina Packer (2020).

4 See *Theatre of the Sphere: The Vibrant Being* (2021) by Luis Valdez.

5 See Cristal Chanelle Truscott's chapter "SoulWork" in *Black Acting Methods: Critical Approaches* (2017) edited by Sharrell D. Luckett and Tia M. Shaffer.
6 Lisa Peck cites Eve Kosofsky Sedgwick's (2003) *beside* relation which "offers an alternative paradigm to the perpetual dualisms that dominate acting (mind/body, inner/outer, self/other)" (Peck, 2021, 204) in her book, *Act As A Feminist: Towards a Critical Acting Pedagogy*. See also, Kosofsky Sedgwick, E. *Touching Feeling: Affect, Pedagogy, Performativity*. London: Duke University Press, 2003, p8.
7 Bella Merlin introduces the metaphor of the gardener training the ivy around a trellis to further explain the relational pedagogy of Active Analysis in her chapter, "'Here, Today, Now': Active Analysis for the Twenty First Century Actor" in *the Routledge Companion to Stanislavsky* (Merlin, 2013, 326) edited by Andrew White.
8 See *Active Analysis* (2021) by Maria Knebel, compiled and edited by Anatoli Vassiliev and translated by Irina Brown.
9 Sharon M. Carnicke offers a concise overview of Maria Knebel's career and her personal struggles with misogyny and antisemitism in her chapter, "The Knebel Technique: Active Analysis in Practice" in Alison Hodge's *Actor Training* (2010).
10 See *The IDC Resource Guide* (First Edition), compiled by Marie C. Percy (2020).

Works Cited

Aston, E. *Feminist Theatre Practice: A Handbook*. London and New York: Routledge, 1999. DOI: https://doi.org/10.4324/9780203981269

Blair, R. "Reconsidering Stanislavsky: Feeling, Feminism, and the Actor". *Theatre Topics*. Volume 12, Issue 2, pp.177–190. Baltimore: John Hopkins University Press, 2002. DOI: https://doi.org/10.1353/tt.2002.0008

Braidotti, R. *Metamorphoses: Towards a Materialist Theory of Becoming*. Cambridge: Polity Press, 2002.

Braidotti, R. *Posthuman Feminism*. Cambridge: Polity Press, 2021.

Carnicke, S M. *Stanislavsky in Focus*. First Edition. Amsterdam: Harwood Academic, 1998.

Carnicke, S M. *Stanislavsky in Focus: An Acting Master for the Twenty-First Century*. Second Edition. London: Routledge, 2009.

Carnicke, S M. *Stanislavsky in Focus: An Acting Master for the Twenty-First Century*. Second Edition: Routledge Theatre Classics). London and New York: Routledge, 2020. (First edition 1998 and Second Edition 2009). DOI: https://doi.org/10.4324/9781003134381

Carnicke, S M. "The Knebel Technique: Active Analysis in Practice". In: Hodge, A. ed. *Actor Training*. Second Edition. London and New York: Routledge, 2010, pp.99–116. DOI: https://doi.org/10.4324/9780203861370

Case, S-E. *Feminism and Theatre*. New York: Methuen, 1988. DOI: https://doi.org/10.4324/9781315024615

Diamond, E. "Brechtian Theory/Feminist Theory: Toward a Gestic Feminist Criticism". *TDR The Drama Review*. Volume 32, Issue 1, pp.82–94. New York: MIT Press, 1988. DOI: https://doi.org/10.2307/1145871

Fowler, B. *Katie Mitchell: Beautiful Illogical Acts*. London and New York: Routledge, 2020. DOI: https://doi.org/10.4324/9781315112572

Gainor, J E. "Rethinking Feminism, Stanislavsky, and Performance". *Theatre Topics*. Volume 12, Issue 2, pp.163–175. Baltimore: John Hopkins University Press, 2002. DOI: https://doi.org/10.1353/tt.2002.0010

Gilson, E. *The Ethics of Vulnerability: A Feminist Analysis of Social Life and Practice*. London and New York: Routledge, 2014. DOI: https://doi.org/10.4324/9780203078136

hooks, b. *Teaching to Transgress: Education as the Practice of Freedom.* London and New York: Routledge, 1994. DOI: https://doi.org/10.4324/9780203700280

hooks, b. *All About Love: New Visions.* New York: William Morrow Paperbacks, 2016.

hooks, b. *Teaching Critical Thinking: Practical Wisdom.* London and New York: Routledge, 2010. DOI: https://doi.org/10.4324/9780203869192

Kamotskaya, K, and Merlin, M. "Re-invisioned directions: Stanislavsky in the twenty-first century". In: Pitches, J. ed. *Russians in Britain: British Theatre and The Russian Tradition of Actor Training.* London and New York: Routledge, 2012. DOI: https://doi.org/10.4324/9780203146590

Knebel, M, and Vassiliev, A. ed. *Active Analysis.* trans. Brown, I. London and New York: Routledge, 2021. DOI: https://doi.org/10.4324/9780203125205

Kosofsky Sedgwick, E. *Touching Feeling: Affect, Pedagogy, Performativity.* London: Duke University Press, 2003. DOI: https://doi.org/10.1215/9780822384786

Lorde, A. *Sister Outsider.* London: Penguin Books, Random House, 2019.

Malague, R. "Stanislavsky's System and Women: A Feminist Reading of New Translations". In: White, A. ed. *The Routledge Companion to Stanislavsky.* London and New York: Routledge, 2013, pp.115–170. DOI: https://doi.org/10.4324/9780203112304-1

Malague, R. *An Actress Prepares: Women and "the Method".* London and New York: Routledge, 2012. DOI: https://doi.org/10.4324/9780203144671

Merlin, B and Packer, T. *Shakespeare & Company: When Action is Eloquence.* London and New York: Routledge, 2020. DOI: https://doi.org/10.4324/9780429292231

Merlin, B. "'Here, Today, Now': Active Analysis for the Twenty First Century Actor". In. White, A. ed. *The Routledge Companion to Stanislavsky.* London and New York: Routledge, 2013, pp.325–340. DOI: https://doi.org/10.4324/9780203112304-27

Merlin, B. *Acting: The Basics.* London and New York: Routledge, 2010.

Merlin, B. *Acting: The Basics.* Second Edition. London and New York: Routledge, 2018.

Merlin, B. *Acting: The Basics.* Third Edition. London and New York: Routledge, 2023. DOI: https://doi.org/10.4324/9781003267270

Merlin, B. *Beyond Stanislavsky: The Psycho-Physical Approach to Actor Training.* London: Nick Hern Books, 2001. DOI: https://doi.org/10.4324/9781315059839

Merlin, B. *Konstantin Stanislavsky.* London and New York: Routledge, 2003. DOI: https://doi.org/10.4324/9781351117180

Merlin, B. *The Complete Stanislavsky Toolkit.* London: Nick Hern Books, 2007).

Merlin, B. *The Complete Stanislavsky Toolkit.* Revised Edition. London: Nick Hern Books, 2014.

Nash, J C. "Practicing Love: Black Feminism, Love-Politics, and Post-Intersectionality". *Meridians: Feminism, Race, Transnationalism.* Volume 11, Issue 2, pp.1–24. Durham NC: Duke University Press, 2013. DOI: https://doi.org/10.1215/15366936-8566089

Peck, L. *Act As A Feminist: Towards a Critical Acting Pedagogy.* London and New York: Routledge, 2021. DOI: https://doi.org/10.4324/9781351130516

Peck, L. *Emma Rice's Feminist Acts of Love.* Cambridge: Cambridge University Press, 2023. DOI: https://doi.org/10.1017/9781009287234

Percy, M C. *Intimacy Directors and Coordinators Presents: The IDC Resource Guide (First Edition).* USA: Intimacy Directors and Coordinators Professionals, 2020. [Online]. [Accessed February 2024]. Available from: https://static1.squarespace.com/static/5e1c12f49383f8245b857d01/t/5f2470bdc8a09c2a6c405251/1596223729318/IDC+Resource+Guide.pdf

Solnit, R. *The Mother of All Questions.* Chicago: Haymarket Books, 2017.

Stanislavski, K. *An Actor's Work: A Student's Diary*. trans. Benedetti, J. London and New York: Routledge, 2008. DOI: https://doi.org/10.4324/9780203936153
Truscott, C C. "SoulWork". In: Luckett, S D. and Shaffer, T M. eds. *Black Acting Methods: Critical Approaches*. London and New York: Routledge, 2017, pp.37–51. DOI: https://doi.org/10.4324/9781315694986
Valdez, L. *Theatre of the Sphere: The Vibrant Being*. London and New York: Routledge, 2021. DOI: https://doi.org/10.4324/9781003107217

4

DISPARITIES IN THE STANISLAVSKY TRADITION

Imperceptible and Dispossessed

Samia La Virgne

Prologue: Between Friends

In conversation with a friend, who is also a Black woman and an actor, I asked her about her experiences with the techniques of Konstantin Stanislavsky and the system during her actor training. She said,

> It's a little bit like a lot of school. It's the white guy that we hold with a certain regard. And it can feel very much like, ah, yes! The Europeans. They do everything so much better! They come up with *all* the innovations.

We both laughed knowingly. She continued by commenting,

> It's almost like he didn't invent anything. He just named and described things. He was more like a scientist. He is the "discoverer" in the Christopher Columbus sense of the word. Something was already there. But now that *he* found it and named it, *he* is then considered the discoverer of this thing.

She concluded,

> When I think of Stanislavsky, I think of books. I think of lots of printed lines on a page. I don't think of it as something vibrant or creative or inspirational.

DOI: 10.4324/9781003411611-5

Introduction: Working from Personal Experience

> [O]ur prime task is not only to portray the life of a role externally, but above all to create the inner life of the character and of the whole play, bringing our own individual feelings to it, endowing it with all the features of our own personality.
>
> (Stanislavski, 2010a, 19)

Although I am an actor and director, and I have a doctorate in the performing arts, I am not a Stanislavsky scholar. Instead, here, I offer insights from my personal experiences of actor training in the United States (US) and the United Kingdom (UK). I will be drawing from lived experience, and so, explaining a few things about myself is necessary for context. I am a six- foot-tall, plus-sized Black woman. I was born in the US, specifically California, where I earned a bachelor's (BA) degree in theatre from a liberal arts university. I moved to the UK in 2014, attended a conservatoire-style drama school and earned a master of fine arts (MFA) degree in the 'British tradition' of acting. I immediately went on to complete a practice-based PhD in the performing arts. My postgraduate research first explored how to foster an environment in which Black women play lead roles on the professional Shakespearean stage, which broadened at a doctoral level to examine how the stereotypical representation of Black women on stage and screen impacts on Black female actors in the UK and the US. I considered both actor training and industry experiences in my analysis. I concluded that actor training in the UK and the US desperately needs change to support Black acting students, particularly Black women, and students from other marginalised and underrepresented groups. Throughout my research, I reflected on my personal actor- training experiences. As a Black woman, it is impossible to separate my womanhood from my Blackness. Thus, my discussion of Stanislavsky and gender for this volume comes from my intersectional experience of gender and race.

The term intersectionality has entered the mainstream, becoming prevalent in contemporary and popularised discourse on identity politics. Kimberlé Crenshaw coined intersectionality as a term in 1989 to identify and describe the nuances of marginalisation, discrimination, and inequality within the intersecting identities of Blackness, womanhood, and class in the US criminal justice system. Crenshaw uses intersectionality to avoid what she explains as "the conceptual limitations of the single-issue analyses"' (Crenshaw, 149). In an interview with *Time* magazine, Crenshaw defines intersectionality as "a lens, a prism, for seeing the way in which various forms of inequality often operate together and exacerbate each other" (Steinmetz, 2020). Furthermore, Patricia Hill Collins and Sirma Bilge explain that intersectionality is an analytical tool that can provide "a way of understanding and explaining complexity in the world, in people, and in human experiences" (Collins and Bilge, 2). And so, my experiences of actor training as a Black woman are nuanced and complex; therefore, I use intersectionality as an analytical tool to inform my discussion in this chapter.

Imperceptible: Visibility and Invisibility in the Stanislavsky Tradition

Stanislavsky's enduring influence in the actor training field is undeniable. Bella Merlin observes that "be it implicitly or explicitly – [Stanislavsky's] terms and theories are on the lips of most Western acting practitioners" (Merlin, 3). Further research by Ross Prior examining actor training across the US, the UK, and Australia identified that acting teachers held "a deeply personal view to actor training, which in every circumstance is shaped by Stanislavsky's thinking or an interpretation of it" (Prior, 153). Both observations I am inclined to agree with, and yet, as a classically trained actor, director, researcher, and most recently, teacher of the mystifying and beguiling discipline of acting, it is difficult to identify any specific techniques that were directly attributed to Stanislavsky in my training. It is an ironic and fascinating phenomenon that something considered crucial to acting is so elusive and imperceptible for me.

When discussing the calibre of their training, actors seem to name-drop famous canonical figures of actor training. They have no problem proudly declaring the techniques and practices that influenced their acting style that are usually European, such as Jerzy Grotowski, the Italian style of Commedia dell'arte, or the French pedagogy of Jacques Lecoq, yet another dead white man's ideals that are preciously held near and dear to the collective hearts of actors and their teachers who want to be taken seriously and considered among the best in the performing arts industry.

As I reflect on my acting training, it's a hodgepodge of various styles, techniques, and approaches that were often indistinct from their specific names, origins, and practitioners. Like many Americans, I assume the principles I encountered that I could attribute to Stanislavsky's system, with only a marginal level of certainty, was 'method acting' and 'emotion memory'. Both terms and their interpretation in the US have been, of course, highly contested.[1] As Merlin and Prior both indicate, most Anglo-American actor training programmes claim to utilise elements of Stanislavsky's system. However, Stanislavsky (the man) is often dissociated from it, further installing each teacher as the purveyor of their interpretation of Stanislavsky (the knowledge). Actors engage with exercises and components of his system when honing their skills with little to no knowledge or critical discussion of the context of its development. Recalling the conversation, I included at the beginning of this chapter, I was surprised to discover that, like me, my friend also struggled to directly attribute exact principles, techniques, and exercises to Stanislavsky.

During my undergraduate study, *An Actor Prepares* (1936) by Konstantin Stanislavsky, translated, and edited by Elizabeth Hapgood Reynolds, appeared as a required reading text. Admittedly, I never read it; I suspect, like many undergraduates studying acting. There were many required readings and recommended texts to navigate independently, and they were often divorced from the teaching I experienced in the classroom. Unfortunately, like others, I often relied on and favoured the in-class practice of techniques – the sole interpretation of an acting teacher. I felt dispossessed from the knowledge that I was supposed to attain. It was also challenging to relate academic literature to my personal experience of the world. What I read on the page did not reflect my reality; its intended real-world application was unclear. Until writing this chapter, I buried my copy of Stanislavsky's *An Actor Prepares* in a box stored away for 'safe keeping'. I hoped one day to absorb some valuable information through osmosis by owning the book and occasionally holding it in my hands. Of course, this has never happened.

Since then, I have become more aware of the complex history of translation, publication, and censorship around *An Actor Prepares* and subsequently *Building a Character* (1950) and *Creating a Role* (1961), significantly impacting interpretations of Stanislavsky in English.[2] I have since encountered Jean Benedetti's edition of *An Actor's Work: A Student's Diary* by Konstantin Stanislavski, translated from Stanislavsky's Soviet editions, which gives an overview of the complexities mentioned earlier of reading Stanislavsky in English and, notably, a brief history of how the system became 'the Method' in the US through the work of the Group Theatre. In *An Actor's Work: A Student's Diary*, Stanislavsky writes his fictionalised (and arguably idealised) account of two years of training in his system from the perspective of a fictional male student Kostya, who represents a young Stanislavsky, taught by esteemed teacher Arkady Tortsov, who represents the older Stanislavsky, a literary device retained across translations and editions that some have found "unnecessary" (Benedetti, 2004, 78). Benedetti contends, "that is the book's purpose: for the reader to experience the students' learning process" (Benedetti, 2010, xviii). Years after completing my undergraduate and graduate actor training, I purchased Benedetti's translation.

I earnestly attempted to read Stanislavsky's writing for the first time, but I was quickly discouraged. In the first two pages of the first chapter, the student Kostya gives his first- person narration of his racist exploration and preparation to perform as Shakespeare's Othello. As Kostya, Stanislavsky writes, "Thus armed, I felt like a proud, majestic, handsome warrior [...] But, Othello is African! There has to be something of the tiger about him" (Stanislavski, 2010a, 6). Not content with characterising a Black person as an animal, Kostya describes his use of Blackface: "Then suddenly I caught sight of a bar of chocolate. [...] It easily spread on my face and turned me into a Moor" (Stanislavski, 2010a, 8). Unsurprisingly, I could not read beyond these moments because of my rage, as Blackness was made synonymous with primitive and animal characteristics. It was all too reminiscent of the human zoos where enslaved Africans were exhibited as colonial objects in the late nineteenth century in Europe. Confronted with explicit racism in the first few pages of Stanislavsky's magnum opus, I was concerned about what else was ahead.

The female characters in *An Actor's Work: A Student's Diary* are stereotypes, illustrated through their "beauty, vanity, and flirtatiousness" (Malague, 2013, 145), and as neurotic and hysterical. The three fictional female students, Marya, Varya (also known as Sonya), and Darya, are included as mere foils to substantiate the plot of *An Actor's Work: A Student's Diary* and to facilitate the focus of the plot, Stanislavsky's intrapersonal narrative device between the characters Kostya and Tortsov, which convey his pedagogical reflections. Tortsov praises the female students display of emotion and Stanislavsky uses their distress as a narrative technique to demonstrate his pedagogy, for example, two female students are berated while walking up and down a corridor so that Tortsov can demonstrate the power of "exaggerated, nit-picking critics" (Stanislavski, 2010a, 174–175). Rosemary Malague argues that the female characters in Stanislavsky's fictional training are the source of what she describes as "the valuation of the weeping woman" in the Stanislavsky tradition (Malague, 2013, 145). In *An Actor's Work: A Student's Diary*, Marya, like Kostya, also gives her first performance in front of the fictional teacher, Tortsov, at the beginning of the plot. Kostya describes Marya as dramatically coming onstage, rushing down a flight of stairs, falling to the floor and crying, "Save me". The rest of her lines are unintelligible, she covers her face in shame and retreats offstage after forgetting her lines (Stanislavski, 2010a, 16). Marya is illustrated as melodramatic and incompetent, though Tortsov praises the intensity of her emotions. In reading the first chapter of *An Actor's Work: A Student's Diary*, I discovered studying such material without adequate context can be challenging for a woman with a marginalised, intersectional identity.

Although Rosemary Malague cites Sharon Carnicke to acknowledge that the male characters are also stereotypes in Stanislavsky's fictional accounts of his training (Malague, 2013, 145; Carnicke, 2009, 5), the female characters are also required to play stereotypical maternal roles, specifically Agnes in *Brand* by Henrik Ibsen (1865), as Malague comments,

> If one were looking for a quintessential example of the kind of female role that worries (and outrages) feminist critics, Agnes would be it; Agnes is also the role that Tortsov's actresses rehearse repeatedly throughout *An Actor's Work*.
>
> *(Malague, 2013, 147)*

Rosemary Malague observes that "by the time the students reach their third year of study in *An Actor's Work on a Role*, it would appear you don't really need any women, for they all but disappear" (Malague, 2013, 143). The fictional women become invisible, and Black women, it seems, are entirely absent in the tradition.

Historically, canonical playwrights, plays, practitioners, and techniques utilised in actor training environments, as well as the directors and instructors working with students, have been male dominated and patriarchal, deliberately, or inadvertently, oppressing women.

While recounting her actor training experience in the 1980s with the Method, Rosemary Malague admits, "we were not assigned any readings, nor were we taught what the Method really was, where it came from, or the theory behind its operation" (Malague, 2012, 6).

Malague explains that she was encouraged and praised to make acting choices that reinforced traditional female gender roles. She describes how often female actors are "routinely rewarded for their 'risk-taking' and they scored points for their 'vulnerability'" (Malague, 2012, 5) in acting only when such risk-taking reinforces and conforms to stereotypical tropes of women being unable to control their emotions. Furthermore, Malague asks an incisive question about seeking to produce a truthful performance using Stanislavsky's system: what happens if the system is "built upon gender-based assumptions and prejudices that reflect a patriarchal worldview?" (Malague, 2012, 11) or, in my case, built upon racial prejudice, too? Feminist academic Sue-Ellen Case also highlights this vital distinction in her writing, that "the woman of colour bears the triple burden of gender, race, and class oppression, while the white woman benefits from her class privilege of colour" (Case, 97). From these perspectives and based on my experience reading *An Actor's Work: A Student's Diary*, engaging with Stanislavsky's system may be more of a burden than I want to carry as a Black woman.

Extensive reading was not the only obstacle in my undergraduate studies. At the time, I was about 19 or 20 years old, the only Black woman in my class, and one of a small handful (maybe three or four) of non-white actors in the Theatre Arts Department of my university. At an age where most people begin figuring out who they are as they enter adulthood, I struggled to find my confidence. I needed an understanding of my identity beyond the stereotypes and assumptions of what a Black woman is or should be. I dealt with a fair share of racism, sexism, and discrimination by this point in my life. These powerful covert forces had started to make me feel invisible. Cheryl Gittens-Jones articulates the paradoxical feeling of in/visibility in her poem My Blackness Goes Before Me. In this excerpt, she writes, "Walking into a room / My blackness goes / My blackness goes / Goes before me / [...] Still do not see / See me as / human / woman / Only / Black" (Gittens-Jones, 2011). Years later, whilst conducting my PhD research, I discovered that the feeling of invisibility was not solely my experience but a systematic occurrence for Black women living in white, hegemonic, patriarchal societies. The dichotomy of being both hyper-visible in the classroom and yet invisible in the literature, traditions, and methodologies I was required to study as an actor is articulated clearly by Audre Lorde, that "Black women have on one hand always been highly visible, and so, on the other hand, have been rendered invisible through the depersonalization of racism" (Lorde, 36).

In March 2010, *the Journal of Experimental Social Psychology* published a psychological study titled "Prototypes of Race and Gender: The Invisibility of Black Women". The article includes findings from two psychological experiments exploring the invisibility of Black women. Both studies addressed "whether Black women go 'unnoticed' and their voices 'unheard,' [...] whether, in fact, Black women are 'invisible' to White people" (Sesko et al., 257). The first study contained 131 white undergraduate student participants in the US. Fifty of the participants were female, and 81 were male.

There were two phases in the study. In Phase One, each participant was shown a series of faces via headshot photos. Each participant viewed 32 photos – 8 photos each of Black men, Black women, white men, and white women. In Phase Two, participants viewed a series of headshot photos that included some of the headshot photos from Phase One and additional photos of people they had not seen before. During the second phase, the participants viewed 24 photos – 6 photos from each of the previously mentioned gendered and racial categories. The experiment required the participants to identify which faces they saw in Phase One and Two. The results revealed that the participants accurately recognised a face from the photos they had previously seen 78.3% of the time. However, "photos of Black women appeared to be the least memorable, a symptom of 'invisibility'" (Sesko et al., 358).

The second study included 65 participants who were predominantly white undergraduate students (81%). Forty of the participants were female, and 25 were male. In this study, participants listened to a pre-recorded conversation of students discussing their plans after graduation. The conversation contained a total of 16 statements. As each statement in the conversation was listened to by the participant, they viewed a photo of a student who made the corresponding statement. After listening to the entire conversation and viewing the photos of the individuals who spoke each of the 16 statements, the participants witnessed an additional 16 statements not included in the original audio conversation, totalling 32 overall. The experiment required the participants to identify which statements were spoken in the original recording and match each statement with the photo of the person who made the corresponding statement. The study aimed to "investigate whether spoken statements made by Black women are less likely to be correctly identified compared to those of Black men, White women and White men" (Sesko et al., 358). The findings showed that participants were more likely to incorrectly attribute statements made by Black women to other people than to misattribute white women's, Black men's, or white men's statements, rendering contributions made to the conversation by Black women imperceptible.

The invisibility of Black women was investigated once more in *the Journal of Psychology of Popular Media Culture* in the article "Gendered Race in Mass Media: Invisibility of Asian Men and Black Women in Popular Magazines" in 2015. The research uncovered that people are "more likely to explicitly and implicitly associate common stereotypes about Blacks with masculinity and common stereotypes about Asians with femininity" (Schug et al., 223), suggesting that gendered and racial bias has fostered the invisibility of both Black women and Asian men within popular media culture because they do not necessarily adhere to the stereotypes of their respective racial and gender group. The study coded 8,124 people shown in 5 issues of 6 magazines of multiple genres. The highest circulation rates, and "the results indicate[d] that proportionally, Asian men and Black women were represented less in both magazines marketed to men and magazines marketed to women" (Schug et al., 228). This study ultimately "provides evidence that Asian men and Black women are rendered invisible in mass media, namely, in popular magazines" (Schug et al., 229). To analyse and contextualise their findings, Schug et al. utilised gendered race theory to argue "that stereotypes about race are gendered, with Asians stereotyped as more feminine, and Blacks stereotyped as more masculine" (Schug et al., 229).

In one of the earliest feminist critiques of the Stanislavsky tradition, Linda Walsh-Jenkins and Susan Ogden-Malouf posit that a feminist approach to teaching Stanislavsky's system could include cross-gender casting to empower women rather than reinforce patriarchal gender roles. They argue that "when actors portray characters of the opposite sex, they confront both their own sex role conditioning and their stereotypical conceptions concerning gender" (Jenkins & Ogden-Malouf, 66–67). Jenkins and Ogden-Malouf further contend that when creating and rehearsing a character, the process ultimately intersects with the actor's personal life, describing how "the growth of a character has parallels with her [...] personal growth, and at some point, in the rehearsal the life offstage imitates or is affected by the life onstage" (Jenkins & Ogden-Malouf, 66). This belief may be true for some female actors, such as the small, petite, soft, or 'girly' types, who society views as falling into specific, traditional, racialised female ideals. As a six-foot-tall, plus-size, Black woman, there are certain stereotypes I have had to confront in the rehearsal room, during casting, onstage or in front of a camera. I often played male roles because directors would not consider me for specific female roles unless they were negative Black stereotypes, such as the 'Mammy', servants, or maids. In her discourse on Black women's bodies, sociologist, and scholar Shirley Anne Tate states that, "the history of the Black woman's body in the European-North American imagination is imbricated within the racialisation of colonialism and enslavement that still remains today" (Tate, 1). Patricia Hill Collins further explains that such stereotypical imagery presents an array of controlling images that constitute part of a generalised ideology of domination, which manipulates the perception of Black womanhood (Collins, 2014). In short, racialisation of the Black female body has created and perpetuated damaging stereotypes that control the visibility of Black women. According to gendered race theory, I am stereotyped as masculine even though I am a Black woman. I have played male roles just as much as I have played female roles, and contrary to Jenkins and Ogden-Malouf, I did not find it empowering. For me, playing a male role by default because my physicality did not fit "the dominant view of ideal women's bodies [which are] thin, frail, and white" (Tate, 3) was not empowering. Playing male roles stripped away an integral part of my identity (my femininity) that I was eager to explore as an actor. When the opportunity has arisen to be visible as a Black woman, these invisible repressive and oppressive forces are constantly at work when I am in an audition room, rehearsals, performance, and learning spaces. The invisible forces of patriarchy and discrimination, coupled with the invisible presence of Stanislavsky's system, are a dichotomy that ultimately created a sense of loss within my overall agency as an actor.

In the conclusion to Rosemary Malague's *An Actress Prepares: Women and "the Method"*, she shares an anecdote regarding Black actress Frances Foster, who was part of the original Broadway cast of Lorraine Hansberry's *A Raisin in the Sun* (1959) and "a founding member of the Negro Ensemble Company (NEC)" (Malague, 2012, 190). Malague quotes an interview with Foster by Holly Hill (1993) as Foster describes a review that alleged "that they allowed me to overact so in the funeral scene" of Philip Hayes Dean's *Sty of the Blind Pig* (1971).

Foster explains in the interview that "when we read that review about how the funeral scene was overacted, we laughed because we understood that the critic didn't know. He had never been to a black funeral" (Foster in Malague, 2012, 190). Though Malague is sensitive to a generalisation of how Black people might behave, she asks,

> How does a white acting teacher judge the "truthfulness" of a black student's performance of a scene? [...] Definitions of believable performances derive from very subjective understandings of *how people behave*, and what is true to an actor or viewer from one culture may seem false to their counterparts from another.
>
> *(Malague, 2012, 191, original emphasis)*

So, it seems that even if the Black actress is to survive the white supremacist patriarchal misogynist world of actor training, succeeding in appearing onstage, she cannot escape what the Pulitzer and Nobel Peace Prize in Literature author Toni Morrison, calls the "white gaze", which she describes as "a burden" (Morrison, 2020).

In conversation at Cornell University, Morrison articulates her experience of writing and resisting the white gaze:

> I thought, "I can't do that." What is the world like if he's not there? And the freedom, the open world that appears is stunning. […] There was this free space opened up by refusing to respond every minute to […] somebody else's gaze.
>
> *(Kelley, 2013)*

In 2011, Morrison reimagined *Othello* from the perspective of his love interest and the play's eponymous titular character, *Desdemona*. The play presents an alternative storyline of the character of Desdemona, raised by her enslaved nurse named Barbary, her name indicating her African ancestry and deliberately invoking the racist connotations of the barbarian that Iago accuses and manipulates Othello to be. The play, directed by Peter Sellars, weaved African traditions with music by Rokia Traoré, who played Barbary singing in Bambara, a dialect of West Africa, notably Mali, where Traoré was born. Morrison further explains:

> I refused to do the play unless Peter permitted me to get rid of Iago all together […] because he's everywhere, he's talking constantly, nobody is telling the truth, he is manipulating everybody, he's gobbling up the play and no one can just live. A friend of mine said "oh no, you can't take Iago out, that is the important role", I said "why didn't he call it Iago? Why did he call it *Othello*?" […] It was so liberating, in the writing and the imagination […] to see what it would be like, what they would say to one another if he wasn't there.
>
> *(Morrison, 2019)*

Discussing the tradition of racism in the history of *Othello*, Morrison describes how "classically trained Black actors love it because they get to be a star on stage in Shakespeare and there is no other place for that to happen, so it's done over and over again pretty much the same" (Morrison, 2019). It is worth noting that there is no female equivalent for Black women to aspire to in the Anglophonic dramatic canon should they wish to.

The author and critical pedagogue, bell hooks, further theorises the possibilities for Black women to be seen and to view themselves and identify their absence in popular media in her essay "The Oppositional Gaze: Black Female Spectators". hooks argues,

> When most black people in the United States first had the opportunity to look at film and television, they did so fully aware that mass media was a system of knowledge and power reproducing and maintaining white

> supremacy. To stare at the television, or mainstream movies, to engage its images, was to engage its negation of black representation. It was the oppositional black gaze that responded to these looking relations by developing independent black cinema. Black viewers of mainstream cinema and television could chart the progress of political movements for racial equality via the construction of images, and did so.
>
> *(hooks, 117)*

hooks further explains that Black women develop a critical praxis of "looking at films with an oppositional gaze" to "critically assess the cinema's construction of white womanhood as object of phallocentric gaze and choose not to identify with either the victim or the perpetrator" (hooks, 122). hooks notes that theoretically, "interrogating black looks were mainly concerned with issues of race and racism, the way racial domination of blacks by whites overdetermined representation. They were rarely concerned with gender" (hooks, 117–8), explaining how Laura Mulvey's (1973) "male gaze" fails to acknowledge the presence and spectatorship of Black women. Thus, hooks argues that "Black female spectators, who refused to identify with white womanhood, who would not take on the phallocentric gaze of desire and possession, created a critical space" (hooks, 122). hooks cites examples of Black cinema such as *Illusions* (1982) and *Daughters of the Dust* (1991) by American filmmaker Julie Dash, and *The Passion of Remembrance* (1986) by Black British filmmaker Maureen Blackwood, to explain how such films "undermine existing grand cinematic narratives. [...] Without providing 'realistic' positive representations that emerge only as a response to the totalizing nature of existing narratives" but instead "offer points of radical departure" (hooks, 130). The nuance and depth offered by these films, hooks writes, "open[s] up a space for the assertion of a critical black female spectatorship" by "imagin[ing] new transgressive possibilities for the formulation of identity" (hooks, 130). She cites cultural theorist Stuart Hall to claim that, cinematically, such representations of Black women provide "new points of recognition" that enable "a critical practice that acknowledges that identity is constituted", quoting Hall, "not outside but within representation" (hooks, 131). A radical expansion and indeed, a rejection of realism, hooks posits, "invites us to see film", quoting Hall again, "not as a second-order mirror held up to reflect what already exists, but as that form of representation which is able to constitute us as new kinds of subjects, and thereby enable us to discover who we are" (Hall, 80; hooks, 131). hooks concludes that "it is this critical practice that enables production of feminist film theory that theorizes black female spectatorship. Looking and looking back [...] using it as a way to know the present and invent the future" (hooks, 131). Thus, decentring the white gaze of the acting teacher who sees himself in Stanislavsky's image as the "the arbiter of truth" (Malague, 2012, 13) can invite the freedom of imagination described by Morrison and the criticality advocated for by hooks.

Rosemary Malague offers the example of how actor, playwright, and professor Anna Deavere Smith presents her hyper-realistic performances of the real people she interviews using verbatim techniques "to embody persons of different races, ethnicities, and genders through her own female, African American body and voice" (Malague, 2012, 200). Deavere Smith rejects psychological realism, enamoured by the Group Theatre in their inspiration from Stanislavsky, and "does not incorporate autobiography into her performance pieces", instead relying on her skills and techniques as an actor to perform the recorded interviews she obtains in person. Though Malague suggests that "Smith's technique borrows elements of the System" (Malague, 2012, 200), Deavere Smith explains,

> When I was trying to write about acting in order to find out why I had trouble with the Stanislavsky technique, I came across a graph of the objectives of the Stanislavsky technique. Super objective. Little objective. It was straight lines with arrows. Quite soon after that I was reading a book about African philosophical systems and saw a picture of a wheel that had all these little spokes with arrows pointing towards the center. I knew then that I wanted to try to find a way of thinking or a structure that was more like that.
>
> *(Deavere Smith and Martin, 51)*

The negative consequences for female actors trained in psychological realism to perform inherently and overtly misogynist roles have been central to the feminist analyses of the Stanislavsky tradition, complicated by the frequent conflation of the system with the Method. The debate on the ethics of realism can be dated back to Plato and Aristotle's conflicting views on mimesis and continues to rumble on. However, as Patricia Schroeder advocates, cited by Malague,

> If we endorse the goal of empowerment for women, and if we accept that feminism is and must be polyvocal and evolving, then it seems crucial to me that we recognize realism as one of the many inherited tools at a feminist artist's disposal.
>
> *(Schroeder, 42, in Malague, 2012, 197)*

In this way, Deavere Smith reconfigures Stanislavsky's idea of the Supertask and the throughline of action from an Afrocentric perspective that is not linear in its destination. In her verbatim performances, she precisely and powerfully demonstrates that a Black female actor can utilise realism to demonstrate her highly skilled and impressive craft.

Hero Worship

> The "system" is a guide. Open it and read. The "system" is a reference book, not a philosophy.
>
> The "system" ends when philosophy begins.
>
> Work on the "system" at home. Onstage put it to one side. You cannot act the "system".
>
> There is no "system". There is nature.
>
> My concern throughout my life has been to find ways to get nearer what we call the "system", that is, to the nature of the creative act.
>
> (Stanislavski, 2010a, 612)

I earlier described and narrated my visceral experience of reading the character of Kostya, who represents a young Stanislavsky, performing in Blackface as Othello in *An Actor's Work: A Student's Diary*. In the continuing *An Actor's Work on a Role*, also translated, and edited by Benedetti, the fictional teacher Tortsov, who represents an elder Stanislavsky, remarks that "*Othello* appeals to everyone, and it is wonderful to cast" (Stanislavski, 2010b, 4). This belief, held by Tortsov, clearly indicates Stanislavsky's naiveté and is demonstrative of its context, dated between 1930 and 1932 by Benedetti, when Blackface was wrongly accepted, popularised, and prevalent, particularly in performances of *Othello*.

In *My Life in Art*, Stanislavsky passionately describes watching his hero, the Italian actor Tommaso Salvini, portray Othello, who performed in Blackface. At first, Stanislavsky admits that Salvini's Othello "left me cold", noticing the artifice of his costume, makeup, and wig before expressing the impact of Salvini's performance: "We were in his power for ever, for the rest of our lives, we knew who this genius was and what we could expect from him" (Stanislavski, 2008, 142). Stanislavsky admits in *My Life in Art*, "What I learned about Salvini marked me deeply for the rest of my career" (Stanislavski, 2008, 144), and later in *An Actor's Work: A Student's Diary*, the fictional teacher Tortsov exemplifies Salvini, remarking that Salvini is "the finest representative of this school of acting" (Stanislavski, 2010a, 19), that is the basis of Tortsov's pedagogy: "the school of experiencing" (Stanislavski, 2010a, 25).

Stanislavsky confesses his obsession with *Othello* after watching Salvini, writing, "From the moment I saw Salvini I never stopped dreaming of playing Othello" (Stanislavski, 2008, 144). He goes on to describe performing as Othello early in his career with the Society of Art and Literature after watching Salvini. He meets in Paris "my new friend, the handsome Arab" (Stanislavski, 2008, 144) and imitates his gestures and clothing to prepare for the role like Kostya in *An Actor's Work: A Student's Diary*. Stanislavsky realises, however, that he has not achieved the "art of experiencing" like his hero Salvini but instead falls foul to the "art of representation" (Stanislavski, 2010a, 22), which he deems antithetical to his acting ethos.

After Kostya's first performance in Blackface as Othello at the beginning of his training in *An Actor's Work: A Student's Diary*, Tortsov admonishes him for his racist portrayal, particularly his animalistic characterisation. During his lecture that explicates the ethics of the "art of experiencing" (Stanislavski, 2010a, 16), Tortsov states,

> So why, apart from one or two moments, was what you did during the show so absurd? Can you actually believe that Moors, renowned for their culture in their time, behaved like wild animals, prowling round their cages? The savage you portrayed snarled, flashed his teeth, and rolled his eyes even during a quiet conversation with his aide-de-camp. Where did such an approach come from? Explain to us how you could possibly arrive at this absurdity. Isn't it because, for an actor who has gone astray, any kind of idiocy is possible?
>
> *(Stanislavski, 2010a, 32)*

Stanislavsky use of Blackface, reflecting on his early autobiography as an actor and as a narrative device to demonstrate Kostya's amateurism, which necessitates training, including the fictional teacher Tortsov's reprimand, lacks the nuance that fully acknowledges the violence of Blackface and needs appropriate framing by educators recommending *An Actor's Work: A Student's Diary* as required reading today.

As Toni Morrison earlier identified, the role of Othello can be fraught for Black actors because it is often considered a benchmark of their skill and contributes to their success and notability, for example celebrated historical figures such as Ira Aldridge and Paul Robeson. Robeson first played Othello at Somerville High School in New Jersey between 1912 and 1915 and in London opposite Peggy Ashcroft as Desdemona in 1930 before making US theatre history in his acclaimed performance with Uta Hagen as Desdemona in 1943, directed by Margaret Webster on Broadway. During the Moscow Art Theatre tours of North America, Paul Robeson met with Aleksandr Arnoldovich Koiransky in New York in 1924, whom both Laurence Senelick and Sharon Carnicke identify as an editor of Stanislavsky's writing for the English language edition of *My Life in Art* (1924).[3] According to Paul Robeson's son and biographer, Paul Robeson Jnr, his father and Koiransky worked together on *Othello* (Robeson, 81). Later, according to another biographer, Lindsey R. Swindall, when Paul Robeson was rehearsing the 1943 Broadway production of *Othello*, "he used the memory of racism on the football field from his Rutgers days to conjure Othello's rage" (Swindall, 103). Robeson's approach caused "friction between [him] and Webster backstage due to their different theatrical approaches" as Webster "in contrast, concentrated more on the external and had trouble relating to Konstantin Stanislavsky's strategies, such as emotion memory" (Swindall, 103). Koiransky's work with Robeson was clearly influential, evidenced by this anecdote and not merely a coincidence. Senelick writes,

> According to the émigré journalist Mark Vishniak, Stanislavsky gave Koiransky "'carte blanche to organize the structure of the book … he allowed him to "abridge" it and make "excisions" wherever he deemed it necessary, for Stanislavsky did not consider himself "a judge of what is interesting and what isn't'".
>
> *(Senelick, xiv)*

Given the extent of Koiransky's editorial power over Stanislavsky's writing, according to Vishniak, and the evident influence of his work with Robeson, it is possible that Paul Robeson, one of the most celebrated Black American actors in history and a pivotal figure in the Black civil rights movement, informed Stanislavsky's writing in some way through his work with Stanislavsky's editor, Aleksandr Koiransky, when they met in 1924.

Dispossessed: Eclipsed by the Stanislavsky Tradition

As the first quarter of the twenty-first century nears completion and almost a century after his death, more intersectional reassessments of Stanislavsky's system are taking place, and his ambition that "[m]y system is for all nations. All peoples possess the same human nature" (Stanislavski, 1968, 170) has been rightly challenged.[4]

Monica White Ndounou describes how "[m]ainstream actor training programs in the United States rarely include the contributions of Black Americans. Instead, they primarily focus on Russian actor, director, and theorist Constantin Stanislavski" (White Ndounou, 2009a, 124). She describes how "Stanislavski-based curricula eclipses the various culturally distinct contributions to the development acting theories and practices throughout the 1,800 US college and university theatre departments offering Bachelor degrees in theatre arts" (White Ndounou, 2009a, 124).

The dominance of European and Stanislavsky-based acting praxis is also challenged by Sharrell D. Luckett and Tia M. Shaffer in their book *Black Acting Methods: Critical Approaches*; they observe,

> The nature of pedagogy is grounded in the questions of what to teach, why to teach it, and then how to teach it. The answers to these questions reveal a complicity of intentions, a foregrounding of particular histories to perpetuate particular realities at the expense of other realities and futures.
>
> *(Luckett & Shaffer, 1)*

They continue to explain how "most acting classes in the United States of America operate within a Eurocentric theoretical framework of performance" and that "White-ness overtly and covertly pervades the texts and linguistic structures," which causes "those who do not share a White lineage or hue" to become "de-centred, misaligned, and exiled from a theatre history that they rightfully co-constructed" (Luckett & Shaffer, 1). Unable to pinpoint and identify, name and articulate precise aspects of Stanislavsky's system that I encountered in my actor training has caused me to feel dispossessed from not only the Stanislavsky tradition but also the contributions of Black people to the art of acting. Both White Ndounou and Luckett and Shaffer present a history of Black American actor training and acting traditions that run parallel to the Stanislavsky tradition, with the book *Black Acting Methods: Critical Approaches* providing "an African-centred origin to theatre and theatre making that broadens the theatrical canon and provides a culturally-specific contribution to performance pedagogy" (Luckett & Shaffer, 1). Luckett and Shaffer credit both Susan Batson and Baron Kelly as "groundbreaking" and "excellent additions to the acting canon", though they comment "their approaches are rooted in Eurocentricity" that draw upon the Stanislavsky tradition (Luckett & Shaffer, 7). It is important to note that Luckett and Shaffer highlight the achievements of two Black American acting teachers while still advocating for necessary change. Comparably, Stefan Aquilina and Jonathan Pitches in *Stanislavsky in the World: The System and its Transformations Across Continents* demonstrate how the Stanislavsky tradition is complicit in colonialism, which complicates the transmission of the Stanislavsky tradition globally. For example, Kene Igweonu discusses the introduction of Stanislavsky as the preferred acting methodology in white-only segregated universities in Nigeria before explaining that Joel Adedeji, who was appointed to the School of Drama, University of Ibadan in 1964, after training at Rose Bruford, also significantly contributed to the transmission of Stanislavsky's system in Nigeria. The volume also demonstrates how Stanislavsky's techniques are adapted and appropriate locally within a variety of specific contexts. While I think it is necessary to describe and explain how the Stanislavsky tradition intersects with white supremacy, it is also fair and accurate to recognise the achievements and contributions of Black people to this revered tradition.

I believe what it comes down to is pedagogy, as Luckett and Shaffer have also identified, and fortunately, there are Black women in the field who are leading this change.

Acknowledging the presence of her Blackness and womanhood in the classroom, Monica White Ndounou explains, "I enter the classroom as an African American woman with production, performance, research, and teaching experiences, all of which guide my pedagogical approach" acknowledging that "I recognize my intrinsic value, as well as the complications of the political, social, and historical intricacies of my identity" which she describes "resembles" – "the contradictions of being black and female in a society historically plagued by racial and gender hierarchies"(White Ndounou, 2009b, 95). She asserts that this gives her a dual perspective on actor training pedagogy or rather, citing W.E.B. Du Bois's concept of "double consciousness", that "as an acting teacher familiar with African American cultural perspectives and performance traditions alongside Western acting methodologies in the American theatre" (White Ndounou, 2009b, 95). White Ndounou shares how she employs "Afrocentric concepts of community" to decentre "the traditional Eurocentric ideologies of theatre and acting by diversifying course materials: dramatic literature, critical theory, and acting methodologies" and as "an effective way to encourage ensemble acting" (White Ndounou, 2009b, 95). White Ndounou articulates how integrating and sharing her culture with students can illuminate dominant acting approaches from the Stanislavsky tradition such as Sanford Meisner and Stella Adler. Ultimately, she contends,

> Complementing modern theories of acting with African American cultural perspectives provides students an opportunity to explore and practice the ways we are connected to the material and metaphysical aspects of our humanity. The recognition of interconnectedness bridges the gap that facilitates the marginalization of blackness. They learn the limitations of predominate techniques like the Method in which actors are encouraged to ignore the audience, which is contrary to African American performance traditions, because they rely heavily on performer/audience interaction (Wiles 172). As a result, students not only learn diverse methods of actor communion and performer/audience interaction, but they also learn that different approaches can be useful tools. In this way, acting functions as a humanistic discipline that aids student understanding of one another as actors, the characters they portray, and, hopefully, the people they encounter outside of the classroom.
>
> *(White Ndounou, 2009b, 98)*

Furthermore, Nicole Brewer has developed her approach to theatre training as Conscientious Theatre Training (CTT). In her article "Training with a Difference", Brewer writes,

> The insidious culture of discrimination is symptomatic of a racialized system of knowledge that privileges the white narrative as superior and universal. For students of color, most of what is taught downplays or ignores their race as a factor in training. The irony is that the industry understands race as a commodity and has no shortage of roles that seek to define us solely based on race. Traditional training therefore does an inadequate job of preparing a vast majority of non-white students for the realities of the industry and the types of jobs they'll be competing for.
>
> *(Brewer, 2018)*

Brewer observes how, not only is the privileging of the white experience in actor training racist, but it is also failing to prepare students who are not white for an industry that appears to be more inclusive and responsive to progress than the training institutions that claim a close alignment with it. Just as Rosemary Malague asserts that "[n]ot to acknowledge difference is to deny the multiplicity of human truth(s)" (Malague, 2012, 195), Brewer is also clear in her pedagogy that "the background and knowledge each student brings must be acknowledged as relevant and pertinent to their development in theatre" (Brewer, 2018).

Brewer states that her approach "creates a spectrum of collaborative, responsive, imaginative, and culturally aware professionals" who have "been given the opportunity to study, apply, and appreciate the diverse contributions within the field of theatre", which she argues "can dismantle practices that are outdated, harmful, and antithetical to the creation of brilliant theatre" (Brewer, 2018).

In the aftermath of George Floyd's murder, the alums of several UK drama schools reported their experiences of racism during their training. This also led to several institutions condemning the murder, as Dermot Daly comments, "There was a raft of statements from many UK drama schools (and indeed public institutions) when in May 2020, George Floyd was murdered by a US Army reservist and Minneapolis Police Department Officer" (Daly, 2022, 554). Recognising that engaging in vocational training at a specialist institution, be it a drama school or conservatoire, Daly concedes that this remains the dominant pathway to an acting career, but that

> [i]n order to build a more equitable, diverse, and inclusive industry, the training offered to those entering the industry needs to mirror and/or begin the conversation that will ensure that those maxims are at the heart of all that is done.
>
> *(Daly, 2022, 556)*

In a further article, Daly discusses Stanislavsky's dominance in the actor training curriculum, commenting, "It is hard to overstate his place and centrality in actor training" (Daly, 2023, 5), while noting the complexity of "additive augmentation and/or gradual replacement" of the so-called actor training canon (Daly, 2023, 12). With its insistence on psychological realism, the augmentation of Stanislavsky's system to become the Method has rightly provoked feminist concern. As Daly warns, there is a danger of "simply remaking the canon in a different image" (Daly, 2023, 12). He cites Daniel Banks' chapter in *Black Acting Methods: Critical Approaches* to exemplify the fusion of "both Afrocentrism and a Stanislavski based approach" (Banks, 141) to demonstrate how synthesising "two seemingly disparate art forms" can "only happen through a thorough interrogation of the canon and not merely through additive augmentation which serves to stifle critical engagement through (often) tokenistic superficial engagement". Such an approach, Daly argues, "will begin to create new unions, new ways of seeing and therefore new and different art" (Daly, 2023, 10).

I must admit that some of Stanislavsky's principles such as the Given Circumstances, the Magic 'If', or Emotion Memory now seem so obvious to me and perhaps they were introduced implicitly into my training without critical discussion, signposting, or reflection. Is it because the influence of Stanislavsky has been carefully maintained in actor training for nearly a century and can no longer be disaggregated from our understanding of acting? Or, perhaps, is it that the system, as Stanislavsky states himself, is not a system at all, but only human nature? Regardless, as Bella Merlin stresses, "we must remain absolutely clear about something: Stanislavsky never intended his 'system' to be gospel" (Merlin, 12). Stanislavsky intended for his system to provide actors access to a greater wealth of creativity. It is now the responsibility of the teachers who cite his influence on their pedagogy to ensure that the system they teach empowers all actors rather than dispossessing some of them from their own creative cultural agency while privileging others. An intersectional and critical discussion of a diverse training curriculum, including required reading, can foster a more nuanced understanding of the connections and complexities of the craft and encourage new knowledge and innovation. As Rosemary Malague recommends, "A multicultural presence in the classroom challenges basic assumptions about the universality of Stanislavsky-based, 'truthful' acting" (Malague, 2012, 194) and, I suggest, can invite students to have a more meaningful and insightful engagement with their training and learning. So, whether you adhere to Stanislavsky's system, augment it, add bits on, challenge, or resist it, as actors and artists may, we all continue to move closer to better understanding creativity and each other, manifesting endless possibilities through art in fascinating and unexpected ways.

Post Chapter Discussion: Samia La Virgne with Maria Brígida De Miranda

Maria Brígida De Miranda Samia, I am delighted to discuss your chapter for *Stanislavsky and Gender* with you, in which you share your personal experiences and research about the intersectionality of gender and race in the performing arts industry in the US and the UK. Though we have never met, your experiences and research resonated with me, evoking memories of studying Stanislavsky's system as an acting student. These similarities struck me despite our subjective differences and contexts.

I am a Brazilian theatre actress, director, and professor of acting and directing in a performing arts department at a public university in the south of Brazil. In Brazil, actor training at a tertiary level of education is offered mainly by public universities supported by federal or state budgets so that students from different backgrounds and social classes attend public examinations to guarantee their entrance to public universities, and courses are free of tuition fees. There are two graduate degrees designed to prepare professional actors and directors to work in the performing arts industry or as performing arts teachers, and occasionally, students follow both pathways. In my department, we deliver a nine-semester full-time course in theatre education at the undergraduate level, though some students embark on a professional acting or directing career. Many of the students are from historically excluded and economically marginalised communities and are dependent on government-funded scholarships to access their training. It has been interesting to observe how the progressive governments of Presidents Luiz Inácio Lula da Silva and Dilma Vana Rousseff and their policies to improve access to education have changed the student demographic in the last two decades.

There has been a significant increase in Black and Indigenous students and transgender and gender non-conforming students, mainly because of these progressive policy changes, which invite and welcome new questions for our field. So, I believe your chapter will connect with young Brazilian acting students.

1 I was interested to read your discussion of Black female practitioners like Monica White Ndounou and Nicole Brewer, who are innovating actor training pedagogy. One of the questions for us in Brazil is, how do we rethink our curriculum, not just by including more diverse people and practices or changing the canon as Dermot Daly, who you cite, argues, but how do we begin to untangle how we learn, teach and act from colonialism and what are your experiences of decolonisation in higher education?

In your chapter, you clearly explain your in/visibility as a Black woman in your respective fields and how gender is racialised and race is gendered. I was considered not white, and often my nationality and gender, 'Brazilian woman' or 'Latino woman', substituted my racial identity when I lived in the UK and Australia. In Brazil, however, I am white. It is interesting to me how these countries of former colonial powers constructed my race and gender differently.

In my doctoral research, which I published as *Playful Training: Towards Capoeira in the Physical Training of Actors* in 2010, I referred to Michel Foucault's idea of 'docile bodies' from *Discipline and Punish* (1975) and gender theories by Judith Butler and Elizabeth Grosz. I question twentieth-century discourses and practices in actor training that make assumptions about bodies and nature. Stanislavsky, for example, discusses correcting the body through physical education, appropriating yoga as a cultural practice and using the female body as a narrative motif that requires correction. The white, male, able and docile actor is considered ideal. I also note how notions of 'nature', 'natural', 'the laws of nature', and 'human nature', often regarded as universal and indisputable, are prevalent in nineteenth- and twentieth-century discourses on training the body. I also argued that a physical practice always carries the cultural politics and beliefs of its origin and the context of its development. For example, if I introduce exercises from indigenous people from the Amazonian forest, I also introduce cultures embodied in gestures, movements, pauses, vocalisations, and rhythms. Thus, there cannot be a universal, politically or socially 'neutral' understanding of what is 'natural', or a universal, politically or socially 'neutral' training to achieve this unattainable ideal.

2 So, I would like to ask you how actors who are gendered female and/or feminine, actors racialised as not white, along with actors who are not non-disabled, actors that are not cis-gendered, white, heterosexual, able-bodied men, can challenge the discourses and practices that propagate notions of 'human nature' and 'the laws of nature' which are misogynist, exclusionary, ableist, Eurocentric and racist?

Samia La Virgne Brígida, I am also delighted to engage in this dialogue with you. I am fascinated and encouraged by the similarity of experience in the performing arts industry that we both have despite having never met each other and coming from very different cultural backgrounds. It reminds me of one of the primary principles of acting, which is the sharing of human experience from various cultures across the globe and the potential power embedded within that act.

Thank you for sharing a bit of your background. It is so interesting to learn about how the public university system works in Brazil. Particularly that, due to the implementation of more progressive government policies, the student demographic has changed, granting access for more students from economically marginalised backgrounds that perhaps would not have had the opportunity to study at university otherwise. Although I applied for scholarships to gain my university education, unfortunately, I had to rely on funded loans from the US government that I, more than likely, will never be able to pay back due to the exorbitant amount. It pleases me to know that your students will not have that issue.

The question you pose about how to rethink curriculum by including more diverse people and practices, as well as untangle the aftereffects of colonialism is a tricky one. Especially because the legacy of colonialism has not only solidified white hegemony but also the eradication, appropriation, and suppression of much of what existed before it came into being. I think it is about defining a new identity for actor training pedagogy. Just as Maria Thais embraces her full "mestizoness" (Thais in De Miranda and Yencken, 102) allowing all three cultures to feed into her practice, on a grander scale, I think the time has come for other cultural practices, divergent of the white hegemonic construct, to feed into the current actor training pedagogy that has been shaped and led by Europe and North America. At the moment, Black practitioners in the US seem to be leading the charge. However, finding ways to highlight and implement work from other practitioners globally, such as Thais, will keep the forward momentum.

The second question you pose is a challenging one. Since 2020, I believe a considerable shift has been initiated. Something is happening on a larger scale that we have not seen in a long time, if ever. The frustration that has been bubbling just below the surface for actors who are not cis-gendered, white, heterosexual, able-bodied men has reached a pressure point that is beginning to release in a powerful way. With that being said, there have been brief moments and/or spaces for some groups of marginalised actors and artists to explore notions of 'human nature' that speak more directly to their lived experience. Modest efforts of activism in theatre that pushed against the overwhelming weight of white, able-bodied, hegemonic, heterosexual patriarchal forces. A couple of examples in the UK include the formation of theatre companies such as the Women's Theatre Group in 1974, renamed the Sphinx Theatre Company in 1999, whose objective is to create roles for women in all aspects of theatre, on stage and off. Or Graeae Theatre Company founded in 1980, whose mission is "to create theatrical excellence through the vision and practice of Deaf, disabled, and Neurodiverse artists"(Graeae Theatre Company). These kinds of artist groups have been few and far between, mainly existing in the fringes. I think with the current momentum of change that has developed since 2020, the performing arts industry has a unique opportunity to seize the moment and bring to the centre certain discourses, practices, and human experiences that encompass the rich and nuanced depth of lived human experience in monumentally impactful and sustainable ways.

With that being said, you asked how can gendered female and/or feminine actors, actors not racialised as white, actors who are Deaf, disabled and neurodivergent, and LGBTQ+ actors challenge training discourses and practices that propagate notions of 'human nature' and 'the laws of nature' which are misogynist, exclusionary, ableist, Eurocentric and racist? I think all actors, including cis-gendered, white, heterosexual, able-bodied men, can, and should, challenge discourses and practices that propagate notions of 'human nature' and 'the laws of nature' which are misogynist, exclusionary, ableist, Eurocentric and racist. How can this be done specifically by actors who are gendered female and/or feminine, not racialised as white, are Deaf or hearing impaired, disabled, neurodivergent, and/or LGBTQ+? I believe it requires the actors to seek out unconventional avenues to explore outside of traditional white hegemonic, ableist, patriarchal contexts and practices that dominate actor training. The experiences they gain via unconventional avenues can then be filtered through the unique lens of the actors' identity and added to their personal 'actor's tool kit'. Combining those experiences with the traditional white, patriarchal discourses and practices they will inevitably encounter, will hopefully synthesise to form a more nuanced actor training experience, and a more well-rounded actor with the knowledge and confidence of their unique skill set, talent, and abilities. Furthermore, what these actors have learned through exploring unconventional avenues has the potential to be disseminated further. We are in an age where actors do not have to be content with the singular label of actor. Actors are exploring and expanding the expression of their artistry through becoming writers, directors, producers, and practitioners as well. More opportunities to 'create your own work' exist than ever before, and more actors are taking advantage of them. Of course, this is much easier said than done. Actors who are exposed to white hegemonic, patriarchal, able-bodied acting approaches, but whose identities differ from aspects of the prescribed white able-bodied male norm, may not know where to find the unconventional avenues that I speak of. Even if these avenues are identified, actors may not have access to them due to various factors such as location, finances, and accessibility. But through the collective consciousness that is rising in the performing arts industry, and the connectivity and accessibility that our modern-day technology offers and provides, I have faith it can be achieved.

Your article with the Brazilian director Maria Thais is presented as an example of cross-cultural exchange in regard to approaches to actor training. I find the idea of cross-cultural exchange in actor training approaches quite interesting because, in my observations, the cross-cultural exchange does not appear to be reciprocal, but rather seems to flow in one direction. By this I mean the European and North American approaches flow out, into other cultures. Very little from other cultures flows into Europe and North America in substantially impactful ways, with the occasional rare exceptions like Augusto Boal and Tadashi Suzuki.

Here are two questions I have:

1. How do you think institutions that train actors in North America and Europe can integrate more culturally diverse actor training practices without a direct connection to that specific culture or practitioners with first-hand experience, or specialist knowledge, of culturally diverse global practices that can feed into, or underpin, actor training?
2. Given the prominence of 'cancel culture' in modern society, how do practitioners draw the line between appreciation and appropriation when drawing from more diverse actor training practices to teach their students?

Maria Brígida De Miranda Thank you for your stimulating answers. They pushed the boundaries of my own perceptions with regards to cross-cultural processes and theatre practices. To answer your first question, I believe that theatre practitioners should, as you said, "*seek out unconventional avenues to explore outside of traditional white hegemonic, ableist, patriarchal contexts and practices that dominate actor training*". As a person who lives in Brazil, I see that we are constantly overloaded with dominant discourses produced in Europe and in the United States of America. So, our process here of decolonising your minds, hearts and bodies is that of looking for counter hegemonic discourses and imagining and testing possibilities that represent ourselves according to our local contexts. If we were to talk about food production for example, we know that native peoples in Latin America have a profound knowledge of food production according to their local ecosystem. If much of this knowledge has been destroyed by centuries of colonisation and industrialisation of agriculture, on the other hand, a lot has been maintained in oral traditions of indigenous, afro diasporic communities and also mestizo rural communities. There are also popular social movements such as the MST (Movimento dos Sem Terra – Landless Workers' Movement) engaged not only in agrarian reform but also to produce food combining local and indigenous traditions with academic research. Since the 1990s, some public research institutions have been addressing these themes offering technical support for social movements such as the MST. This movement is the biggest producer of organic and non-transgenic rice consumed in Latin America. Their attitude challenges agro-business and transgenic seeds corporations but MST, founded in 1984 resists and creates alternatives for a country with huge social gaps. So, if we go back to the theatrical terrain, we might engage in collective actions that start from detecting our dependency on literature, philosophy, and theories from dominant countries and dominant cultures. After that, we might draw our own questions and strategies to create new possibilities. And as far as I understood, that is already happening as you pointed out.

Surely the answers will be in consonance to the complexities of the communities involved, the political agenda of the group and the capacity for dialogue with other groups and communities. To answer your question more directly, I believe that European countries and the USA have a lot of minority groups and cultures that have been marginalised, and silenced: indigenous peoples, afro diasporic descendants, and immigrants from all over the world. Many of these non-white people are inside the university system and can dig on their buried cultural heritage. I bet there is performing arts knowledge there that can help to imagine how a new set, a new script, a new way of preparing the body and of performing can be developed. But I also recognise that these processes take time and find resistance from different segments of the institutions they operate in. But we can be inspired by each other and by the solutions of social movements such as MST.

Regarding the issue of cancel culture. As a person working in education, I believe we must create ways of dialogue. So, if I agree with the idea of cancelling someone because the person has a view that is politically incorrect, I cannot enter a classroom and organise a circular gathering for debating with all the students. As a teacher I have to listen to everybody's argument and try to use my best knowledge to counsel a person/group that what she/he/they is/are saying is offensive or harmful. I know that it is emotionally demanding for a teacher to be in this situation; still, that is somehow the very nature of teaching.

I cannot ignore that we are facing a turbulent era with climate change intensely affecting the poorest and the most vulnerable populations in the globe, the failure of post-war international institutions, mass migration, and the effects of hybrid wars. In this apocalyptic scenario, what can theatre artists do but create possibilities of dialogue between different cultures? I am glad that we are already doing that through this chapter. In a theatrical production we are physically present in the same space, we are facing each other. Members of cast and production have to talk and to make alliances, to negotiate time and space with each other, so dialogue must prevail. And to deal with conflict and cancel culture, I think that Augusto Boal had developed effective methods to create room for people to talk and workshop solutions for social and political problems. Can we use some of his Theatre of the Oppressed methods such as Forum Theatre to address sensitive issues? I believe that he created ways that theatre becomes a place for engagement and negotiation, ultimately for dialogue instead of war.

Notes

1 For a more detailed explanation of how Stanislavsky's ideas influenced the work of the Group Theatre and the development of 'the Method', see Jean Benedetti's translator's foreword in *An Actor's Work: A Student's Diary* (2010a), also "Strasberg, Adler and Meisner: Method Acting" by David Krasner in *Actor Training* edited by Alison Hodge (2010), and *Stanislavsky in Focus* by Sharon M. Carnicke (2009).

2 See "An Actor Prepares/Rabota aktera nad soboĭ, Chast' I": A Comparison of the English with the Russian Stanislavsky" (1984), "Stanislavsky: Uncensored and Unabridged" (1993), "The Effects of Russian and Soviet Censorship on the Practice of Stanislavsky's System" (2013) in *The Routledge Companion to Stanislavsky*, and *Stanislavsky in Focus* (2008) all written by Sharon M. Carnicke. Also "A History of Stanislavski in Translation" by Jean Benedetti (1990).

3 See "Stanislavsky's Double Life in Art" by Laurence Senelick in *My Life in Art* by Konstantin Stanislavski, translated and edited by Jean Benedetti (2008), and *Stanislavsky in Focus* (2003, 71–79) "An Actor Prepares/Rabota aktera nad soboĭ, Chast' I": A Comparison of the English with the Russian Stanislavsky" (1984) and "Stanislavsky: Uncensored and Unabridged" (1993) by Sharon M. Carnicke.

4 See "A System for all Nations? Stanislavsky's Transmission in the World" by Jonathan Pitches in *Stanislavsky in the World: The System and Its Transformations Across Continents* (2017) edited by Stefan Aquilina and Jonathan Pitches.

Works Cited

Aquilina, S. and Pitches, J. *Stanislavsky in the World: The System and its Transformations Across Continents*. London: Bloomsbury, 2017. DOI: https://doi.org/10.5040/9781472587916

Banks, D. "The Hip Hop Theatre Initiative." In: Luckett, S. D. and Shaffer, T. M. eds. *Black Acting Methods: Critical Approaches*. London & New York: Routledge, 2017. DOI: https://doi.org/10.4324/9781315694986

Benedetti, J. "A History of Stanislavski in Translation". *New Theatre Quarterly*. Volume 6, Issue 23, pp. 266–278. DOI: https://doi.org10.1017/S0266464X00004577

Benedetti, J. *Stanislavski: An Introduction*. London & New York: Routledge, 2004. DOI: https://doi.org/10.4324/9780203998182

Benedetti, J. trans. ed. "Translator's Foreword". In: Stanislavski, K. *An Actor's Work: A Student's Diary*. London & New York: Routledge, 2010, xv–xxii. DOI: https://doi.org/10.4324/9780203936153

Bilge, S and Hill Collins, P. I*ntersectionality*. Second Edition. New York: Polity Press, 2020.

Brewer, N. "Training with a Difference". *American Theatre*. Online: https://www.americantheatre.org/2018/01/04/training-with-a-difference/, 2018.

Carnicke, S. M. "An Actor Prepares/Rabota aktera nad soboĭ, Chast' I": A Comparison of the English with the Russian Stanislavsky". *Theatre Journal*. Volume 36, Issue 4, pp.481–494. Washington DC: John Hopkins University Press, 1984. DOI: https://doi.org/10.2307/320673

Carnicke, S. M. "Stanislavsky Uncensored and Unabridged". *The Drama Review (TDR)*. Volume 37, Issue 1, pp.22–37. New York: New York University, 1993. DOI: https://doi.org/10.2307/1146268

Carnicke, S. M. "The Effects of Russian and Soviet Censorship on the Practice of Stanislavsky's System" In: White, A. ed. *The Routledge Companion to Stanislavsky*. London & New York: Routledge, 2013. DOI: https://doi.org/10.4324/9780203112304-20

Carnicke, S. M. *Stanislavsky in Focus: An Acting Master for the Twenty-First Century*. Second Edition. London & New York: Routledge, 2009. DOI: https://doi.org/10.4324/9781003134381

Case, S. E. *Feminism and Theatre*. London: Methuen, 1988. DOI: https://doi.org/10.4324/9781315024615

Collins, P. H. *Black Feminist Thought: Knowledge, Consciousness, and the Politics of Empowerment*. 2nd edition New York: Routledge, 2014. DOI: https://doi.org/10.4324/9780203900055

Crenshaw, K. "Demarginalizing the Intersection of Race and Sex: A Black Feminist Critique of Antidiscrimination Doctrine, Feminist Theory and Antiracist Politics". *University of Chicago Legal Forum*. Issue 1, Article 8, pp.139–167, 1989. DOI: https://doi.org/10.4324/9781315582924-3

Daly, D. "Actions Speak Louder than Words. An Investigation Around the Promises and the Reality of Representation in Actor Training". *Theatre, Dance, and Performance Training*. Volume 13, Issue 4, pp.554–572. London: Taylor and Francis, 2022. DOI: https://doi.org/10.1080/19443927.2022.2078873

Daly, D. "The Canon and the Contemporary: Change, Challenge, Conceit". *Theatre, Dance, and Performance Training*. Volume 14, Issue 4, pp.462–477. London: Taylor and Francis, 2023. DOI: https://doi.org/10.1080/19443927.2023.2182830

Deavere Smith, A. and Martin, C. "The Word Becomes You". *The Drama Review (TDR)*. Volume 37, Issue 4, pp.45–62. New York: New York University, 1993. DOI: https://doi.org/10.2307/1146292

Foster, F. *In: Hill. H. Actor's Lives: On and Off the American Stage*. New York: Theatre Communications Group, 1993.

Graeae Theatre Company Homepage. [*Online*] [Accessed February 2024] (n.d.), Available from: https://graeae.org/

Gittens-Jones, C. "My Blackness Goes Before Me: A Poem and Commentary on Racism and Reproductive Justice". *Rewire News Group*. Online: https://rewirenewsgroup.com/2011/05/04/blackness-goes-poem-commentary-racism-reproductive-justice-0, 2011.

Hall, S. "Cultural Identity and Cinematic Representation". *Framework: The Journal of Cinema and Media*. Volume 36, pp.68–81, 1989.

Hooks, B. *Black Looks: Race and Representation*. New York: Routledge, 2015. DOI: https://doi.org/10.4324/9781315743226

Kelley, S. "Morrison speaks on evil, language and 'the white gaze'". *Cornell Chronicle*. Online: https://news.cornell.edu/stories/2013/03/morrison-speaks-evil-language-and-white-gaze, 2013.

Krasner, D. "Strasberg, Adler and Meisner: Method Acting". In: *Hodge, A. Actor Training*. Second Edition. London & New York: Routledge, 2010. DOI: https://doi.org/10.4324/9780203861370

Lorde, A. "The Transformation of Silence into Language and Action". *Sister Outsider: Essays and Speeches*. New York: The Crossing Press, 1984.

Luckett, S.D. and Shaffer, T. M. eds. *Black Acting Methods: Critical Approaches*. London & New York: Routledge, 2017. DOI: https://doi.org/10.4324/9781315694986

Malague, R. "Stanislavsky's System and Women: A feminist reading of new translations". In: White, A. ed. *The Routledge Companion to Stanislavsky*. London & New York: Routledge, 2013. DOI: https://doi.org/10.4324/9780203112304-12

Malague, R. *An Actress Prepares: Women and "the Method"*. London & New York: Routledge, 2012. DOI: https://doi.org/10.4324/9780203144671

Merlin, B. *The Complete Stanislavsky Toolkit*. London: Nick Hern Books, 2007.

Miranda, M.B. "Training Actions to Convey Theatrical Emotions: An Interview with Brazilian Director Maria Thais". Translated by Daniel Yencken. *Australasian Drama Studies*. Issue 49, pp.101–109. Bundoora: La Trobe University, 2006.

Miranda, M.B. *Playful Training: Towards Capoeira in the Physical Training of Actors*. Saarbrucken: Lambert Academic Publishing, 2010.

Morrison, T. Hay Festival. *Toni Morrison on her re-imagining of Othello*. Online: https://youtu.be/1-k-O2yLYOo?si=ic-zHadgjQR-XjHj, 2019.

Morrison, T. The Connecticut Forum (CT FORUM). *Toni Morrison On Writing for Black Readers Under the White Gaze*. Online: https://www.youtube.com/watch?v=oP_-m7V58_I, 2020.

Ogden-Malouf, S. and Walsh Jenkins, L. "The (Female) Actor Prepares". *Theater*. Volume 17, Issue 1, pp.66–69, North Carolina: Duke University Press, 1985. DOI: https://doi.org/10.1215/01610775-17-1-66

Prior, R.W. *Teaching Actors: Knowledge Transfer in Actor Training*. Chicago: University of Chicago Press, 2013.

Robeson Jr, P. *The Undiscovered Paul Robeson: An Artist's Journey 1898–1939*. New York: John Wiley & Sons, 2001.

Schroder, P. R. "American Drama, Feminist Discourse, and Dramatic Form: In Defence of Critical Pluralism". *Journal of Dramatic Theory and Criticism*. Volume 7, Issue 2, pp.203–207. University of Kansas, 1993. DOI: https://doi.org/10.17161/jdtc.v7i2.1871

Schug, J., et al. "Gendered Race in Mass Media: Invisibility of Asian Men and Black Women in Popular Magazines." *Psychology of Popular Media Culture*. Volume 6, Issue 3, pp. 222–236. Educational Publishing Foundation, 2017. https://doi.org/10.1037/ppm0000096

Senelick, L. "Introduction: Stanislavsky's Double Life in Art". In: Stanislavski, K. *My Life in Art*. London & New York: Routledge, 2008. DOI: https://doi.org/10.4324/9781315823720

Sesko, A. K., et al. "Prototypes of Race and Gender: The Invisibility of Black Women". *Journal of Experimental Social Psychology*. Volume 46, Issue 2, pp. 356–360. Elsevier, 2010. DOI: https://doi.org/10.1016/j.jesp.2009.10.016

Stanislavski, C. *Stanislavski's Legacy*. trans. E Hapgood. London: Methuen, 1968.

Stanislavski, K. *An Actor's Work on a Role*. London: Routledge, 2010b. https://doi.org/10.4324/9780203870921

Stanislavski, K. *An Actor's Work: A Student's Diary*. London: Routledge, 2010a. https://doi.org/10.4324/9780203936153

Stanislavski, K. *My Life in Art*. London: Routledge, 2008. https://doi.org/10.4324/9781315823720

Steinmetz, K. "She Coined the Term 'Intersectionality' Over 30 Years Ago. Here's What It Means to Her Today". *Time Magazine*. Online: https://time.com/5786710/kimberle-crenshaw-intersectionality/, 2020.

Swindall, L. R. *Paul Robeson: A Life of Activism and Art*. New York: Rowman and Littlefield Publishers, 2013.

Tate, S. A. *Black Women's Bodies and the Nation: Race, Gender and Culture*. London: Palgrave Macmillan, 2015. DOI: https://doi.org/10.1057/9781137355287

White Ndounou, M. "Being Black on Stage and Screen: Black Actor Training Before Black Power and the Rise of Stanislavski's System". In: Perkins, K. A. Richards, S. L. Craft, R. A. DeFrantz, T. F. eds. *The Routledge Companion to African American Theatre and Performance*. London: Routledge, 2009a. DOI: https://doi.org/10.4324/9781315191225

White Ndounou, M. "Encountering Black Culture in Acting Classrooms and Beyond". *Theatre Topics*. Volume 19, Issue 1, pp. 95–102. Baltimore: John Hopkins University, 2009b. DOI: https://doi.org/0.1353/tt.0.0056

5

COMMINGLING QUEERNESS AND STANISLAVSKY

Developing and Practising a Slippery Pedagogy to Shift Perspectives on Actor Training

Barry Fitzgerald

I'm Cis.
But Sissy.
And for the longest time that sissy was in
hiding. Or hidden.
I found myself so firmly fixed around my
sexuality – a good gay schooled in a kind
of silence. Suppressing those sissy signs and
systems at play in my body.

But the camber of my construction
screamed sibilant sounds.
It said – I'm going off script. I'm scrapping.
I'm sissifying. I'm sissiest.

Childhood memories are seen in a clearer,
truer light.

The flamingo flounce of my youth, which
scandalised and provoked new middle
names – gay, bender, poof – is finally
embraced. Albeit as a thirty-something
juvenile re-finding their femininity. I'm
looking outside myself.

DOI: 10.4324/9781003411611-6

I'm no coward.

I am strong.

It's not a loss of masculinity but my
volunteering to have it dismantled.

I'm Cis.
But Sissy.

(Outbox Theatre, 48)

I am a queer performer, maker, director, and acting teacher. I make work that is often queer-focused, interdisciplinary, and increasingly experimental. My practice is evolving; it purposefully moves and shifts, encompassing autobiographical work and the politics of intersectional representation, it evolves with me and my identity. I have taught, created, and directed projects in a variety of settings and mediums across communities and the higher education sector, including conservatoires and drama schools such as Arts Educational School (ArtsEd) and Mountview, and most regularly at the Royal Central School of Speech and Drama (Central), for over a decade.

I wrote the preceding speech during the rehearsal period for *And The Rest of Me Floats* by OUTBOX, a show that interrogates the "messiness of gender" (Buratta, xix). We created a rehearsal space that facilitated and embraced new ways to work with gender expressions and identities. It was 2019, and although I had graduated from drama school nearly 15 years earlier and had been making my own work for nearly a decade, performing in this show further expanded my creative practice and was a pivotal point in my personal relationship with gender. The gender penny had truly dropped.

In this chapter, I consider how my work as a queer performer and performance maker and my experience leading creative educational spaces have commingled with the Stanislavsky tradition, evolving to facilitate a queer-inclusive pedagogy. These reflections are from the artist's perspective, informed by my own training and interactions in rehearsal rooms and learning spaces and through collaborative and devised work with other artists and LGBTQIA+ community projects.

Queer in the Conservatoire: Commingling with the Stanislavsky Tradition

I am from a small town in the Irish countryside, and I grew up with no explicit knowledge of actor training and its traditions. Ireland is known for its literature, art, and a long line of prolific dramatic writers; however, it often surprises people that the school curriculum does not include drama and theatre and performance studies as specific subjects, and there are limited options at the third level of education. As such, I do not recall hearing about Stanislavsky before I was 18 and studying at a university in the UK. More recently, the Department of Education in Ireland announced that they will introduce drama, film, and theatre studies as brand-new subjects for leaving certificate students in Ireland from 2025 onwards. Nevertheless, I had many opportunities to perform. I participated in school plays, wore shiny lamé costumes at town hall variety shows, and danced and sang in festive community celebrations. I also attended Saturday drama club classes in a local school hall. If I were to pin down the training methods of my early years as a performer it would amount to learn your lines, speak louder, and be bolder in your choices. All sound advice if you need to be heard by those standing at the back of the town hall. In his autobiography, *My Life in Art*, Stanislavsky reflects on his formative childhood experiences of performing with his community, planting the seeds for his now-renowned techniques. He recalls an early experience: "I have known, on the one hand, the living pleasure success can give, of being onstage and performing meaningful actions, and, on the other, the misery of failure, of just sitting in front of an audience" (Stanislavski, 2008, 5). I learned a great deal about rigour, creativity, and community from my early experiences, which formed the foundations for my work as an artist.

My first experiences of actor training at university coincided with my moving away from rural Ireland to the UK and coming out as queer. Through these experiences, Stanislavsky's techniques have featured in my creative learning, beginning with a Contemporary Arts degree in university, followed by drama school training, to being an openly queer performer and maker in the acting industry, and, finally, as a practitioner, teaching a new generation of performers and makers. I first encountered the fundamentals of the Stanislavsky tradition as a young performer and found many elements helpful – for example, examining Given Circumstances and grasping Objectives or Tasks, analysing the text, and breaking it down into units or Bits, plotting the actions for each section, and developing a physical practice to relax and bring a sense of ease and bodily connection to the performance. These tools aimed to provide a structure and methodology to deepen characters, examine texts, and immerse myself in imaginary worlds.

Like many queer people, this point in my life was a time of transformation. I was experiencing the freedom to finally be myself, simultaneously with the of joy of becoming others through performance. Growing up across the 1980s and 1990s into the new millennium, if there was any understanding or conversation about gender, sexuality, diversity, inclusivity, and representation, it was mainly explored through clichéd, problematic, and binary stereotypes. I also exploited these stereotypes in my early years of actor training when I did not have the language or knowledge to articulate what I was experiencing. Ironically, Stanislavsky was against the "actors' clichés" (Stanislavski, 2010, 28). Exploring or embodying queerness through actor training felt light years away.

In my early years of actor training, I came across some skilled and influential teachers who created spaces where I felt supported. These teachers allowed me to develop my passion for performance; however, my training lacked positive explorations of queerness and how an embodied understanding of my identity would allow for my performances to be more connected, expansive, and alive. Character analysis and interpretations were rigid, especially regarding LGBTQIA+ characters. I encountered teachers who exploited emotion without any sense of aftercare, using the Stanislavsky tradition to justify their approach. Feedback shamed or denied me the opportunity to inhabit a sense of queer authenticity in my acting work, and criticism was often given by acting teachers from a heteronormative, cis-gender perspective that viewed queer characters as one-dimensional and homogenous. These perspectives limited me, at best, and were deeply damaging, at worst. There were times that the learning atmosphere felt hostile towards my queerness, though I did not consciously have the language to express or challenge this at the time. I learned that following my instincts and impulses did not lead to success in such environments. Instead, I was encouraged to disinvest in my embodied experience. Teachers coaxed me to transform 'convincingly' into other characters in ways that felt counterintuitive to my understanding of the techniques they were offering. Being openly queer in these environments also meant I received more scrutiny than others; teachers would regularly comment on how I needed to 'ground' myself or how exploring flamboyance was futile as I was 'flamboyant enough'. I was left feeling that my queer body had failed me once again. It was not a space to embrace or explore queerness, and certainly not one that celebrated or gave me the agency to deepen my understanding of the intersections of gender and sexuality and my embodied experiences of being queer. As a child and teenager, I quickly learned to dim, hide, and shun my instinctive physicality, with varying degrees of success. This led to a hyper-awareness of how my body was observed and positioned within group settings. Getting something 'wrong' could result in looks, commentary or even physical harm. LGBTQIA+ students often carry this hypervigilance with them when they begin their training and then on into the acting industry.

The opportunity to explore and celebrate the embodied experience that Stanislavsky advocates for in his pedagogy is rarely available to queer performers, who often hear advice such as "we know you can play yourself, but you need to be versatile". In many training environments queer people rarely get to play queer; and when they do it can result in a copied version of queer, a 'type' or as Stanislavsky identifies, "playacting stereotypes" as "stock-in-trade, ham, and exploitation" (Stanislavski, 2010, 35) authored from, and for, a normative perspective. Furthermore, when queer performers finish their formal training, they then move on to negotiate an industry that continues to laud accolades upon non-queer performers for portraying queer characters. Of course, Stanislavsky contends,

> Whatever dreams you may have, whatever you may have experienced in reality or in your imagination, you are always yourself. Never lose communication with yourself onstage. Act from your own personality as an actor/ human being. You can never run away from yourself. If you deny your "me", then you cut the ground from under your feet, and that is the most terrible thing that can happen. The moment when you lose communication with yourself onstage is the moment when experiencing ends and playacting begins. So, however many performances you give, whoever it is emotion memory you are portraying, you must use your own feelings, always. Infringement of this law is tantamount to the actor murdering the character he is playing, depriving it of the pulsating, living, human soul which alone gives life to a dead role.
>
> *(Stanislavski, 2010, 209–210)*

As Sharon Carnicke attests, Stanislavsky's influence on actor training is "indisputable", and "[t]o this day, theatre professionals tend to position themselves in relationship to him" (Carnicke, 2009, 9). However, my experiences have been more ambivalent. Reflecting on my training experiences, I have found techniques attributed to Stanislavsky's system helpful. Still, I am also mindful of exploitative and unsafe pedagogies that are excused or justified by invoking his name. Commingling suggests a more ambivalent relationship to Stanislavsky, acknowledging the pervasiveness of his influence in most actor training contexts but consciously as mutual coexistence.

Engaging the Haptic: Feeling Language and Developing and Practising a Slippery Pedagogy

Much of what we search for when working on a scene or exploring a character in rehearsal is subjective and fleeting; it can feel slippery. Practitioners often search for words momentarily to explain and illuminate the human experience. However, the language of training, rehearsal, and creative spaces is often indicative of culture and society where being heteronormative is centred and rewarded.

One example commonly used in actor training is the search for 'neutrality'. The word 'neutral' is rarely questioned in the teacher's vernacular and renders the term as 'universal'. This is problematic, as it means student actors of all cultural backgrounds and identities (gender, class, disability, race, sexuality, etc.) are aspiring to the same version and idea of 'neutral', usually established and created by the white, privileged, heterosexual and the binary and highly gendered, abled body. The instruction to perform with 'neutrality' illustrates how the predominant language of actor training pedagogy implements normative assumptions and puts restrictions upon acting students. I find the search or demand for 'neutrality' ineffective in my work today, as it so often obstructs the performer rather than a word that invites and encourages receptivity, liveness, openness, and engagement. This is an example of how language in acting pedagogy can potentially oppress rather than empower.

Stanislavsky recognised the importance of the "creation of the living word" (Stanislavsky 2000, 262). He also believed that "[i]n the theatre, knowing means feeling" (Stanislavski, 2010, xxiv). Actor training arguably aims to create a space to nurture impulses and sharpen instincts. The vocabulary must then bolster this objective, to hold the performers with care rather than diminish or shame them. Acting teachers must strive for language that expands an understanding of the human experience to create spaces where performers feel open and supported enough to reach their full potential. Though Stanislavsky intended the actor to demonstrate technical proficiency in language and speech, the teacher should show the same awareness and sensitivity to language. After all, Stanislavsky emphasised the importance of subtext for the meaning and authorship of words. He explains,

> The meaning of a work of art lies in its *Subtext*. Without it words are ineffectual onstage. When we create a performance the words are the author's and the subtext is ours. If it were otherwise, the audience wouldn't make an effort to come to the theatre to see the actor. They'd stay at home and read the play instead.
>
> *(Stanislavski, 2010, 403, Original emphasis)*

Reframing Stanislavsky's advice not for the actor but for the acting teacher is an invitation for the practitioner to consider the subtext of their own language in giving instruction, direction, guidance, and feedback. The words they use might be Stanislavsky's when explaining a concept or teaching a technique, however the acting teacher gives Stanislavsky's words meaning and authorship in their respective pedagogies, and therefore, the subtext, whether it diminishes or empowers the student, is crucial. An openness and sensitivity to language is vital, as it influences how students embody Stanislavsky's system. Otherwise, the student might as well stay home and read Stanislavsky instead.

Words reverberate in our bodies in palpable and personal ways and an unexamined or neglectful use of language from a practitioner can result in physical tension in the performer. Physical action is essential to the system; however, physical *tension*, as Sharon. Carnicke comments, according to Stanislavsky "is creativity's greatest enemy, not only paralysing and distorting the beauty of the body but also interfering with the mind's ability to concentrate and fantasise" (Carnicke, 2010, 8). In my earlier experiences as a queer performer, physical tension often brought rigidity and contained my movements. It could set my heart racing, disconnect my imagination, and inhibit the sense of flow. If Stanislavsky's techniques on muscular release aim to cultivate creativity and to inhabit oneself and a character comfortably with a sense of ease, as Carnicke suggests, then the facilitation of acting techniques, including the language used by teachers, must be considered. Unfortunately, in my experience, when a queer person highlights these problems in training, it can often lead to them being labelled as 'resistant' or 'blocked'.

The feeling of language engages the idea of the haptic. Summarising Jack Halberstam's discussion of the transgender body as a "fragmentary site", Sophie Chapuis explains,

> A haptic perspective encourages one to see not only with their eyes, but to sense with their whole body. Since it focuses less on sight than touch, viewing is no longer limited to the visual, but depends on a variety of senses.
>
> *(Chapuis, 3)*

This haptic perspective engages and strengthens our awareness of the senses, directing the performer away from focusing on their external presentation and the merely observational and inviting them to feel words from a deeper, more embodied perspective. Words like tingle, rough, hot, and embrace, are examples of words that might cultivate a haptic understanding for the actor. These examples are not an exact science, as words vibrate differently for everyone and every body. It is part of my attempt towards a 'slippery pedagogy' that remains open and fluid. This pedagogy is invested in the sensual and visceral experience of being human. It is delicate and something to be held with care; if grasped too firmly, it may slip right out of the hand.

In my work, I now pay more attention to the *language* of training. I aim for vocabulary that encourages a psychophysical approach; psycho-physicality recognises and embraces that body, mind, and soul are all interconnected and impossible to separate. These techniques invite anybody, or indeed *any body*, to draw upon their physicality and imagination in expansive and connected ways. According to translator and editor Jean Benedetti, Stanislavsky intended to use "ordinary, everyday words, what he called his 'home-grown' vocabulary" (Benedetti, xviii), creating his own lexicon of acting, introducing through his writing and the system, what he called "actor's jargon" (Stanislavski, 2010, 73). This approach offers a gender-neutral vocabulary for training and rehearsal. For example, he appropriates music terminology such as *staccato* and *largo lento* to demonstrate his technique of tempo-rhythm, which he asserts "cannot only prompt the right feelings and experiences intuitively, directly and immediately, it can help create characters" (Stanislavski, 2010, 476). However, the subtext of these words can still further reinforce gender stereotypes, even unintentionally. When acting teachers use the Stanislavsky lexicon of the Magic 'if' or the Given Circumstances, they must remain open to the difference and subjectivity these techniques and principles invite.

The psychophysical work of practitioners within the Russian tradition, like Michael Chekhov's sense of ease, can also be generative and inclusive.

The language of movement has become central to my creative practice. I lean towards movement frameworks, including Laban's effort actions, which Joan Littlewood combined with Stanislavsky's Bits and Tasks, and I also use Viewpoints (Mary Overlie, Anne Bogart and Tina Landau). The methodologies encourage words, including direct, with flow, bound, and high tempo, allowing the performer to explore a spectrum of bodily sensations that are not binary or gendered. I should note that it is not that I never use feminine or masculine words when working, but I interrogate whether these words are the most useful ones for character development. When working with a performer, I try to remain aware and sensitive to an evolving language that is engaging and appropriate for the individual to amplify and enliven their connection to the work, themselves, and each other. This inquiry into the language I use when creating and collaborating is ongoing, and it is not something I am looking to complete or set in stone. Paradoxically, Stanislavsky, when reluctantly writing *An Actor Prepares*, became cautious about the permanence of the written word, the precision of language, and pedantry, tending to over explain and repeat himself (Benedetti, xv–xxii). Sometimes, I feel unsatisfied with the words available to me; the way the words resonate in the space doesn't quite feel enough, sometimes. In these moments, I comfort myself, knowing that a meaningful creative practice should not aim for a final or fixed position, something Stanislavsky also warns against in his discussion of the "art of representation" (Stanislavski, 2010, 22). This slippery pedagogy moves and flows through the work as we do, and akin to my own relationship with queerness, it continues to evolve and shift over time.

Shifting Perspectives

TransActing

> Being trans has held me back from going into a career as an actor, to begin with, because I felt I couldn't personally, at school, pursue it.
>
> Being trans has always been a bit of a – sort of barrier for getting into acting. In fact, before I started doing this course, it was never really – I'd always kind of just crossed it off my list […] very early on I was just like, well there's just no way that you could be trans and act […] it was only after starting to go to these workshops that I've actually thought about getting back into performing and going to auditions.
>
> (My Genderation, 2015)

In the years since I trained as an actor, there has been more openness and inclusivity in actor training spaces; however, this work is gradual and can feel slow-moving and there continues to be reverence and mystery in some acting institutions for actor training traditions, protecting them from interrogation or an acknowledgement of progressive societal shifts. Recent projects have been transformative and instrumental in shifting my actor training and performance-making pedagogy.

The TransActing project started in 2015 as a collaboration between Gendered Intelligence, a "trans-led and trans-involving charity that exists to increase understandings of gender diversity and improve trans people's quality of life" (Gendered Intelligence, 2024); *My Genderation*, a trans-led film and resource project founded by Fox Fisher and Lewis Hancox "that celebrates trans lives and trans experiences" (My Genderation, 2024) and the Royal Central School of Speech and Drama (Central), one of the leading drama schools in the UK and where academic Prof. Catherine McNamara began the project. OUTBOX, a company of LGBTQIA+ creatives that "creates spaces where queer people can dream and imagine" (OUTBOX, 2023), became a partner in 2016 with a particular focus on providing masterclasses and workshops for participants across the UK.

I have been a visiting lecturer at Central since 2012, and I was asked to lead sessions there as an acting tutor for TransActing when the project began as a series of workshops in the summer of 2015. The workshops which included voice, movement, text, improvisation, and audition techniques aimed to create a safe, gender-inclusive performer training space for trans, non-binary, and gender non-conforming (GNC) people, during which we also introduced some techniques from the Stanislavsky tradition – for example, Circles of Attention, Tasks, and Physical Actions.

The aforementioned comments are from recorded interviews with TransActing students included in a film produced by My Genderation. Their testimonies give insight into the barriers people can experience accessing actor training simply for being themselves. The students identified the many obstacles that trans, non-binary, and GNC people face when trying to access training opportunities or engage with the performing arts industry.

Although acting institutions are often well-intentioned, promising graduates a close alignment with the performing arts industries, they can sometimes replicate normative structures of broader society. Until recently, casting, and associated services such as Spotlight (the UK's most well-known casting directory) also categorised performers based on binary genders. For trans, non-binary, and GNC people, there were signals everywhere that you did not have a place in the performing arts industry unless you tidily conformed to these categories. There has been some progress with professionals like Spotlight and Equity collaborating with organisations such as Gendered Intelligence, OUTBOX, and the Queer House, an artist development agency for queer, trans, non-binary and GNC actors, writers, and performance makers, to advise on casting and working with LGBTQIA+ characters and performers, including inclusive language. Still, there is much more room to grow.

I approached the first sessions I led for TransActing by building a sense of ensemble through warm-up exercises and games before moving on to more detailed work on character and text. Across the sessions, we explored a variety of methodologies, including Laban's Effort Actions and Bogart and Landau's Viewpoints, along with Stanislavsky-based exercises, such as Circles of Attention and analysing text using Bits, Tasks, and Physical Actions. I had never been in an acting class with an openly queer and trans majority before. This queer environment created a sense of ease among the participants, and I soon became aware that traditional actor training language required my attention. I began to question my vocabulary and reimagine it, bolstered by this sense of community.

Using Stanislavsky's Circles of Attention gained new significance in a queer-inclusive environment. The technique guides the actor's awareness through different degrees of attention, first introspectively listening to their inner life; then externally, outside of themselves, to the people and things immediately around them; and, finally, to the wider world and universe. Concentrating on their inner life in a queer environment, the actors found and described a sense of ease, something rarely afforded in their everyday lives, supporting them to begin engaging their inner creative state. Their description of ease manifested physically and was observable in their bodies; their shoulders dropped, their breath became full, and their imaginations flourished. As a witness to these changes, I no longer began to think about individual exercises but how my pedagogy facilitated these techniques with an attention to language and the haptic as my perspective shifted in this new learning environment.

The TransActing project was a success; we went on to run many more workshops and were invited to share work at festivals, including the Scottish Queer International Film Festival, BFI Flare Film Festival (British Film Institute, London), and Transarte (Rio de Janeiro, Brazil). OUTBOX collaborated with Gendered Intelligence in the following years to lead some of the TransActing projects. This phase of work included organising a TransActing summer school at the Southbank Centre in 2019, which was led by an all-queer and trans team. My involvement in the TransActing project allowed me to think more deeply and expand my practice. The project highlighted how unwelcoming and unsafe training spaces can be for trans, GNC, and queer people and it became clear that more gender-inclusive practices and spaces were (and still are) urgently needed. Such spaces must include practices that can remedy the highly gendered, binary, and rigid nature of many teaching environments and acting practices.

And The Rest of Me Floats

The speech I included at the beginning of this chapter is from *And The Rest of Me Floats*, created and performed in 2019 by OUTBOX. I have worked with the company as a performer on their productions since 2013 and became an associate artist in 2016. The company aims to create work where queer people feel centred and seen, and I lead their participation projects, working with LGBTQIA+ organisations and queer people of all ages across the UK.

Originally devised and performed in 2017 at the Rose Lipman Building, a brutalist community centre in East London, *And The Rest of Me Floats* was programmed as a main house show in 2019 at the Bush Theatre in London before touring. I was a cast member alongside six other performers from across trans, non-binary, and queer communities working with the company's artistic director, Ben Buratta, and a creative team to devise the show.

> *And The Rest of Me Floats* is all about the messy business of gender. Performers from across the trans, non-binary, and queer communities weave together autobiographical performance, movement, pop songs, stand-up and dress-up in this anarchic celebration of gender expression and identity.
>
> Playful and powerful *And The Rest of Me Floats* explores how it feels to live in a society where you are regularly categorised and policed. "Do you see me?" Beyond the questions, the confusion, and the anger: "Do you really see me?".
>
> *(Outbox Theatre, backcover)*

And The Rest of Me Floats reordered traditional narrative chronologies to queer form, resisting an autobiographical dramaturgy that was artificially 'straightened out' for legibility. Transitions became more blurred, becoming increasingly more central to the action than fixed 'scenes'. The director, Ben Buratta, explains,

> The play is form-busting; swerving realism means that the linear, causal narratives that see trans and queer people victimised, in trauma and in danger could be re-authored by the performers […]
>
> In a normative process, the transition in theatre acts as the connective tissue between scenes, it is clearly defined and takes us from one section of a play to the next […]
>
> The supple plasticity of the transition harnessed the shifting form of the stories being told until, near the end of the play, the transition is completely ruptured.
>
> *(Buratta, xix–xx)*

Making *And The Rest of Me Floats* involved some traditional actor training and making approaches – constructing biographies, voice techniques, and objectives; Ben found a way for the company to have agency in these decisions. Approaching the creative process in this way shifted our perspectives, giving performers ownership of the work with an understanding that not all queer experiences are the same. This environment allowed each performer to explore and deliver more connected and nuanced performances and enlivened their own relationship to queerness rather than conforming and delivering the director's interpretation.

I recognised a lot of the exercises during rehearsals for the show. However, this was my first time experiencing these techniques as a performer in a creative space so intrinsically queer, so alive with an embodied understanding of gender. We wrote and performed scenes about or inspired by our lives, and the rehearsal environment brought a renewed sense of clarity to our emotions and memories. A powerful moment for me was exploring an early childhood memory from when I was 5. It was a different take on a story my family had told for years.

BARRY Five
I'm the youngest of eight children, three girls and five boys. Mammy cuts all of our hair short. Bowl-around-the-head kind of job, to keep things easy

Daddy is the Del Boy of our small country town

He's in a business meeting in our kitchen

And I'm in my sister Brenda's Communion dress.

(Outbox Theatre, 39)

At age 5, I was obsessed with wearing my sister's dresses and could not understand why boys were not allowed to wear girls' clothes. The pinnacle of my sister's wardrobe was her communion dress, a beautiful, flowing, feminine garment.

- **Who's this then?**
- **This is. Mary.**
- **Hello Mary.**

BARRY I'm not Mary
- **That's a lovely dress.**

BARRY I'm Barry
- **Out you go then, Mary**

BARRY I'm not Mary.
- **We're in a meeting.**

BARRY It's me, Daddy. It's Barry.
- **Run along then, Mary.**

(Outbox Theatre, 40)

For years, I viewed this memory as an early indication of my gayness or sexuality. This perspective mirrored how my younger explorations of gender were labelled as gay by others before I had any understanding of what this meant. As a young adult, even after I had come out, I would recount the story to friends, unknowingly replicating the normative viewpoint of my family, which did not allow for the nuance of gender. This perspective shifted in the flux of rehearsals for *And The Rest of Me Floats*. I realised that the family memory of the story and its emotions differed from my internal experience and memory. The simple story of me in my sister's dress had very little to do with sexuality (who I was attracted to) and everything to do with gender (how I felt and wanted to express myself).

The queer-inclusive space allowed for unlocking and embodied understanding of that memory. In the performance, I could recall the emotions differently, re-experiencing the wonder and joy of wearing my sister's dress for the first time. I remembered how my body responded to the fabric, enlivening my movement as I wore it. I believe this ultimately created a more connected and textured performance. I may have employed a Stanislavskian technique of Sense and Emotion Memory as I touched the dress again in my imagination and remembered how it felt and made me feel. The inclusive, communal, and supportive environment of creating and rehearsing *And The Rest of Me Floats* and experiencing this exercise queered my memory, shifting my perspective as a performer, queering not only my recollection of the memory which became the basis of my performance but the Stanislavskian technique too.

As a young child, I explored and connected my femininity with performance. I went through childhood, adolescence, and early adulthood, learning that this was 'incorrect' for my body, and it had taken until my mid-thirties for these mental pathways to unravel and for me to realise that my relationship with gender had been so alive as a child. It was a powerful reawakening personally and creatively, as I further saw how society's heteronormative, cis-centred perspective extends into most training, practice, and content. Stanislavsky informed some work in the room but commingling the technique with the openness and aliveness of a queer creative space, allowed for more connection and authenticity in the work. These rehearsals were a powerful moment for me as a performer that I have endeavoured to bring into my pedagogy. The experience allowed me to embrace a more fluid identity and reconnect and reform a relationship with my gender identity and expression; the dresses finally returned.

Opening the Seams

TransActing and my work with OUTBOX, including making, rehearsing, and performing *And The Rest of Me Floats*, are experiences that have allowed me to deepen my thinking around language and the haptic in my pedagogy. The role as a performer within a queer company and the way I now facilitate actor training spaces is reciprocal. These projects traverse the experiences of performer, teacher and maker and there is a slipperiness to the creative roles that impacts, shifts, and informs my creative perspective.

These queer-led projects and my other work in queer spaces have reshaped my pedagogy to embrace a more fluid approach to address not only the lack of meaningful representation for trans, non-binary, GNC, and queer people but also the exclusivity and prescribed cisgender heterosexuality that pervades our classrooms, stages, pages, and screens. Halberstam, marking the passing of two GNC performers, David Bowie and Prince, encourages us: "Let's look at forms of gender, idioms of gender, gender practices and ask all the while how gender shifts and changes through all bodies and how it might be imagined in the future" (Halberstam, xiii). Everybody has a relationship to gender; for most people, however, the elements of this construct have rarely been reflected on or fully explored.

When the experiences of trans and queer people are welcomed and endorsed within actor training spaces, it has the power to shift and broaden an understanding of gender for everyone in the room. We may start with inclusivity for students and performers, but we should open up the seams of actor training and creative spaces to include practitioners and methodologies from a diverse range of identities and experiences. This will be a generative process that moves beyond tokenism and brings true depth, texture and feeling to the work for all. A practice commingling traditions and queer practices can enrich pedagogy and the creative imagination, providing a more inclusive environment for all performers and makers. These projects contributed to my practice, which is live and evolving, and continues to be responsive – it is not concrete or conclusive, it is a slippery pedagogy that centres care, inclusivity, and expansive curiosity.

Post Chapter Discussion: Barry Fitzgerald with Ray Young

Barry Fitzgerald Hi, Ray! Firstly, thanks so much for having a read through the chapter.

Ray Young Of course.

Barry Fitzgerald So, I thought we'd see where this goes, and of course, you might have questions for me. I wanted to chat to you about your experience as a performer and maker. As someone who has experience of training and its spaces but also an artist who leads and curates queer spaces now. I also thought it might be interesting for us to cast our minds back and reflect on what it was like for us to train as performers, actors, whatever you might want to call it.

Ray Young Yeah, great. I think one of the things that really struck me when I was reading your writing was that although I work in institutions where they are training people to be performers or makers, I'm not really teaching on anything that might be considered traditional. What really struck me when I was reading your chapter was that in the more traditional setting [...], when you're non-binary or you don't sit in a specific place on the gender spectrum, then going into a drama school must feel like an experience where you can't be you. Or you have to be a really fixed or rigid version of you. And then you'll probably encounter roles (I know I did) that historically everyone views as one thing, which of course is often white, straight, cis-gendered, and so on. So how do you bring a sense of authenticity to the work, to a role, when you've been told for years that there isn't space for you within it?

Barry Fitzgerald Diving in deep! The big questions first.

Ray Young Yeah, diving right in there. But really, I think that's why the work that you've been doing with projects like TransActing is so necessary. Is that why it came about?

Barry Fitzgerald Yes, I think so. TransActing was about breaking down barriers for people who are trans, non-binary, GNC. When I went to drama school training spaces were, and in some cases still are, very rigid in their view of what a performer should be. What qualities they should possess. They were rigid ideas around character too. In a way, whether said or unsaid, you had to fit into those neat boxes.

Ray Young Yeah, let me draw my mind back [...] drawing back to drama school. I feel like maybe there were unspoken things, a bit like you've said, and for me, there was a sense of knowing that certain roles would not be available because I would not sit within their ideas of what that role should be. A whole range of things were in that [...] ideas around beauty, Blackness, gender [...] because everything is very, very rigid, isn't it? There's no real way out of it.

Barry Fitzgerald Exactly.

Ray Young Thinking about it now feels different. [...] I have more of a sense of the spectrum of gender that I didn't have before. Whatever the archetype of woman or girl [...] I think there's always been something where I felt like I don't fit. Maybe if I'd had the language then, I might have been able to figure out why all of that was so uncomfortable.

Barry Fitzgerald That language or having a space to explore that feels important.

Ray Young On that, I also wanted to ask you [...] you talk about the use of your language in those spaces, and how you became more aware of language from the experience of projects like TransActing and your work with OUTBOX. It feels that language is something that continues to shift or evolve. So how have you gone about adapting your language?

Barry Fitzgerald It's an ongoing thing for sure and can feel challenging at times. But I guess it's an openness or a curiosity, a fluidity that I try to embrace. And of course, language I used previously, in the past, I may not use now, and I'm open to the idea that the language I use now, given time, I may need to adapt or expand on depending on the work and the world. I've heard people talk about their fear of getting things 'wrong' or about saying the incorrect thing, and how this fear stops them engaging with gender at all. But of course, you trip up, you make 'mistakes', and in that moment your heart definitely sinks. It's the last thing you want. But if you can lean back, and sometimes I'll actually physically lean back, often it's simply about acknowledging and then moving on. Not centring yourself in that 'mistake' moment. Then you might take that moment as an opportunity to learn or shift ideas, to change your process if that makes sense?

Ray Young Yeah, it does.

Barry Fitzgerald And in terms of my own experiences as a younger performer, I'd like to think that the teachers I was working with [...] that when there were moments that felt less inclusive or even damaging...that their intentions weren't to damage or stifle me. It was, I'm sure, the exact opposite. It was likely their perspective and, in some cases, quite limited perspective on these things, meant their way of teaching or holding space was always from that normative, cis-centred viewpoint.

Ray Young So how did that play out?

Barry Fitzgerald I mean various ways [...] it could be that they'd comment on my body or way of moving in space or speaking in a way that dulled anything that was queer. Ironed that out. Even if they weren't aware of that. Sometimes it was very direct and about moulding you into something palatable. Other times, it was more nuanced. They might talk about being neutral or centred or something along those lines, and I'd know or feel that the comment had been in reaction to some sort of movement or flourish in my body. The lasting impression was that it needed to be dulled, not explored. Certainly not celebrated.

Ray Young When I think of training, things were so rigid – there's one way to be this and another way to be that. There was no nuance. But then when you think about people, the people you actually know in the world, you find all sorts of play with masculinity or femininity. People might not even be queer; you know what I mean? There's lots of ways to show up in the world.

Barry Fitzgerald You're making me think about how I wanted to, in part, highlight how my experience may be in teaching people across different identities [...] a lot of the work that I reference in the chapter happened in queer spaces [...] but I think we have to realise, as you've said, that everyone has their way of showing up. Everyone has a relationship to gender. So, we need to be thinking about how we embrace ideas around gender, not limit them. How ideas around it could be something generative for everyone. Something that enlivens their training and performance. Makes them more understanding. But so often, it's not spoken about in that way. Deeper conversations around gender, like those we might have in queer spaces or with queer friends [...] I don't think they happen as much outside of those environments.

Ray Young It feels like we could invest more in language and in those conversations.

Barry Fitzgerald But thinking about the physical nature of your work, the movement in your work – how do you go about rehearsing or working on performance, and does language play a part?

Ray Young I guess when I'm working with the body [...] because I don't come from a dance background, I often think about movement in terms of what we might be moving through. So, I might think about moving through different materials or emotional states [...] moving through water, moving through thick air, or moving through fear, through oppression or how might the performer move if they really want to be seen? It's then our job to explore how each of these states might cause us to move differently, and they should feel different, right? Or with gender, I might think about the idea of how masculinity can take up space, or we've been taught that masculinity is allowed to take up space in a room, and then use that to build a movement language. This is how we worked when we were building my show, *Nightclubbing*; we played a lot with the idea of taking up space. Playing with perspective, from which vantage point might I appear bigger or smaller and how we could use the object in the space to support this. You've got all of these years of being a practitioner, all of these books that you've read, and all the things that you've learned. So, you pull from all that work, all those tools at any point.

Barry Fitzgerald You adapt things. Use what's useful.

Ray Young I found it was really interesting reading your work and thinking about going into a creative space and the idea of re-working or adapting things. Maybe using more traditional practices or approaches that can feel like they've excluded certain people or identities. When you do that, how do you still make the space playful? I feel like that's important, right? Making it feel like a space of possibilities and bringing out the best in each performer.

Barry Fitzgerald I guess it's about meeting the individual. Even in queer circles, we have these ideas around what it is to be queer, trans, non-binary, transmasc, transfemme, and these become boxes in themselves. So, it's about meeting those individuals and seeing the breadth of their experience. Of course, someone might have an identity that feels quite firm and at their centre. But often, there's fluidity and potential. So, for me, it's about facilitating exercises in a way that allows people to slowly reveal who they are or where they could lean into, if that makes sense?

Ray Young It makes loads of sense. I really like the idea of revealing. Revealing more of yourself and creating a space for that. Because I think that's partly about what it is, right? We talk about the idea of having these safe spaces, and I know that safe spaces really don't exist. Maybe it's about a space of generosity or something like that.

Barry Fitzgerald Yes exactly […], and it's not my phrase, but at the moment, I like using the term 'brave spaces'. As you say, there's no such thing as a truly safe space, but we can acknowledge that. We can discuss what systems we have in place when we encounter something. When there's a bit of a jolt or rub or whatever that might be, big or small […] that we then have our systems in place to acknowledge that. The idea being it might allow you to be braver in the work. To lean into things and reveal more parts of yourself.

Ray Young So that's with a group or an ensemble, but I know you make a lot of solo work too. Or work that has elements of you in it […] so when you're in a space and you're making work alone, does that feel really different from when you're rehearsing with a group or training people?

Barry Fitzgerald It feels very different. […] I really enjoy working in a group setting, in that ensemble way. Just in its very nature, there's a whole set of different experiences that you can observe. When it's just me in the space, and maybe you feel like this as well, you have to use two sides of your practice. Your performer side and then that outside eye, directorial side […] and of course you have collaborators involved, other creatives around so they can be an outside eye. But I've definitely had times in a room where I'm rehearsing alone and staring at the wall. It's a real challenge, and it's often easier to feedback on someone else's work and draw that performance out. You have that distance.

Ray Young That perspective.

Barry Fitzgerald It's a practice though, isn't it? You have to flex it and keep that muscle going. If I haven't made something or performed for a long time, then I find it hard. It takes a while for me to get back into it.

Ray Young And do you use any of the exercises, like the ones that you mention in your chapter? Are you able to work on those when it's just you?

Barry Fitzgerald I might do some yeah. I'll certainly, if I'm working on text, break it down and think about objectives and so on. What that journey might be. The subtext. I'll think about tempo, inner and outer [...] I'll work in imaginary exercises. Exploring those Circles of Attention [...] that inner, more reflective energy and the connection to other characters or the audience. Then out to the wider world or universe. If there's not another character or performer, I'll ask who could the audience be to me? Are they a friend, a confidante? Things you would do with an actor if it was a solo show.

Ray Young That connection to the audience feels important in my work to. You want to take them on a journey, right?

Barry Fitzgerald When you're working, especially if the work is queer focused, how important do you think it is to have queer people in the room, as practitioners or collaborators who have that embodied knowledge?

Ray Young God, hugely important, I would say. I'm not saying that absolutely everybody in the room has to be queer. But if we're making work and it has queerness as its centre then those collaborators should be from those communities, right? But also, I think there is some viability in having people that are outside of that because if you're thinking about your audiences, then it might be interesting to have somebody who doesn't have that experience sit in as an outside eye. And if they feedback that something is unclear or it's resonating with them then you can make a decision. You can make the call on whether it is important, whether it isn't, whether you want to include it, or how you might need to tweak something so that everybody understands it. But that said, it's fine to make work that you only get if you're queer.

Barry Fitzgerald Of course.

Ray Young But I think that queerness isn't just about the people in the work, it's about how we're making the work, the structure of the work. It's about how we're building the teams and who gets input. All of these different things.

Barry Fitzgerald Yes, I think that's so important [...] I mean, we're discussing Stanislavsky in this book. Someone who is integral to Western actor training. At some point, someone who is training to be an actor will encounter something Stanislavskian, and it can feel like there's still this reverence to that, and a lack of wanting to shift or change. A resistance to allowing other ways of working in. I know things have become more inclusive but at times that inclusivity can feel very surface and that's what needs to be interrogated. It's not just about the actors who are coming out of these institutions; that's important of course, but it needs to go deeper. It's about who is leading the spaces, who are the writers or artists that they're studying and whose methodologies? It's about who can access those spaces or ways of working?

Ray Young Yes exactly.

Barry Fitzgerald We need to have practitioners with different experiences, identities, cultural backgrounds bringing their own work and ways…and informing, adapting, or challenging traditional work. But it can feel like once we've found something then just stick with it.

Ray Young Yeah, and that's it forever. We'll never deviate from it.

Barry Fitzgerald It doesn't mean we can't use those things. And we do in different ways, but we need to keep alive and curious about other potential. But that takes time.

Ray Young I was thinking about OUTBOX and the work that you do. I just really loved watching your show *And The Rest of Me Floats*. I don't think I'd ever seen an ensemble of queer people making work in that way before that time. I just really thought the work was beautiful. It really did stay with me. And following on from what you're talking about in terms of actor training… how those spaces or projects are so valuable and how we need different approaches. Who starts to pick up the mantle for that? How can we have more of this kind of work?

Barry Fitzgerald More funding? Less cuts.

Ray Young Yeah, that'd be nice.

Barry Fitzgerald But that's another conversation. It's true but it's another conversation […] it's about valuing that work. Knowing that there's a place for it, and it has real value and power. In terms of who is going to create it, well, so often it's an individual or smaller organisation that leads the way. That takes a lot of energy and time, and funding, so projects come and go. They're transient. But I think they do have lasting influence on larger institutions or ways of working.

Ray Young Yeah.

Barry Fitzgerald And look, sometimes it's really important for a certain group of people to have that space to explore. That's what was brilliant about working with OUTBOX and on

TransActing. At that time, and I can't speak for everyone, I don't think there had been a space where everyone felt as included in that way. That gave people confidence and a way of seeing themselves in the larger picture or industry if you like. For some people, the experience meant they started making and valuing their own work, and some of them went into or back to training.

Ray Young That's amazing.

Barry Fitzgerald So, I think both of these things can exist. We need to strive for training spaces that are properly inclusive for all, and that's a complex and evolving thing. Just because it's challenging doesn't mean we shouldn't do it though. And then there also needs to be spaces, specific projects for people from different communities who can learn with and from each other – where there's that unspoken, embodied understanding.

Works Cited

Benedetti, J. "Translator's Foreword". In: *Stanislavski, K. An Actor's Work: A Student's Diary.* London: Routledge, 2010. DOI: https://doi.org/10.4324/9780203936153

Buratta, B. "A Note on the Play". In: *Outbox Theatre. And The Rest of Me Floats.* London: Oberon Modern Plays, 2019.

Carnicke, S.M. "Stanislavsky's System: Pathways for the Actor". In: Hodge, A. ed. *Actor Training.* Second Edition. London: Routledge, 2010. DOI: https://doi.org/10.4324/9780203861370

Carnicke, S.M. *Stanislavsky in Focus: An Acting Master for the Twenty-first Century.* Second Edition. London: Routledge, 2009. DOI: https://doi.org/10.4324/9781003134381

Chapuis, S. "Lecture by Jack Halberstam: "Trans*: Bodies, Gender Variance and Power". *Transatlantica.* Issue 2, pp.1–5. Paris: French Association for American Studies (AFEA), 2016. DOI: https://doi.org/10.4000/transatlantica.8286

Gendered Intelligence, "About Us". [*Online*]. 2024. Available from: https://genderedintelligence.co.uk/about-us. [Accessed February 2024].

Halberstam, J. *Trans: A Quick and Quirky Account of Gender Variability.* Berkeley: University of California Press, 2017.

My Genderation. (2024), Homepage. [*Online*] [Accessed February 2024]. Available from: https://mygenderation.com/

My Genderation. Trans Acting Course. [*Online*]. [Accessed December 2023]. Available from: https://youtu.be/5Cio_9kia8k?si=HL8tFmXXc5neJniM. 2015.

Outbox Theatre. *And the Rest of Me Floats.* London: Oberon Modern Plays, Bloomsbury Publishing, 2019.

OUTBOX. (2023), Homepage. [*Online*]. Available from: https://outboxtheatre.com/About. [Accessed December 2023].

Stanislavski, K. *An Actor's Work: A Student's Diary.* London: Routledge, 2010. https://doi.org/10.4324/9780203936153

Stanislavski, K. *My Life in Art.* London: Routledge, 2008. DOI: https://doi.org/10.4324/9781315823720

Stanislavsky, K. *Creating a Role*, trans. Elizabeth Reynolds Hapgood, London: Methuen, 2000.

EPILOGUE

Stanislavski's Dog

It's said an actor used to bring her dog to rehearsal where it would nestle into a corner
and remain uninterested by the human world of performance but as the day's
work drew to a close the dog would be at the door lead in its mouth
Stanislavski believed the dog knew it was time to leave as the actors began talking
naturally once more from this came his challenge to his cast to all actors
forever get the dog to stand by the door

No matter how many ways I say *mate* it doesn't lift an eye but my brother says
faggot by accident and it's scratching up the woodwork howling to escape

Spencer Wood

DOI: 10.4324/9781003411611-7

INDEX

For Product Safety Concerns and Information please contact our EU representative GPSR@taylorandfrancis.com
Taylor & Francis Verlag GmbH, Kaufingerstraße 24, 80331 München, Germany

www.ingramcontent.com/pod-product-compliance
Ingram Content Group UK Ltd.
Pitfield, Milton Keynes, MK11 3LW, UK
UKHW020053160325
456294UK00017B/185
* 9 7 8 1 0 3 2 5 3 3 5 0 6 *